Developing Application Frameworks in .NET

XIN CHEN

Apress™

Developing Application Frameworks in .NET

Copyright © 2004 by Xin Chen

ISBN-13 (pbk): 978-1-59059-288-5

ISBN-10 (pbk): 1-59059-288-3

eISBN-13 (pbk): 978-1-4302-0677-4

Printed and bound in the United States of America (POD)

Trademarked names may appear in this book. Rather than use a trademark symbol with every occurrence of a trademarked name, we use the names only in an editorial fashion and to the benefit of the trademark owner, with no intention of infringement of the trademark.

Lead Editor: Julian Skinner

Technical Reviewer: Basiru Samba

Editorial Board: Steve Anglin, Dan Appleman, Ewan Buckingham, Gary Cornell, Tony Davis, Jason Gilmore, Jonathan Hassell, Chris Mills, Dominic Shakeshaft, Jim Sumser

Project Manager: Nate McFadden

Copy Manager: Nicole LeClerc

Copy Editor: David Kramer

Production Manager: Kari Brooks

Production Editor: Ellie Fountain

Compositor: Diana Van Winkle, Van Winkle Design

Proofreader: Greg Teague

Indexer: Carol Burbo

Cover Designer: Kurt Krames

Manufacturing Manager: Tom Debolski

Distributed to the book trade in the United States by Springer-Verlag New York, Inc., 233 Spring Street, 6th Floor, New York, NY 10013 and outside the United States by Springer-Verlag GmbH & Co. KG, Tiergartenstr. 17, 69112 Heidelberg, Germany.

In the United States: phone 1-800-SPRINGER, e-mail orders@springer-ny.com, or visit http://www.springer-ny.com. Outside the United States: fax +49 6221 345229, e-mail orders@springer.de, or visit http://www.springer.de.

For information on translations, please contact Apress directly at 2855 Telegraph Avenue, Suite 600, Berkeley, CA 94705. Phone 510-549-5930, fax 510-549-5939, e-mail info@apress.com, or visit http://www.apress.com.

The information in this book is distributed on an "as is" basis, without warranty. Although every precaution has been taken in the preparation of this work, neither the author(s) nor Apress shall have any liability to any person or entity with respect to any loss or damage caused or alleged to be caused directly or indirectly by the information contained in this work.

The source code for this book is available to readers at http://www.apress.com in the Downloads section.

This book is dedicated to the countless mentors
who have helped me in my career.
Without them, this book would not have been possible.

Contents at a Glance

Contents

About the Author

 **Xin Chen** is the founder of Xtremework, Inc. Since the inception of .NET, Xin Chen has helped customers in a wide range of industries turn their business ideas into software products using .NET technology. Leveraging his expertise in .NET and EAI, Xin Chen has also worked with several technology leaders, such as Microsoft and Accenture, to bring winning solutions to their customers. When not working overtime, Xin enjoys reading books, writing books, and resting. He is the author of another Apress book, *BizTalk 2002 Design and Implementation*. Xin Chen earned his M.A. in statistics from Columbia University and is currently living in New Jersey. He can be reached at xchen@Xtremework.com.

About the
Technical Reviewer

Basiru Samba has more than a decade of experience designing and building reli-able software solutions for a variety of industries. He has spent more than half of his professional career on Wall Street building financial systems using Microsoft Technologies. He has extensive technical skills in distributed systems design and operations. He has a Masters degree in Computer Engineering, and he is currently working for a major Wall Street firm as a Systems Architect.

Acknowledgments

For me, computer programming is not just a job, but a passion. Software is more than just making database calls and displaying data to users. It is about creating something new, something better, something that people can point to and say, "Yeah, that would solve my problem!" Of course, to create new and better applications, you must be well versed in computer languages and various APIs, but the real fun is not about getting something done. Everything can be done in the field of computer technology. That is not the point. The point is how to do it better, how *you* can do it better.

This book is about doing it better. It is about how to develop application frameworks that help make your applications more reusable and extensible. Different readers may take away different things from this book. You may learn about some interesting .NET technologies, a new approach to application development, or the design of framework components. However, above all else, I want you to take away at least one point from this book: When it comes to software design, the sky is the limit. When you are developing your next application, use your creativity, use your imagination, use the techniques you have learned throughout your career, and don't just settle for getting things done. Aim for doing things better. Don't rush to judgment just yet; don't fire up your VS.NET just yet: You may be missing out on the most enjoyable part of your job.

Many individuals have expended considerable effort in bringing this book to you. I want to thank Gary Cornell, Karen Watterson, and Julian Skinner for their enthusiasm and support; Basiru Samba for his unmatched expertise in software design and the .NET framework, which he shared with me during the technical review process; David Kramer for his excellent editing, which has made this book a much more enjoyable read; and Nate McFadden for making the book publishing process incredibly effortless for me. I also want to give special thanks to Steve Halliwell of Microsoft for providing invaluable opportunities from which I learned about BizTalk and .NET, the topics of two of my books. Last, but not least, I want to thank Hugh Ang of Avanade, who mentored me on .NET and software design many years ago and who continues to be an excellent source of technical advice for me.

Introduction

APPLICATION FRAMEWORKS, which provide a base of common services on which applications are built, offer the benefits of extensibility, modularity, and reusability of both code and design to your applications. This book explains what frameworks are and how they fit into applications, and offers many object-oriented techniques used in application frameworks. This book also shows readers how actually to develop application frameworks through a concrete framework example called Simplified Application Framework (SAF). The SAF framework was developed by Xin Chen in C#. It consists of common services needed by many applications, such as a class factory service, configuration service, event notification service, security service, and transaction service. The book goes into detail on each of these services to explain its benefits, as well as its design and implementation in C#. Through a discussion of each service, readers will also learn about many advanced .NET techniques employed by the framework, such as .NET remoting, reflection, custom attribute, multithreading, and ServicedComponent. Many of the services discussed in the book also use design patterns as their blueprints. The book discusses these design patterns in depth and shows how to implement them in a real-world scenario. Accompanying the book are the complete source code of the sample framework and sample executable projects (downloadable via the Internet), allowing readers to actually test out each framework service/component of SAF and learn about the development of frameworks, .NET technologies, and design patterns in a more interactive fashion.

CHAPTER 1

Introduction to Application Frameworks

As THE AUTHOR of this book I have a single goal, which is to sell you on the idea of application frameworks. Throughout this book, I will talk about many aspects of application frameworks. I will explain, for example, why a framework is important in application development, and what techniques can be used in developing an application framework. I believe in explaining through concrete examples, so I will show you how to develop an application framework through a sample framework that I have developed, called SAF, which is short for *Simplified Application Framework*.

The SAF sample framework is written in C#, a computer programming language that provides object-oriented features for the development of an application framework. Some good hands-on experience with the Microsoft .NET Framework, C#, and object-oriented programming would undoubtedly be of great benefit in understanding the technical aspects of this topic. Many characteristics of .NET technologies to which we will refer in discussing application frameworks are advanced topics that you may have read about but have not yet used yourself, and you can take this opportunity to see how many of those .NET features are actually implemented and used in the sample framework. The "gang of four" (GOF) design patterns discussed in this book are another area in which you can learn a great deal about good application design. Application frameworks often rely on those patterns for the reuse of their designs. You will learn more about many of the GOF design patterns as I show you how they are implemented in the framework throughout the book. If you buy into the idea of application frameworks, and at the same time learn about many .NET technologies and design patterns that you can use in your projects after reading this book, you will make me a happy author.

What Is an Application Framework?

Before I start selling you on the idea of application frameworks, we first need to define what it is. Let us start with the definition of *framework* from the *American Heritage Dictionary*: "A structure for supporting or enclosing something else, especially a skeletal support used as the basis for something being constructed; a fundamental structure, as for a written work or a system of ideas."

The term "framework" can mean different things to different people. Politicians use the word to describe certain policies and certain approaches to problems. Architects (the ones who design buildings) use the word to describe the skeleton or frame of a building. Software architects use the word to describe a set of reusable designs and code that can assist in the development of software applications. It is this meaning of "framework" that we will discuss in the rest of the book.

The word "structure" is really at the heart of any framework. Structure exists everywhere. When you see that a new construction is underway, the first thing you observe is that its structure is built first. When I am writing a book, I first come up with a structure, or outline, for what I will be discussing in the book. By developing a "structure," we are forced to look at the big picture. In the case of a building, a focus on the big picture forces the architect to focus on how one portion of the construction affects every other aspect. In the case of writing this book, such a focus forced me to think about how chapters and topics are organized to make the whole book easy for readers to understand.

Structure also plays an important role in application development. A fairly complex application can contain so many moving and changing parts that no human being can keep track of their interrelationships. Structure helps us organize those moving parts into a few major ones that you can easily track. As we start developing the application, we can rely on structures to provide us with a context for detailed implementations. An application framework provides developers with a structure and template that they can use as a baseline to build their applications. Such a framework often consists of abstract classes, concrete classes, and predefined interaction among the classes throughout the framework. Developers can then build the application on top of the framework and reduce the development effort through reuse of code and designs provided in the framework. Figure 1-1 provides a high-level overview on how an application framework relates to a business application.

Of course, many applications have been developed without using a framework, so you can probably do the job without even knowing the concept of a framework. In the world of application development, everything can be done, with or without a framework. However, by taking an application framework approach, you can take advantage of the many benefits that a framework can offer your application. It is these benefits that lie at the heart of the promotion of application frameworks.

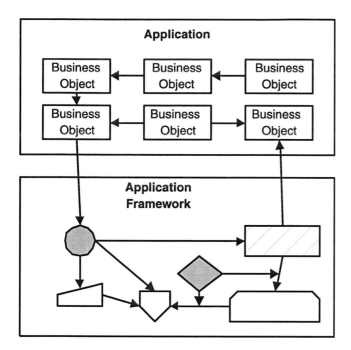

Figure 1-1. High-level overview of the relationship between an application and the application framework

A History of Application Frameworks

The concept of the application framework is not new, and various types of frameworks have been around for a couple of decades. The first widely used framework was the Model-View Controller (MVC), a Smalltalk user interface framework developed by Xerox. The approach of MVC, which depends on the Observer design pattern, has been adapted in many user interface systems. In addition to the Smalltalk MVC, other user-interface frameworks have emerged to assist in the development of applications running under several operating systems. Some of the well-known user-interface frameworks are MacApp and MFC, which assist in application development on Macintosh and Windows systems, respectively.

Although the concept of a framework has been widely adopted in user-interface development, it is not limited to the user-interface framework. The framework concept is also used in generic application development. Taligent, a company that develops object-oriented operating systems, alerted the software industry to the possibilities of the framework concept. Taligent was formed in 1992 as a result of collaboration between IBM and Apple to create new operating systems that would run on any hardware platform. However, as time went by, the industry became less interested in such new operating systems. Taligent shifted

3

its focus to developing framework layers that sit on top of existing operating systems. CommonPoint, a framework developed by Taligent, aims to reduce application development effort by providing developers with a comprehensive programming environment, similar to what Sun's Java environment offers today through its Java language and runtime virtual machine.

Sun's Java environment and Microsoft's .NET environment provide their own frameworks along with the new languages and virtual machines. Those who work with Java or .NET can fully appreciate the benefits what those two frameworks have offered to application development in the past several years. Java and .NET are both frameworks that target all types of applications, and thus such frameworks must not contain any business-domain–related classes and designs. However, there exist frameworks that sit on top of such generic frameworks and provide services and expertise for certain specific business domains, such as supply chain systems and financial applications.

IBM (which later bought Taligent) also developed its own business-domain–orientated framework, called the San Francisco Project. San Francisco was developed using Java, and it consists of the application frameworks for various business domains, such as order management, warehouse management, and general ledger management. Unlike general-purpose frameworks such as Java and .NET, the San Francisco framework is designed especially for specific business domains.

Why Use an Application Framework?

There are five major benefits of using application frameworks: Modularity, Reusability, Extensibility, Simplicity, and Maintainability.

Modularity

Modularity, the division of an application into structural components, or modules, allows developers to use the application framework in a piece-by-piece fashion. Developers who want to use one component of the application framework are shielded from potential changes to other parts of the framework. As they build applications on top of the framework, their development is better insulated from changes occurring in other parts of the application framework, resulting in a significant boost to their productivity and a reduction in the amount of time spent on fixing code affected by other parts of the application. By dividing the framework into modules, we can maximize productivity by assigning a developer the specific part of the application that would benefit most from that developer's expertise. The advantage that accrues from modularity can be seen, for example, in Web applications: developers who are expert in presentation user interfaces can be more productive when assigned to the front-end portion of the application, while developers who are expert in the development of application business logic can be more productive when assigned to the middle tier and back-end portion of the application. Similarly, developers can leverage the framework module related to the user interface during their development of the presentation tier of the application, while other developers can leverage the framework module related to the development of business objects during their development of the middle and back-end tiers of the application.

Reusability

Reusability of code is one of the most important and desirable goals of application development. An application framework provides such reusability to the application built on top of it not only by sharing its classes and code, but by sharing its designs as well. Applications usually contain many tasks that are similar in nature. However, different developers on the team often create their own implementations of these similar tasks. The result of such duplicated implementation is not only the unnecessary waste of resources on the duplicated code, but also the problem of maintainability further down the road, since any change to the task must be duplicated in multiple places throughout the application to ensure its integrity. On top of that, each developer might use a different design approach during implementation. This opens the application to risks of poor software design, which could lead to unforeseen issues down the road. With an application framework, however, we can move much of the duplicated code and commonly used solutions from the application layer to the framework components. This reduces the amount of duplicate code developers have to write and maintain, and significantly boosts their productivity. The application framework is also the place where we can bake many well-tested software designs into the components. Developers may not always be experts in software design, yet as they start using these framework components to build their applications, they unavoidably reuse many good software design approaches, such as design patterns that underlie the framework components.

Extensibility

Extensibility, the ability to add custom functionalities to the existing framework, allows developers not only to use the framework component "out of the box," but also to alter the components to suit a specific business scenario. Extensibility is an important feature for the framework. Each business application is unique in its business requirements, architecture, and implementation. It is impossible for a framework to accommodate such variation by itself, but if a framework is designed in such way that it leaves room for some customization, then different business applications can still use the generic features of the framework, yet at the same time developers will have the freedom to tailor their applications to the unique business requirements by plugging the customized logic into the framework. With a high degree of extensibility, the framework itself can become more applicable to different types of business applications. However, in creating a framework, its extensibility should always be determined in the context and assumptions of the application you are trying to develop. Each time you increase the extensibility of the framework, your developers may need to write more code and require more detailed knowledge about how the framework operates, which will have a negative impact on their productivity. An extreme scenario of a highly extensible framework is Microsoft's .NET framework itself, which is designed for development of a wide variety of applications. Indeed, there are few constraints in developing applications using the .NET framework, but as a result, you lose the benefits of what an application framework can provide. The key is to add the flexibility and extensibility to the places in the framework that are more likely to change in the particular type of application you are developing.

Simplicity

The term "simplicity" here means more than just being simple. Simplicity refers to the way the framework simplifies development by encapsulating much of the control of process flow and hiding it from the developers. Such encapsulation also represents one of the distinctions between a framework and a class library. A class library consists of a number of ready-to-use components that developers can use to build an application. However, developers must understand the relationships between various components and write process flow code to wire many components together in the application. On the other hand, a framework encapsulates the control of such process flow by prewiring many of its components so that developers do not have to write code to control how the various components interact with each other. Figure 1-2 illustrates the difference between a class library and a framework.

As you can see from the figure, in a class library approach, the developer must provide the code to manage the flow of control between different instances of the components in the class library. In order for developers to "wire" the object correctly, they must have a full understanding of each component involved and the business logic needed to make all the components work together. In the framework approach, developers have only very lightweight wiring to code inside the application, since most of the process flow is managed by the framework itself. By hiding such process flow between different components, developers are freed from writing the coordination logic for the components and going through the learning curve required to write such coordination code. By moving the process flow logic from the application to the application framework, the framework designer can use his or her architecture and domain expertise to define how components should work together inside the framework. As a developer starts using the framework, he or she can be highly productive in developing the application knowing very little about how the framework components work together.

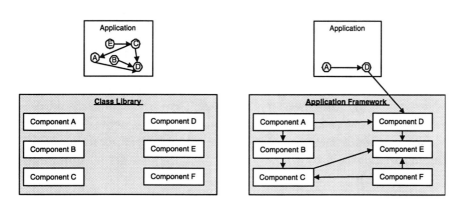

Figure 1-2. Comparison between a class library and an application framework

Maintainability

Maintainability, the ability to effectively support changes to the application as a result of changes to the business requirements, is a welcome side effect of code reuse. Framework components are commonly shared by multiple applications and multiple areas within a single application. Having a single copy of the framework code base makes the application easy to maintain, because you need to make a change only once when a requirement changes. The application framework may also contain many layers. Each layer makes certain assumptions about the business the application is intended to serve. The bottom layer consists of framework components that make no assumptions about the business. They are also the most generic components in the framework. As you move higher up the stack of the layers, its components depend on more business assumptions than do the previous layers, and hence are more susceptible to change when business requirements and rules change. When changes do occur, only the components at the layer where the business assumption is broken need to be fixed and tested. Therefore, by injecting different levels of business knowledge into different levels of the framework layers, you can reduce the cascade effect of changing business rules and requirements to the application. This also leads to the reduction of maintenance costs, since you need to touch only the code that is affected by the business rule change. You will learn more about the framework layers in Chapter 2.

While application frameworks offer benefits as described above, they also follow the No-Free-Lunch rule. Application frameworks also carry a set of additional costs to the development process.

The Economics of Application Frameworks

You have just seen what wonderful things frameworks can do for our applications; however, while application frameworks are the best choice in many circumstances, that doesn't mean they are always the right choice. In exploring the possibilities offered by application frameworks, we must not lose sight of what we are trying to accomplish with the application we are developing. There are two areas in developing and using application frameworks that you need to consider in determining whether an application framework will help achieve your objectives: framework development and user training.

Framework Development

Developing an application framework is not an easy and inexpensive effort. In order to develop a highly usable and extensible framework, you need first to find individuals who are not only expert in the business domain, but also expert in software design and development. It is important that those who are developing the framework be competent in both business knowledge and software development. Without business expertise, you cannot create the business-domain–specific framework layers that developers rely on to offset their lack of knowledge of the business domain. Without the technical expertise in software development, you cannot transfer the concept of the framework from theory to the concrete framework code that developers can reuse and extend. Finding people who have expertise in both the business domain and software development is the first hurdle to leap over in the development of a high-quality framework.

Clearly, the design and implementation of the framework demands a significant amount of human resources. Developing the application framework requires different skills from those used in developing an application. The framework designer must determine how developers can benefit from the services and architecture provided in the framework, how to abstract certain common logic in the application so that developers can reuse such logic throughout the framework, and how to provide the hot spots, or flexibility points, at the right place in the framework so that developers can plug in their code to achieve specific results.

Some of the work involved in creating a framework is abstract and relies heavily on assumptions about how developers will use the framework to build the application. It is difficult to get everything right on the first try, since the design can only guess at how the final application will look and how it will be built to solve the business problem. Certain framework components that were originally thought of as shared by multiple parts of the application may turn out not to be, and they should be taken out of the framework. Certain bits of application code that were originally supposed to be unique in different scenarios may turn out to share certain common abstractions, and they should be added to the framework to be shared throughout the application. After the framework has been deployed, new business requirements or changed requirements may result in the addition of new components to the framework and a modification of the existing framework components. As you may imagine, it takes a series of iterations to get the framework right for the applications that are built on top of it. The development cycle for a framework is similar to that of a regular application, namely, Analysis, Design, Development, and Stabilization in a reiterative fashion. Framework development is very much an evolving task, and it demands continual development and support efforts to ensure its relevance.

User Training

Because the users of the framework are the developers who are building the application, user training for the framework means training the developers to use the application framework. In order to take advantage of what the framework offers, developers must have sufficient knowledge about the application framework and how to use it in their development. However, learning about a framework can be a time-consuming process. There are several factors that contribute to the difficulties in learning an application framework.

By its nature, the application framework is an incomplete application. Many missing parts of the framework will need to be filled in with application code written by the developers. However, before the application is complete, the framework itself may look obscure to many developers, since not every piece in the framework is well connected from beginning to end.

Application frameworks also contain much wiring needed to control the process flow throughout the framework. Although one of the goals of the framework is to hide such complex wiring from the developer, during training, developers may have a harder time understanding how the framework works as it does, because much of this wiring and the dependencies among classes in the framework are indirect and complex.

As with any new product and programming model, an application framework contains many APIs, services, and configuration settings that are strange to developers, and it will take some time for developers to work with the framework before they become fluent with it and fully productive in developing applications based on it.

Despite this learning curve, we can speed up developers' adaptation of the framework by creating well-written documentation and samples that show developers how the framework is used in various scenarios. In the case of programming, an example is worth a thousand words and pictures.

With the potential development cost and efforts in mind, we can weigh whether we need an application framework. Not every application needs to be built on an application framework, and many applications have been successfully developed without one. There are situations in which you want a quick solution produced on a limited budget, and thus the savings on the development effort through the framework may not cover the extra development effort invested in creating the framework. In contrast, there are situations in which an application framework is shared by multiple applications and would significantly reduce the overall development effort. There are also situations in which you want to invest in the application framework today so that it can provide an extensible and reusable foundation for future development. What it comes down to is whether an application framework will help you achieve the objective you set for your project. Developing an application framework is like investing in the stock market; good investments are not judged on whether they are making money today, but on whether they support your investment objectives.

Summary

In this introduction to application frameworks, you have learned the definition of the application framework and have read a brief history of it. We then looked at how we can leverage a framework in application development to reduce the overall development effort. We discussed the benefits of using an application framework as a starting point for the business application we are developing: modularity, reusability, extensibility, simplicity, and maintainability. We also discussed some of the cost of developing and using a framework, such as additional development effort and developer training issues. Knowing both the benefits and costs of developing an application framework helps us make the right choice whether one should be used in a particular scenario. In the next chapter, we will look at what is inside a framework, and see how to develop an application framework that is both reusable and extensible through the use of object-oriented techniques.

CHAPTER 2

Dissection of an Application Framework

WE LOOKED BRIEFLY in the previous chapter at what an application framework is, and we considered its benefits and costs. In this chapter, we will dive more deeply into the details of the framework. We will look specifically at what is in a framework, how we can develop a framework for our application, and what object-oriented techniques we can leverage in developing the framework.

To better understand how we can develop an application framework, we need first to understand what goes in an application framework and its relationship to other parts of the system.

Framework Layers

You learned in chapter one that an application framework is a "semifinished" application that can act as a starting point for a business application. Applications that are built on top of the framework consist of two layers: the application layer and the framework layer. The framework layer may consist of numerous components, which can be again grouped into domain-specific components and cross-domain components. Figure 2-1 illustrates the different participants in an application and their relationship to each other.

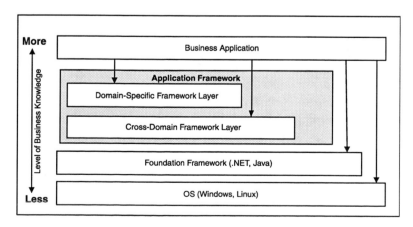

Figure 2-1. Multiple layers within an application

The following is a brief description of what each layer represents and what role it plays in the overall system.

The Business Application

The business application represents the custom application that developers are responsible for. It implements the detailed business knowledge for the specific application under development. Developers build the business application according to the particular scenario described by business analysts. As the business logic and rules change, it is this level at which changes will mostly likely occur, particularly when such changes are minor and isolated.

The Application Framework

The application framework represents the semifinished application that architects have developed as a basis for developers to use to construct their business applications. The application framework can be broken down into two layers: a domain-specific framework layer and a cross-domain framework layer.

The Domain-Specific Framework Layer

The domain-specific framework consists of specialized framework components that target a specific business domain. In comparison to the business application layer, the domain-specific framework layer implements knowledge that is common to all applications of a particular business domain, in contrast to the business application layer, where the business knowledge and logic are targeted to a particular application.

You can think of a domain-specific framework as corresponding to a country's constitution and a business application as analogous to the laws of a particular state or local government. The constitution doesn't describe the specific laws that the state has to implement, but instead it describes the principles under which the system of laws should be framed. Each state may pass its own laws, but all those laws must be based on the principles set out in the constitution. However, as long as the state law is in conformity with the constitution, the state is free to create laws that are best suited to that state. Like the constitution, a domain-specific framework doesn't mandate how each business application should be built; instead, it provides a set of components that encapsulate the core business characteristics and processes of a particular business domain. For example, a shopping cart component describing a customer's selected product items, the quantity of each, and the time of selection can be considered a domain-specific framework component for the on-line B2C business domain. Different business applications (an on-line shopping site in this case) may use the shopping cart component differently in separate scenarios, but they all share a common trait: They all need an object that provides information on the customer's product selection, quantity of each selection, and time of the selection.

Unlike the business application, where developers are in charge of design and implementation of the actual application, the domain-specific framework layer is designed and implemented by persons who have expertise and deep understanding of a specific business area and know how to encapsulate and abstract business-domain knowledge in a form that can be easily adapted by developers in building the actual business application. Although software architecting skill is important in developing a business-specific framework, the business expertise is especially critical in the success of this layer of the framework.

The domain-specific framework layer contains business-domain knowledge that is much less volatile than that in the business applications and it expects few or no changes as the business rules change throughout the application.

The Cross-Domain Framework Layer

The cross-domain framework represents framework components that contain no business-domain knowledge. Because the business-domain knowledge is absent from this layer of the framework, it can be shared among multiple applications in different business domains. In other words, this layer hosts the components and services that are commonly found in most applications, regardless of their business domain.

There are many common themes among applications of different business domains that we can "package" into the cross-domain framework layer. For example, every application needs some way of managing the configuration information used by different parts of the application. A configuration service and architecture greatly reduces the development effort of numerous applications, regardless of the business domain of the application. In a distributed application environment, one application often needs to talk to another application residing on a different system, so an event notification service will also benefit the development effort of such applications by presenting a ready-to-use system that transmits information among the different applications. As you can see, if we can identify the common themes among different types of applications and develop services and components to take care of such common requirements, we can significantly increase code and design reuse throughout the applications.

Those who develop cross-domain framework layers are individuals who have developed a large number of applications and have a good understanding of software design as well as a knowledge of the features that are common to many applications. These individuals don't have to know a great deal about particular businesses, but they must have good object-oriented skills so that they can build the framework in such way that application developers can easily plug in their custom business logic to solve application-specific problems.

Since the cross-domain framework layer contains no specific business-domain knowledge, it may be thought of as generic to most applications. It is thus unaffected by changes to business rules and requirements. However, this layer will be affected by the recognition of new common themes that arise during the development process, for such themes will be implemented in this layer. Moreover, if it turns out that certain aspects of the framework's design interfere with the adaptation of the business application, the cross-domain framework will have to be modified.

The Foundation Framework

The foundation framework represents the programming model on which the application framework and business application are built. This layer is developed by the software vendor. Some of the best-known foundation frameworks are Sun's Java environment and Microsoft's .NET Framework. The foundation framework is used to develop a wide variety of applications, and it contains no specific business-domain knowledge. Changes to the foundation framework are driven primarily by the need for higher performance or the support of newer technologies.

OS

The OS layer represents, as its name implies, the operating system level. It provides access to system resources, such as CPU, memory, and disks, and to all the layers that sit on top of it.

With a basic understanding of the different layers in the overall picture and how they are positioned in an application, let's take a look at how to actually build an application framework. First, we will look at the application framework's development process.

The Framework Development Process

After you have decided that you need an application framework, you should first determine the major phases involved in a framework development process. Figure 2-2 shows four majors phases: analysis, design, development, and stabilization.

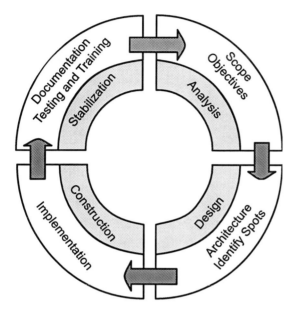

Figure 2-2. Framework development process

The gray inner circle indicates the phase, and the outer circle indicates some of the major tasks involved in each phase. Let's take a look at what is involved in each phase.

Analysis

As we start the process of developing an application framework, the first phase we enter is the analysis phase. As with application development, framework development starts by first setting the scope and objectives of the project or framework. We need first to identify the key features that are to be included in the framework. What types of business applications will be relying on this framework? What use cases will the framework support? In other words, how will developers be able to develop their business applications on top of this framework? The framework is built to support the development of the business application, so it is important to figure out what business domains the framework will able to support. Many questions will be asked during the analysis phase of framework development to set the scope and objectives of the framework.

During the analysis phase, we also need to create an iteration plan for improving the framework over time. Framework development involves complex and abstract tasks, and you shouldn't expect to get everything right on the first iteration. You may discover that certain items need to be added to or removed from the framework as you start implementing it. You may also decide to modify how some parts of the framework work to help developers become more productive in adapting the framework. You need to set up a plan to collect ideas for enhancements and fixes as developers start using the framework for use as the input to the next iteration. In addition to such an iteration plan, you will also need to draft a project plan and establish a timeline and documentation of major milestones for all phases of the process.

Design

After we have set the objectives for the application framework, the next phase is the design phase. The design phase for framework development involves two major tasks. First, we need to identity the common spots and the hot spots in both the domain-specific layer and the cross-domain framework layer. Second, we need to devise an architecture for the framework that will be used as a blueprint during the construction phase.

"Common spot" and "hot spot" are special terms relating to framework development. You will learn more about them later in the chapter. In a nutshell, a common spot is an area in the framework where variation is unlikely. A common spot is often a framework component or service that is ready for use without significant customization by application developers. On the other hand, a hot spot is an area in the framework where variation is frequent. Developers must provide their specific business logic in those hot spots in order to use the framework component. A hot spot is an abstract method that requires the developer to implement specific business logic. Identifying the common spots and hot spots in a business application allows you to identify the specific components and services in the framework. Identifying what is variable and what is fixed in a business domain is not an easy task. The business experts and software architects need to work together to identify those spots among the different layers of the framework in order to design a framework that is both easy to use and extensible.

After the business experts and software architects have come up with a list of components and services and identify which are common spots and which hot spots, the software architects can start designing the blueprint of the framework. As part of the architectural design of the framework, you need to create a number of design deliverables, such as class diagrams and activity diagrams, which will be used during the construction phase of the framework. Software architects also spend their time thinking about the techniques they can use on various components and services, such as design patterns, to maximize code reuse and extensibility in the final framework.

During the design phase, you can also begin to create a prototype of the application framework and then build a sample application on top of it. Testing the prototype with a sample application helps you learn how the framework you develop will be used to build the business application and gain insight into potential improvements in the design of the framework.

Implementation

After the framework design is done, the next phase is to actually code the application framework. The implementation phase has one goal, which is to develop a framework that meets the requirements and time constraints. If you have done a good design job on the framework, implementing it is no different from regular application development. As with application development, where different team members can work on different parts of the same application simultaneously, you can have work progressing on different pieces of the application framework simultaneously, as long as the framework is partitioned into well-defined modules. Unit testing on the newly created functionality can be tricky during framework development. In the case of application development, developers will simply test the use case on the newly created functionality to see whether it works as desired. However, unit testing of frameworks is much less direct and visual than that of business applications, since the application that uses the framework simply hasn't been created yet and all the business data needed by the application have not been generated.

As with application development, you can create number of milestone releases during the implementation phase. You can create several incremental releases so that you can get part of the application framework to developers and start getting feedback on any potential improvements and fixes for the next release.

Stabilization

The stabilization phase, the last phase before the next iteration starts, focuses on testing, bug fixing, developer feedback, documentation, and knowledge transfer.

Testing the framework in this phase is often driven by developers instead of professional quality-assurance testers or business end users, since developers are the primary users of the framework. During the stabilization phase of the framework development, the design and construction of the actual application have not yet started, so developers haven't yet created much application code. In such a situation, you need to identity at least one usage scenario in the business application for each framework component and service and ask the development team to write a small portion of the application based on such usage scenarios. Although it is not possible to test every framework usage scenario of an application that has not yet been built, you can effectively test your framework through the selective implementation of part of a business application that is representative of the usage pattern of the framework.

Of course, in order for developers to develop part of an application based on the framework, they must know how to use the framework productively. As the creator of the application framework, you will initiate developer training in the stabilization phase. The better job you do educating developers about the framework, the better the developers will be able to test your framework and the more productive they will be when they start using your framework extensively in application development.

Besides conducting frequent training sessions on how to use the application framework, you also need to produce good documentation of your framework, which will be an invaluable tool in helping developers learn to use the framework.

Typical documentation created to help developers consists of four parts:

- An overview of the framework that explains the purpose of the framework and the major components and services available in the framework.

- Some pictures, diagrams, and descriptions of the framework that help developers grasp the framework and its design philosophy.

- An API reference for the functionalities inside the framework that enables developers to look up the framework's functionalities during the development process.

- A collection of examples that show how the framework is used. Concrete examples of the framework in action best demonstrate the usage scenario of the application framework and help shorten the learning process for developers.

The stabilization phase is also where the framework designer will continually collect developers' feedback on the framework for the next iteration of framework development. After developers start using the framework, the framework designer must also participate in the effort of application development by providing assistance to the developer team, answering questions and solving problems related to the usability of the framework.

With a development process in place for framework development, let's look at some common approaches and techniques for developing a framework that we will use in the rest of the book

Framework Development Techniques

In order to develop an effective application framework, you need to know some common techniques for framework development. The following list shows some useful techniques and approaches that can help you develop a framework that is both easy to use and extensible.

- Common spots

- Hot spots

- Black-box framework

- White-box framework

- Gray-box framework

- Design patterns

Common spots, hot spots, and design patterns are some of the techniques used in framework development. Black, white, and gray boxes represent the approaches you can take to developing the framework.

Common Spots

Common spots, as the name suggests, represent the places in the business application where a common theme is repeated over and over again. If certain parts of the application repeat without much variation throughout the application, we can extract such common spots out of the application and package them into components in the framework layer. By moving such common spots into the framework, you avoid the duplication of such common spots throughout the application, and hence promote code reuse. This reduces the development effort when developers can simply referencing to the common spot in the framework from their applications. Figure 2-3 shows how the common spots relate to the framework and business application.

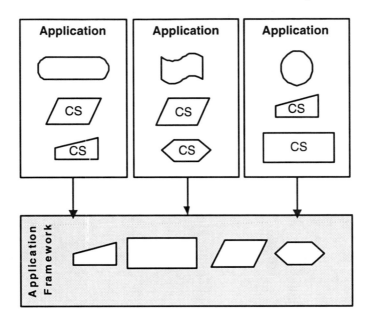

Figure 2-3. Common spots

In Figure 2-3, the application framework contains the components that provide the implementation for various common spots found in the application. When developers start building applications, they will reference the common spots implemented in the framework component instead of developing them themselves. As a result, the amount of application code they have to write is reduced.

To qualify as a common spot, a theme does not have appear in exactly the same way throughout the application. As long as the variations are small, you can still treat them as common spots and handle the small variations through parameterization and/or configuration settings.

The actual task of moving the common spot theme into a framework component is not hard. The difficult task is to identify in the analysis phase the common spots throughout the business application that have not yet been developed. It is not always easy to see through the common theme embedded in the application, and it usually takes a few tries to get it right.

Common spots can exist in both the domain-specific framework layer and the cross-domain framework layer. For example, the exchange of business documents is the central theme of B2B applications. A business document object would be considered one of the common themes that can be turned into a framework component for the domain-specific framework layer. Another example is a data cryptography service. Regardless of the type of application, data encryption and decryption are often applied at different parts of the application. A data encryption/decryption component, which simplifies and reduces the amount of code developers have to write to support cryptographic needs in the application, would be considered one of the components in the cross-domain framework layer.

From a technical point of view, implementation of common spots is straightforward. After identifying a common spot, the framework designer can develop the components that encapsulate the theme and logic in the common spot. Such components often take the form of concrete classes or executables. To accommodate the small variations in the component, some configuration data may also accompany the component. For example, you can allocate certain sections in the configuration file for parameterization of the framework components. In terms of adapting such framework components, developers need to write little or no code to use the component within the application.

Common spots capture the themes that are repeated throughout the application; however, each business application is unique, and there are as many spots where each application varies significantly due to the nature of the application as there are common spots. As a framework designer, you need to take account of those variations when designing the framework and make sure that developers can take advantage of the framework not only when there are common themes among applications, but also significant variation and customization between applications. This leads us to the next topic: hot spots.

Hot Spots

A hot spot is point of flexibility in the application framework. Another way to look at the hot spot is that it is a placeholder embedded in the framework where application-specific customization occurs.

Hot spots are the opposite of common spots. In a common spot, the framework implements the common themes inside the framework component; however, in the case of hot spots, there is nothing for the framework to implement except to leave an empty placeholder, which is later filled with a custom implementation by the business application built on top of the framework. Because each business application is responsible for providing its own implementation for the hot spot in the framework, the framework will behave differently for each business application. This is how a framework can be designed to suit different business applications in spite of significant variations among these business applications. Figure 2-4 illustrates how an application framework achieves flexibility through hot spots.

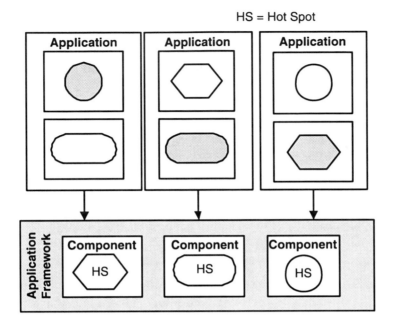

Figure 2-4. Hot spots

In Figure 2-4, components in the application framework layer consist of different hot spots, or empty placeholders for customization. Each application may use a number of framework components throughout the application. When the application uses a framework component that contains the hot spot, it needs to provide the implementation only in the hot spot in order to use the framework. The different designs and shading of the hot spot shapes shown in the figure represent the different implementations among various applications. As you can see, by implementing different logic inside the hot spots, each application will elicit different behaviors from the framework components.

As with common spots, identifying the hot spots may not be easy. To identify a potential hot spot, you must understand the business domain inside out and understand which points in the business application will potentially need to be customized. Having too many unnecessary hot spots in the framework will lead to extra coding effort for the developer team. Having too few hot spots makes it harder for the developer team to adapt the framework when desired customization becomes difficult due to the inflexibility of the underlying framework. Although it is possible to achieve such customization by overriding most or all the virtual methods in the base class, doing so would diminish code reuse and the purpose of inheritance.

Creating hot spots in the framework is not as straightforward as creating common spots. There are two approaches on how hot spots are enabled in the framework: the inheritance approach, and the composition approach. Let's look at the inheritance approach first.

The Inheritance Approach

The inheritance approach is driven by two important object-oriented concepts: hook methods and template methods.

Hook Methods

A hook method is a placeholder that will be filled by the application-specific logic. It is the manifestation of a hot spot concept in an actual class. The terms "hook method" and "hot spot" are interchangeable in many publications. However, a hot spot doesn't necessarily take the form of a method; it can also be in the form of a class or application, although the method form is the most common manifestation of a hot spot. Although a hook method can also appear in a concrete class (as we will see later in this section), it often appears in the form of an abstract method inside an abstract class.

An abstract class, by definition, is a class that contains abstract methods. An abstract method defined in the abstract class doesn't contain its method implementation. In order to use an abstract class, a class must inherit from the abstract class and implement the abstract methods in the parent class. Because of this feature, the derived class has the opportunity to inject some customized logic to make it behave according to some specific business requirement. The following example shows how abstract methods work:

```
public abstract class BasicBusiness
{
    protected float income;
    //the template method
    public void ReportTax()
    {
        float sTax = CalculateStateTax();
        float fTax = CalculateFedTax();
        bool ok = CheckBankBalance(sTax + fTax);
        if (!ok)
        {
            FileBankruptcy();
        }
```

```
        else
        {
            SendMoneyToGov(sTax + fTax);
        }

    }

    protected abstract float CalculateStateTax();
    protected abstract float CalculateFedTax();
}
```

The BasicBusiness class is an abstract class containing three methods:
ReportTax, CalculateStateTax, and CalculateFedTax; the latter two are abstract
methods. BasicBusiness is used to report income tax to state and federal government, and it contains the fictitious business-domain knowledge about the action
taken at the time of tax filing. ReportTax determines whether the bank balance can
cover the total tax. If the balance can cover it, a check will be sent out to the government; otherwise, the account holder will file for bankruptcy.

The ReportTax method depends on two pieces of information in order to
determine whether to pay the tax or file for bankruptcy: the tax amount to be paid
to the state government and the tax amount to be paid to the federal government.
The creators of the BasicBusiness component have no knowledge of the tax law
that applies to each situation. For example, depending on the location and type of
business, different tax brackets may apply. Since BasicBusiness doesn't know how
to calculate the tax amount, it will leave such tasks to someone who knows. The
two abstract methods will act as placeholders to be filled later with code that generates the final tax amounts. Although CalculateStateTax and CalculateFedTax are
abstract methods, they can be called just like regular methods. As you can see in
the previous sample, the CheckBankBalance method takes the return values of two
abstract methods as its parameters even though the two abstract methods have
not yet been implemented.

Of course, someone has to implement the CalculateStateTax and CalculateFedTax
abstract methods before the ReportTax method can provide any meaningful functionality. In fact, because BasicBusiness contains the abstract methods, it can't be
used by instantiating it. Instead, you will need to create a concrete class that
derives from the BasicBusiness class and implements its two abstract methods.
The following example shows a class that extends BasicBusiness and implements
its two abstract methods:

```
public class NewYorkBusiness : BasicBusiness
{
    //implementation of abstract method
    protected override float CalculateStateTax()
```

```
    {
        return income * 0.1F;
    }
    //implementation of abstract method
    protected override float CalculateFedTax()
    {
        return income * 0.2F;
    }
}
```

NewYorkBusiness is a concrete class that provides the tax calculation methods for New York State. With the custom implementation in the NewYorkBusiness class, ReportTax defined in BasicBusiness can perform some meaningful actions, as shown in the next example:

```
BasicBusiness nyBusiness = new NewYorkBusiness();
//ReportTax now will use the tax calculation algorithm defined for New York.
nyBusiness.ReportTax();

BasicBusiness caBusiness = new CaliforniaBusiness();
//ReportTax now will use the tax calculation algorithm defined for California.
caBusiness.ReportTax();
```

Abstract methods are a very powerful concept in both application development and framework development. Imagine that the BasicBusiness class is a framework component and the NewYorkBusiness is an application component. BasicBusiness leaves the hot spots (CalculateStateTax and CalculateFedTax) for the application to fill. Each application will fill those spots according to its specific requirements.

Although the application provides the implementation for the abstract method, it often doesn't invoke the abstract methods directly. Abstract methods are often invoked through the template method.

Template Methods

A template method, one of the GOF design patterns, describes a skeleton or process flow for certain operations rather than prescribing how each operation is carried out. In the example of our BasicBusiness component, ReportTax is a template method. The ReportTax method describes what steps are involved in reporting tax, but it does not describe how every step is performed, since some of the methods it references haven't been implemented. The template method emphasizes how the coordination between different objects/methods is carried out. In framework development, template methods contain the business-domain knowledge on how different methods should work together, whereas abstract methods provide a means of custom method implementation that is referenced in the template method. It is important to realize that template methods and hook methods embody two different concepts; Figure 2-5 illustrates the relationship between an abstract method (or hook method) and a template method in a framework.

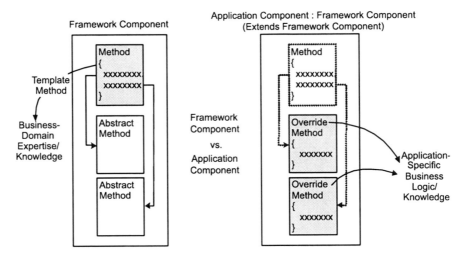

Figure 2-5. Template method and abstract method

The left side of the figure represents a framework component, which contains the concrete template method that contains the business expertise and knowledge for a specific business domain. The framework component also has a number of hot spots, represented by the abstract methods. The arrows that point from the template method to the abstract methods indicate that the template method calls several abstract methods for their application-specific behaviors.

On the right side of the figure, an application component extends the framework component and implements the abstract methods in the framework component with the application-specific business logic and knowledge. Because the application framework inherits the functionalities of its framework component parent, its overridden methods (or hook methods) and the template method in its parent class together should be able to provide a combination of business-domain expertise/knowledge and application-level business logics.

Hot spots can be enabled not only through the hook and template methods as we just saw, but also through the concept of pluggable objects in a composition approach.

NOTE *A term has been used in several technical papers to describe this framework approach as the "Hollywood principle" or the "don't call me, I'll call you principle." Such terms describe the characteristic that a template method in the framework calls the application code instead of the application code calling the framework. However, this terminology is somewhat misleading. The reason such terms are used to describe a framework is that they stress that it is the template method in the framework that calls the implemented abstract methods and controls the process flow in the application. In most cases, the application always calls the framework. Although it may appear that a template method is calling the application code, it is the application code that first invokes the template method.*

The Composition Approach

The inheritance approach is a simple approach to enabling hot spots inside a framework, but because developers must know what data and methods are available inside the parent class as well as their interrelations in order to implement the abstract method, they often are required to have a very detailed knowledge of a framework in order to use it.

For example, in the NewYorkBusiness class, as easy as the implementation of CalculateStateTax and CalculateFedTax may seem, in order to implement these two methods, the developer must know that there is a protected float variable called income and that its value must have been set somewhere else prior to invoking either of the CalculateXxxTax methods. Also, exposing the internal details of the child class diminishes the encapsulation of the parent class, which can lead to the uncontrolled access and modification of the class's internal state by developers that are beyond the intent of parent class's designer. The following code segment shows the filling of the "hot spot" in an inheritance approach:

```
public class NewYorkBusiness : BasicBusiness
{
    protected override float CalculateStateTax()
    {
        return income * 0.1F;
    }
    protected override float CalculateFedTax()
    {
        return income * 0.2F;
    }
}
```

As you can imagine, as the method grows more complicated, developers may need to reference more data and methods inside the parent class and understand what the consequences are of setting the values of such data and calling such methods to change the overall state of the object.

Requiring developers to know such detailed information about the parent class stretches their learning curve for the framework and is burdensome to developers using the framework. One way to keep developers from having to learn the internal details of framework components is to define the hot spots as a set of interfaces that are well connected with the framework. Developers can create components by implementing such interfaces, which can then be plugged into the framework to customize its behaviors.

Pluggable Components

To enable hot spots through pluggable components, the application framework must first define the interface for the hot spot. An interface describes a set of methods a class must implement to be considered compatible with the interface. The interface describes what the methods inside the class look like, such as the method names, the number of parameters, and the parameter types, but not how they should be implemented. The following is an example of an interface definition in C#:

```
public interface ICalculateTax
{
    float CalculateStateTax();
    float CalculateFedTax();
    float Income
    {
        get;set;
    }
}
```

You can then create application components that support ICalculateTax by creating a concrete class and implementing every method/property defined in the interface, such as the NewYorkBusiness class shown as follows:

```
public class NewYorkBusiness : ICalculateTax
{
    private float income;
    public float Income
    {
        get { return income; }
```

```
        set { income = value; }
    }
    public float CalculateStateTax()
    {
        return income * 0.1F;
    }
    public float CalculateFedTax()
    {
        return income * 0.2F;
    }
}
```

Because NewYorkBusiness implements the ICalculateTax interface, it now becomes compatible with or pluggable to any hot spot in the framework that can work with the ICalculateTax interface. With the help of interfaces, application developers can compose the custom behaviors into the underlying framework by loading the pluggable application components in the hot spots of the framework. Figure 2-6 illustrates how the composition approach enables the hot spots in the application framework.

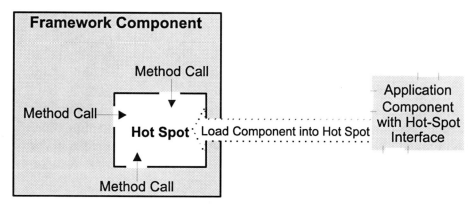

Figure 2-6. A pluggable application component

In using the composition approach to enable the hot spot, developers will need to create pluggable application components that have matching interfaces with the hot spot in the framework. The developer can then plug the component into the hot spot by binding the application component and the framework component together.

This composition approach for enabling hot spots is based on yet another GOF design pattern called "strategy." You will learn more about the strategy pattern in Chapter 5.

Now let's convert the tax example so that the hot spot is enabled through the composition approach. First, we need to modify the `BasicBusiness` component. Instead of making it an abstract class, this time we will make it a concrete class. The following code snippet shows the new `BasicBusiness` component:

```
public class BasicBusiness
{
    public void ReportTax (ICalculateTax calculator)
    {
        float sTax = calculator.CalculateStateTax();
        float fTax = calculator.CalculateFedTax();
        bool ok = CheckBankBalance(sTax + fTax);
        if (!ok)
        {
            FileBankruptcy();
        }
        else
        {
            SendMoneyToGov(sTax + fTax);
        }
    }
}
```

The `ReportTax` method now takes an input parameter of `ICalculateTax` type. This input parameter will provide the custom tax calculation mechanism, which is also a hot spot in the `BasicBusiness` framework component. As you can see, by plugging in the custom application component, we effectively "fill up" the hot spot with application-specific business logic/knowledge.

The following example shows how we can plug the application component into the framework from the application code:

```
ICalculateTax nyBusiness = new NewYorkBusiness();
ICalculateTax caBusiness = new CaliforniaBusiness();

BasicBusiness basic= new BasicBusiness();
basic.ReportTax(nyBusiness);
basic.ReportTax(caBusiness);
```

In the previous example, each `ReportTax` call will result in a different outcome, since the framework component is bound to a different `ICalculateTax` component on each call.

In order for the framework component to load the pluggable object, you can either use the approach described in the previous example or store the application component's type information inside a configuration file, then load the appropriate component through reflection and plug it right into the framework component dynamically.

Identifying and enabling common spots and hot spots are the central themes of application framework development. Depending on how you enable such spots, you create either a white-box framework, a black-box framework, or a gray-box framework.

White-Box Frameworks

A white-box framework is a framework that consists of abstract classes. Adapting a white-box framework requires developers to create concrete classes that inherit the abstract classes in the framework. White-box frameworks take on the inheritance approach to enable their hot spots. Figure 2-7 shows a white-box framework.

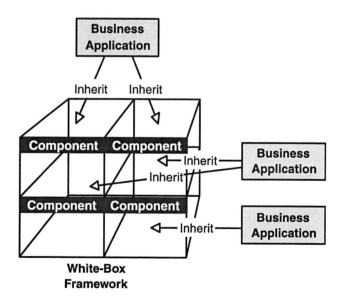

Figure 2-7. A white-box framework

A white-box framework is relatively easy to develop. You can start developing the abstract class by looking at some of the similar applications you have developed before, identifying their hot spots, and making them the abstract methods. When developing white-box frameworks, you are making an assumption about the pattern of process flow involved in each framework component through the template method. You often base these assumptions on business-domain expertise and prior business-application development experience. As developers start adapting the white-box framework, they need to program only a small number of "override" methods in the derived class and don't have to worry about the overall process flow or how the abstract method is used inside the framework. This allows developers to focus solely on the abstract method without worrying about how the methods they are overriding relate to the rest of the framework.

Of course, there is a tradeoff in almost everything. White-box frameworks are very easy to design and develop, but they have their drawbacks. The first drawback is their inflexibility. In a white-box framework, when you determine how the process flow occurs inside a component through the template method you effectively hard-code the process flow and coordination logic in the component. Although developers who adapt the component may change the logic of the component's hot spot, the overall process flow is nevertheless fixed. This "hard-coded" process flow is reflected as inflexibility when a change in business rules triggers a change in the process flow in the component. Because the process flow and coordination logic are fixed, you would have to update the existing component or write a new one that carries the process flow and coordination logic.

Another drawback of a white-box framework is that it often requires the developer to know many implementation details of the framework component. As the developer is implementing the abstract method in the framework component, he or she often needs to reference the abstract class's methods and variables in the implementation code. This makes the understanding of internal details of the framework component an important prerequisite for correctly adapting the component.

A black-box framework often takes a composition-style approach to solving some of the challenges of the white box, but it has its own share of drawbacks.

Black-Box Frameworks

Black-box frameworks consist of concrete and ready-to-use classes and services. Although developers can extend the existing framework components to achieve customization in a black-box framework, they more often adapt the framework by combining a number of components to create the desired result. A black-box framework may contain many common spots, and it employs the composition approach to enable its hot spots. Figure 2-8 illustrates a black-box framework.

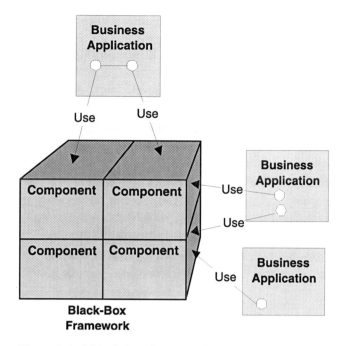

Figure 2-8. A black-box framework

Because of the composition approach in a black-box framework, it provides a greater range of flexibility than that of a white-box framework. Developers can pick and choose different components to achieve specific application requirements with infinite possibilities. Unlike white-box frameworks, where a developer often needs to know the detailed implementation of the framework component for adaptation, black-box frameworks consist of components that hide their internal implementation. Adaptation of such components is done through well-defined interfaces, such as certain public methods and properties. Developers need to be familiar with only these public members in order to use the framework.

Compared with white-box frameworks, black-box frameworks are harder to develop. Encapsulating business-domain expertise into components that are generic enough to be used in many application scenarios is not an easy task. Encapsulating too much will lead the domain expertise inside the component becoming less fit in many application scenarios. Encapsulating too little will lead to developers having to work with a large number of components and more complex coordination logic in order to build the application.

The extra flexibility of black-box frameworks doesn't come for free. When using a black-box framework, developers must implement their own process flow and coordination logic needed to link multiple components together. Because developers now control how and what components need to work together, they are responsible for the extra workload on "wiring" the components together along with the extra flexibility provided by the black-box framework. In contrast, white-box frameworks automatically handle the "wiring" for you in the template methods of their components.

Although developers don't have to deal with learning the internal implementation of the abstract class as they do with a white-box framework, they do have to be familiar with a greater number of components and their use when using a black-box framework, since the developer now has more "moving" parts to deal with in order to combine them into something they need.

When developing an application framework, there is no requirement that the framework contain either all abstract classes or all concrete classes. In fact, neither pure white-box nor black-box frameworks are practical in the real world. Having a mix of both the inheritance approach and composition approach gives you the freedom to use whatever approach is best for the design of a particular component. By mixing white-box frameworks and black-box frameworks, you effectively create a gray-box framework.

Gray-Box Frameworks

Gray-box frameworks take both inheritance and composition approach, is usually made up with combination of abstract classes and concrete classes. The approach of enabling its common spots and hot spots is determined on a component-by-component basis. Figure 2-9 shows a gray-box framework.

> **NOTE** *Because a concrete class that contains virtual methods can either be used directly or inherited by another class that overrides the virtual methods to alter its behavior, it is possible for a gray-box framework to consist of only concrete classes, as long as the approach taken by the classes is a combination of composition and inheritance.*

In the real world, the application frameworks you will be developing will most likely be gray-box frameworks. The decision whether a given components will follow the inheritance approach or composition approach is decided by which approach is best suited for what the component is trying to accomplish and how developers will likely use the component in their business applications.

As we are choosing the inheritance approach, the composition approach, or a mix of the two, we should consistently keep in mind the tradeoffs and implications for performance, maintenance, and usability with each approach.

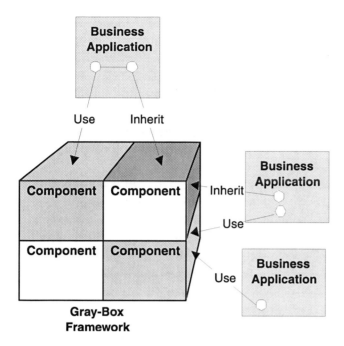

Figure 2-9. A gray-box framework

From the performance point of view, the composition approach tends to be slower than the inheritance approach, primarily because of the extra components it has to load and access at run time to produce the desired results. As you are gathering the features from multiple components, you may also add a number of extra calls to bridge different components. In the inheritance approach, however, an inherited class often contains most of the required features within itself, hence reducing the number of objects the program needs to create and access to produce the same results and eliminating as well much of the extra code that would be needed to bridge different components if the composition approach were used.

Maintenance is another area in which we see the tradeoffs in both approaches. In the composition approach, developers work with a set of highly decoupled framework components, which makes their application more adaptive to changes, and hence more flexible and extensible. However, after the application is deployed, those who provide postproduction support will have to deal with many more "moving parts," which leads to extra maintenance effort. For example, a change in a business requirement may result in the modification of framework components. With a composition approach, such requirement changes may potentially affect a series of framework components that participate in a certain business feature, since the business requirement is supported by the collaboration of a number of components. Such changes in multiple components may also multiply the effort in testing and deployment of the application framework. On the other hand, the inheritance approach may be less flexible than the composition approach, but in compensation, it introduces fewer moving parts. When business features are served by a hierarchy of classes, a change in business requirements can often be resolved with changes to far fewer classes on the hierarchical tree. Of course, the real maintenance cost of your application framework depends on the design of the framework as well as the type of business-requirement changes involved. But generally speaking, you have less overhead on maintenance if you have fewer moving parts to deal with.

Usability is yet another area you need to consider in designing the application framework. The framework component that takes on the inheritance approach usually hides the complex coordination logic and process flow inside the parent class or abstract class, so the developer often needs only to implement or override a few methods to achieve the desired result. Hence, inheritance provides very good usability as long as developers aren't required to learn overwhelming details of the parent class or abstract class they inherit. Usability for the composition approach, on the other hand, depends considerably on how much composition developers have to support to achieve certain results. Having a set of highly decoupled components often requires developers to learn and code their own coordination logic and process flow to wire such components together to produce the desired results. However, if you are willing to sacrifice flexibility and create a few coarse-grained components so that developers need to work with only a small number of components to get what they want, then the framework will become easier to use and developers will be much more productive, since the composition approach significantly reduces the coordination logic developers have to learn and write.

As you approach many framework design decisions, you must keep in mind that there is no silver bullet. There is often a tradeoff between different approaches. It is your job to decide how to balance them and create an application framework that fits your objectives.

Design Patterns

As you are architecting and developing the application framework, you will often run into design challenges on recurring scenarios, such as how to improve handling of changes to the process flow and how to improve application-specific customization. Design patterns, which describe the solution to common software development problems, can assist you in solving some of these common problems in developing an application framework. Many commonly used design patterns are documented in the classic book *Design Patterns: Elements of Reusable Object-Oriented Software*, by Erich Gamma, Richard Helm, Ralph Johnson, and John Vlissides, the "gang of four" (GOF). Some design patterns are especially useful in application framework development. The following list describes some of these patterns and the problems they can solve:

Strategy: a design that handles the variation of algorithms in the application. It allows the developer to customize the framework by "plug and play"-ing different application-specific algorithms.

Bridge: a design that decouples the abstraction and implementation in the application. It allows developers to provide different implementations for part of the application without affecting other parts of the application.

Decorator: a design that provides a layer approach in processing data. It allows developers to easily assemble multiple components to process data.

Observer: a design that provides a publish–subscribe communication model. It allows developers to disperse information easily to multiple objects.

Mediator: a design that keeps objects from referring to each other explicitly. It allows developers to create loosely coupled communication between different objects.

Template method: a design that provides the skeleton of the algorithm it operates. It allows developers to define process flow and coordination logic without having to define how the algorithm is implemented.

Visitor: a design that lets you define a new operation without changing the existing ones. It allows developers to decouple an operation from the coordination logic that is constantly changing.

Singleton: a design that ensures that only one instance of the class is created. It allows developers to have better control of the creation of the object.

Abstract factory: a design that provides an interface for creating families of objects without specifying their concrete classes. It allows developers to reduce the reference to concrete classes throughout the application, and hence reduce the amount of code changed when the concrete classes change.

For the rest of the book, we will look at how these design patterns can help us develop our application framework and how these patterns are implemented in .NET.

Summary

In this chapter, you have learned about processes and techniques of application framework development. We first looked at the different layers that make up the application framework and how each layer is related to the others. Then we looked at the framework development process, which involves analysis, design, development, and stabilization stages in an iterative fashion and specific tasks involved in each of these stages. Following that, you learned about the several approaches in framework development, such as white-box, black-box, and gray-box frameworks. We also looked at some key framework development techniques through discussion of common-spot, hot-spot, and design patterns. For the rest of book, we will consider how to actually design and implement an application framework through examples. We will use a sample framework as reference to show you how you can develop your application framework using .NET technology and design patterns.

CHAPTER 3

An Overview of the Simplified Application Framework

IN THE PREVIOUS TWO CHAPTERS we discussed some of the key concepts regarding application frameworks. Now we will begin to develop some concrete examples for you to test your understanding as well as to provide you a jump start for applying these ideas in a real-world situation. To this end, I have created a sample application framework project to provide a concrete view of what a framework look like and what it offers to application development.

What Is SAF?

I began brainstorming about this sample framework and gathering some ideas from existing software products and my previous experience. I finally decided to create a framework for business-to-business (B2B) applications. It is relatively easy to identify the common services used in most of customized applications, but it is more difficult to identify some of the domain-specific framework components, since they are visible only to those who have an extensive understanding of the business domain. To make this book complete, I felt that I had to come up with a good example for domain-specific components that are easy to understand. I had worked with the Microsoft BizTalk Server (a server product Microsoft first released in 2000 that allows companies to quickly set up a system to exchange and process business documents with their business partners) on several projects and written a book on it, and I have a number of ideas about what is involved in a typical B2B application, so I chose the B2B application as the model on which to base the sample framework. I jotted down a list of a number of items that are commonly found in B2B applications and used it as part of the sample framework I created for this book.

I named this framework Simplified Application Framework, or SAF. My goal was to create a framework project that was easy to understand, with just enough code to achieve its intended goals and get my points across.

SAF consists of two groups of framework components. The first group consists of generic cross-domain components, while the second group contains the domain-specific components. The first group includes some of the generic components such as class factory service, caching service, and event notification services. These services are commonly found in every application regardless of the business domain, and little domain-specific knowledge resides in such components. The second group, on the other hand, consists of the domain-specific components that are commonly found in a B2B application. The essence of a B2B application is the exchange and processing of business documents among business partners. A component that makes possible the application of multiple processing layers on the document object would be very useful in development of many B2B applications. One of the SAF components achieves precisely that goal.

In Chapter 2 we looked at the different layers that exist in an application framework. SAF has a similar layer structure. Figure 3-1 illustrates the SAF's layer structure and the components that belong to each layer.

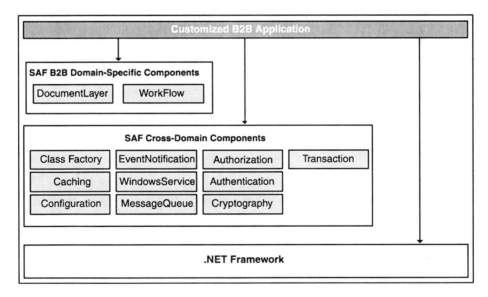

Figure 3-1. Layer structure of SAF

At the bottom of the structure is the .NET framework, which consists of sets of classes that provides the fundamental functionalities on which every. NET application is built. In fact, every .NET application will have the .NET framework as the lowest layer of the structure. The layer on top of the .NET framework is the home of SAF cross-domain components. There are currently ten components that provide common services in many .NET applications. We will briefly look at each of them later in this chapter. I will also use the next ten chapters to discuss each of the components in detail. The layer on top of the SAF cross-domain component layer is the home of SAF B2B domain-specific components. The components in this layer are specialized components that target B2B applications. The very top layer is the customized application layer. It is where the customized application is located. Developers create their applications by coding against the .NET framework, SAF cross-domain components, and SAF B2B components.

As illustrated in Figure 3-1, SAF contains ten foundation components and two domain components. I want to use it as a model to show you how to design and develop an application framework by giving an in-depth discussion on each of these twelve framework components. In the next 12 chapters, I will talk about these components by listing the goals and benefits for each component. I will then talk about some of the .NET technologies that are involved in developing these components. For example, I will explain .NET remoting and .NET reflection when we cover the class factory service, XML when covering the caching service, ServicedComponent when covering the transaction service, etc. Some of the .NET technologies used by the framework components are basic, while others are a bit tricky; either way, I will try to give a concise tutorial on those technologies before diving into the actual code of the framework. Design patterns are commonly used inside frameworks to solve many of their design problems. They are wonderful things that allow you to unravel the intricacies of relationships among different pieces inside the application. Many of SAF's components rely on design patterns as their underlying object-oriented techniques to make them more flexible and customizable. As you read through the chapters, you will learn about these design patterns, see their implementation in the SAF components, and most importantly, understand why using a particular pattern makes sense for a particular SAF component.

SAF Foundation Components

The rest of this chapter will be a quick rundown of each of the SAF components.

The ClassFactory Service

As developers are developing applications using the business class they have created, we want to reduce the need for them to specify the concrete business class as much as possible. The SAF.ClassFactory service allows developers to obtain a concrete object without specifying the concrete business class in their code during the development of their applications, thereby reducing and possibly eliminating the code changes associated with changes in the underlying business object. Because

ClassFactory extracts the creation of business objects from the programs that use these business objects, we can now also add special object instantiation logic into the class factory service, hence alter the behavior of the object without significant code changes and extra attention from developers.

Two of the major .NET technologies used in SAF.ClassFactory to achieve such goals are *.NET reflection* and *.NET remoting.* The *abstract factory* and *singleton* patterns are used as the blueprint for this framework component. We will cover its design and implementation in Chapter 4.

The Caching Service

SAF.Cache provides the object-caching ability for the framework. During application development, developers will often want to boost the application's performance by eliminating excessive object creation within the application. They often need to store existing business objects and retrieve them later to access their properties and methods. The need for object caching is universal across all types of business applications. Creating an easy-to-use object caching mechanism will eliminate the effort for developers to "roll their own" object-caching techniques. By creating a caching service as part of a framework component, we are able not only to reduce the developers' workload, but also to standardize the way object caching is performed throughout the application.

SAF.Cache provides an object-caching service for the framework. It has two major features: First, it has an XML flavor to it that gives the cached objects a hierarchical structure. This feature allows developers to manage the cached object more easily. Second, it has a built-in hook that allows developers to change its caching behavior and an algorithm to fit specific business requirements without changing the framework code.

Some of the major .NET technologies used in SAF.Cache are XML and XPath supports in the .NET framework. We will look at how SAF.Cache is implemented using these technologies as well as the strategy design pattern in Chapter 5.

The Configuration Service

SAF.Configuration provides a consolidated service for providing application-specific configuration information at runtime. A business application is often composed of several separate applications and is perhaps developed by multiple teams. Establishing a standard configuration storage and retrieval mechanism helps reduce the management overhead and make the code easier to read, since patterns of retrieving configuration information are the same across different part of the application.

SAF.Configuration is built on top of the .NET configuration and provides an easy way for developers to define application-specific configurations. SAF.Configuration enables developers to consolidate and centralize their configuration settings. SAF.Configuration also introduces the concept of strongly typed configuration objects, which should simplify reading configurations within an application's code.

Some of the major .NET technologies used in SAF.Configuration are .NET configuration file/concepts. We will learn more about this configuration component as well as strongly typed configuration objects in Chapter 6.

The EventNotification Service

The EventNotification service provides an event-notification model for business applications. It is very common that one part of application's actions are based on events fired from another part of the application, usually from a separate process or remote system. Without predefined event-notification architecture, each team of developers would create its own event-notification system. This would result in a difficult integration process among the different event-notification implementations from separate teams. SAF.EventNotification solves this problem by providing an event-notification service as a component at the framework level. It reduces the need for each development team to create its own event-notification implementation. Because each development team can now use the same standard in sending and receiving the fired events, extra integration effort will not be required during development.

SAF.EventNotification is built on top of two .NET technologies: delegates and .NET remoting. There are two major goals for SAF.EventNotification. First, it should provide developers a standard way to send and receive events across process boundaries. Second, it should eliminate integration effort when multiple applications are involved in event notification. SAF.EventNotification's architecture is based on the "observer" and "mediator" design patterns, which we will learn in depth in Chapter 7.

The WindowService Service

One of the most common ways to start and continue running an application on a Windows platform is through a window service. For example, you can create a window service to host a listener object that constantly watches incoming data at a message queue, network port, etc. Window services integrate very nicely with the service console under the administrative tools and can be configured to automatically start when the operating system is launched. However, for each window service, there is a service installation project that has to be created and deployed. If your application requires multiple window services, the result will be additional overhead to the development and deployment effort. SAF.WindowService solves this problem by creating a consolidated window service that allows the developer to add additional background processes through a simple change to a configuration file. With SAF.WindowService, developers are no longer required to create and deploy multiple window service projects and its installation projects. Instead, they can simply create multiple business classes and modify the settings in the configuration file. These business classes will be loaded and will run continuously in the background after system startup.

The key .NET technologies used in SAF.WindowService are .NET window services, .NET reflection, and .NET threading. The template method design pattern is also used to create the hot spots where developers can plug in their own business logics for the running services. We will cover them in depth in Chapter 8.

The MessageQueue Service

Message queues are one of the most underrated technologies in application development. Its ability to decouple the client and server applications allows you to build an asynchronous application that is highly scalable and fault tolerant. Message queues are also commonly used in application integration development where applications in heterogonous environments send and receive data via message queues. In order to take advantage of message queues, developers are often required to learn different sets of APIs associated with various message queue technologies, such as MSMQ, MQSeries, and in-house custom queuing technologies. The SAF.MessageQueue service provides one set of APIs that developers can learn to program against message queues regardless of the type of underlying queuing technology. The SAF.MessageQueue service also allows you to plug in your own implementation of the queuing mechanism without having to make developers learn new sets of APIs.

SAF.MessageQueue uses the System.Messaging namespace to access MSMQ and .NET's interop feature to access the MQSeries's COM DLL. It relies on the Bridge design pattern to decouple the client interface from the underlying implementation of various queuing technologies. We will look at how SAF.MessageQueue works in depth in Chapter 9.

The Authorization Service

Authorization is a process of determining whether a caller may access a specific underlying resource based on the caller's identity or group. The SAF.Authorization service provides developers an easy way to add an authorization check to the application without coupling the security code to the application code. By using SAF.Authorization, developers can perform security checks, such as role-level checks or user-level checks on methods simply by adding the attributes on the methods. It provides a declarative security feature similar to that of COM+ security, in which you can define the security attributes of a component as a separate layer on top of the component.

Unlike the out-of-box .NET security attribute, which requires you to define the user/group access permission inside the application code, SAF.Authorization is designed to remove such a requirement. Using SAF.Authorization, developers can change the security permissions of a business object by modifying the settings of a configuration file without any change to the application code.

The technologies used to implement the SAF.Authorization service include .NET declarative security, .NET attributes, and .NET reflection. The SAF.Authorization service also allows developers to change the way the security permission check is performed through the use of strategy patterns. You will learn more about the SAF.Authorization service in Chapter 10.

Authentication Service

Authentication is the process of identifying who the caller is. The ability to identify a caller is a prerequisite of any security feature in an application. An application often consists of many subsystems, and each has its own way of identifying a particular caller, usually with a separate set of credentials such as user name and password. This presents a problem when a caller's request has to go through multiple subsystems. The call would have to carry and present multiple sets of credentials at every step of the way. This often adds a significant development burden and makes each subsystem heavily coupled with the authentication logic of other subsystems within an application. The SAF.Authentication service solves this problem by creating a single-sign-on feature for the whole application. With SAF.Authentication, the caller is no longer required to present multiple credentials. Instead, the caller needs to carry only one credential to gain access to all other applications/subsystems. SAF.Authentication performs the credential mapping on behalf of the callers and eliminates the need for developers to code such logic inside their applications.

SAF.Authentication achieves this single-sign-on feature through technologies such as the .NET security Web service. You will learn more detail about this service in Chapter 11.

The Cryptography Service

SAF.Cryptography provides the data encryption and decryption service for the application. Whether it is the password or data that needs to be transmitted over the network, application developers often need to encrypt certain sensitive data within the application. SAF.Cryptography offers a simple tool developers can use to achieve such goals without extensive study of security-related technologies

SAF.Cryptography uses .NET Cryptography, Web Service Enhancement, and .NET remoting. You will learn about it in Chapter 12.

The Transaction Service

SAF.Transaction provides a flexible way for developers to make an application transactional. Distributed transactions are supported through COM+ components in .NET. However, it is difficult to implement transactions across multiple method calls without rearranging the flow of the method calls and creating an excessive number of COM+ components. SAF.Transaction makes transaction support across multiple method calls easier and keeps the number of COM+ components down regardless of the number of transactions that need to be supported within the application.

SAF.Transaction is implemented using COM+ in .NET. We will look at the SAF.Transaction service in depth as well as the ServicedComponent class and other COM+ features in the .NET framework in Chapter 13.

SAF B2B Domain-Specific Components

I will introduce the last two framework components in the last two chapters of this book. The business requirement for this B2B application is very simple. I want to create an application that can accept an incoming document from a business partner over the Internet, and then apply several services to it to prepare it for internal business processes, some of which are data decryption, document schema transformation, and document logging. Then the document will be passed to a workflow or a series of business tasks to be processed. After the document has been processed, the B2B application may generate an outgoing document or receipt and send it back to the original sender via various protocols. Figure 3-2 illustrates a high-level process flow for this B2B application.

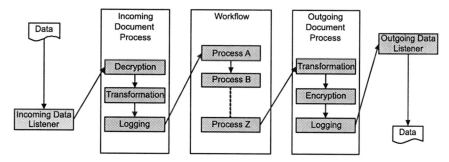

Figure 3-2. Process flow for the B2B application built on SAF

This typical B2B process diagram consists of three major categories: incoming document process, workflow process, and outgoing document process.

The incoming document process consists of a series of document processing layers that apply a number of services to incoming documents. Some examples of document processing layers are document decryption, document schema transformation, document logging, and services that inject some application-specific data into the document.

The concept of outgoing document process is very similar to that of the incoming document process, except that services are applied to the document in reverse order. However, this certainly doesn't always have to be the case. Services that apply to the document can be added, removed, or reordered according to the application's business requirements.

The real "business" tasks such as updating inventory, processing new orders, and updating databases are preformed inside the workflow process. Processing of a business document often touches multiple applications and systems inside an enterprise. Being able to identify the participating applications and link them all together to automate the process of a particular business document is the central task of the workflow process.

Because B2B applications can more or less fit into this model, we can use it as a blueprint to develop some domain-specific framework components for B2B applications that would make B2B applications easier to develop, yet be flexible enough to react to changes in business rules and requirements more gracefully.

SAF has two domain-specific framework components for B2B applications: the DocumentLayer service and Workflow service.

The DocumentLayer Service

The SAF.DocumentLayer service provides developers with an easy way to create individual document process layers that are decoupled from one another, yet work together to process incoming documents as well as outgoing documents. Using the SAF.DocumentLayer service, developers can easily define in a configuration file how a particular document should be processed through each layer. As new processing layers are introduced into the system, developers can also inject the new processes into the existing layers through the configuration setting changes without touching the existing application code.

The core of the SAF.DocumentLayer is the decorator design pattern, which gives you the ability to apply services to an object in a layer-by-layer fashion. We will take a closer look at this framework component in Chapter 14.

The Workflow Service

As a business document is passing through a B2B application, many business components will participate in processing the document. You have to manage the coordination among these business components to ensure that the document is processed in the correct order. As the number of these business components increases, such coordination logic will become more complicated, because more components need to be wired to each other to make everything work. Both the components and the sequence of components involved in processing a business document can change dramatically as the underlying business rules for processing the documents change.

The SAF.Workflow service reduces the complexity of such processes by decoupling the business logic for processing the document from the coordination logic that controls the sequence of the process flow. If a rule changes or a new rule is added for the way multiple components collaborate with each other, we only have to change the coordination logic of the workflow. On the other hand, if a rule changes on how one particular component should process the document, we then only have to change that particular component.

SAF.Workflow is based on the visitor design pattern to separate the workflow's business logic and coordination logic, and make it easy to introduce the new coordination logic and business component into the workflow. We will look in detail at SAF.Workflow and its implementation in Chapter 15.

Testing Projects for SAF

Each of the twelve framework components in SAF is accompanied by an executable C# project that demonstrates the purpose of the framework component as well as how the component can be used in the application. After reading each chapter, I encourage you to load the testing project into VS.NET and test it out. You will also find a "code walkthrough" section on the key code segments as I talk about each framework component, but nothing better explains the code than running it through debug mode and stepping into each line of code to see exactly what is happening behind the cover. The source code for each framework component is located in an appropriately named folder. For example, source code for the SAF.ClassFactory component is located in the "SAF.ClassFactory" folder. The testing project for SAF.ClassFactory is located in the "Test.SAF.ClassFactory" folder.

If you want to look at the source code of all the SAF components at once, you can load the solution file "SAF.sln" in VS.NET, which will load the entire SAF.* project into the IDE.

A Few Words About the SAF Source Code

SAF was created as a companion to the book. I created SAF to show you different services you can develop in an application framework and to use it as an example of a framework implementation that shows different .NET technologies and design patterns that you can leverage when developing your own frameworks. I have tried to keep the code as concise as possible so that it is easy to read and understand. I omitted a lot of code for exception handling, thread safety, and various validations that would normally be required for an application in a production environment. SAF is intended for educational purposes and not for actual production use. However, you are welcome to use SAF as a starting point and modify it to fit your particular scenario. There is no restriction on how you can use and modify the SAF source code provided with this book.

Summary

In this chapter we have presented a brief overview of SAF, describing its purpose and architecture and how it can be used to build a customized application. We also looked at each individual component inside SAF. Through a brief introduction to the ten cross-domain framework components and two domain-specific framework components, you have learned about the idea behind each component and its added values, as well as the .NET technologies and design patterns involved in these components. In the next chapter, we will look at the first component of SAF: the `ClassFactory` service.

CHAPTER 4

Class Factories

ONE OF THE THEMES of object-oriented programming is to identify the responsibilities involved in an application and decouple the tasks that are to carry out different responsibilities. Decoupling tasks based on responsibilities can insulate us from a possible chain reaction when change occurs. The difficult part is to identity boundaries between responsibilities and where we can stop decoupling. The drawback of decoupling responsibilities is the increased effort in establishing connections between the decoupled parts. Hence, application architects need to find a balance between decoupling too much, which makes the application harder to write, and decoupling too little, which makes the application inflexible to changes and difficult to extend. Besides its affect on the development effort, the degree of decoupling in the application also affects the postproduction maintenance effort. For instance, an application that is less decoupled usually contains fewer moving parts that maintenance and support staff have to deal with.

In a simple scenario, in which a client application calls a business component, how many responsibilities do you see in that picture? It is easy to see that there are at least two. The first responsibility is owned by the business component, which is in charge of performing some predefined service upon request. The second responsibility is owned by the client application, which is in charge of commanding the business component to perform certain specific tasks by calling methods on the business component. However, there is one more possible responsibility in the picture. Who is in charge of preparing the business object to service the clients? We can name this extra "thing," which gets the object ready for the server, a *class factory*. In this chapter, we will talk about why we need a class factory and how to create one.

Motivation and Goals

Identifying responsibilities is a matter of human judgment. The simple action of writing may be considered a single responsibility, but you can't say that I am wrong if I see it as two separate responsibilities: one for muscle movement and another for the cerebral activity that decides what to write. Or I might see it as combination of three separate responsibilities: muscle movement, nerve signal transmission, and cerebral activity.

Creating a class factory is not justified simply because we see a certain activity as a separate responsibility on some logical level. No matter how lofty the logical and theoretical concepts, they must eventually descend to earth at the end of the day to meet the low-level application code. We must determine how exactly a class factory can help us build a better application. We will talk about class factories using SAF.ClassFactory as an example.

There are three major goals that we want SAF.ClassFactory to achieve:

- Reduce the need to specify the concrete class.

- Hide the complexity of object creation from the developers.

- Make the creation of objects, remote or otherwise, transparent with respect to location, version, and culture. In other words, the class factory should resolve class location, version, and culture based on the underlying configuration.

The first goal is to remove the class reference of the concrete class from the application code as much as possible. Normally, we create an object and call its services in the following fashion:

```
BusinessObject bo =new BusinessObject();
bo.DoWork();
```

BusinessObject is a concrete class. This means that if we want to replace BusinessObject later with something else, for example, SpecialBusinessObject, we would have to replace the name of the class and the variable type throughout the application. It is impossible to completely remove a concrete class name when you need to access the methods that belong to the specific concrete class exclusively. However, you should try to reduce direct references to concrete classes as much as possible so that code changes are minimal when there happen to be some changes to the concrete class. We will see an example of this later in the chapter.

The second goal is to hide information. The BusinessObject example we saw earlier requires no special catering to create an object. It has a default constructor and returns an object instance when we call new BusinessObject(). There are situations in which quite a lot of work is involved in creating an instance of a class. There are classes that may need additional information to create an object. For example, a database connection class normally needs the database name, user name, and password information before the connection object can be created properly. You want application developers to concentrate on the business logic rather than pay too much attention to such infrastructure-level information. Through the class factory, you can now have one place to create objects that may require additional initialization information before the object is ready for use. Because developers no longer need to write repetitive object creation code, you can also benefit from code reuse. For example, you can get an object ready with one line of code from the client side no matter how complicated it is to set up the object:

```
IBusinessObject bo =
ClassFactoryService.GetBusinessObject.GetComplexBusinessObject();
```

For the rest the chapter, we will look at how SAF.ClassFactory is implemented in .NET and some of the design patterns it uses.

.NET Technology Overview

SAF.ClassFactory is implemented using the following two key .NET concepts:

- .NET reflection;

- .NET remoting.

.NET reflection provides an alternative way for creating an object and calling its methods. It is cumbersome to code your application using reflection, and you need to write a lot more code using reflection to achieve something that can be done with much less conventional code. However, putting reflection code in the right place in your application will significantly boost its flexibility.

.NET remoting is the technology for accessing objects located in different AppDomains that are either local or remote. It provides features to .NET components similar to those that DCOM provides to COM components. Compared to DCOM, .NET remoting gives you more control over network transport, message customization, and the way objects are created on the remote server when calls are made. Along with the extra flexibility come the extra configuration effort and knowledge needed to make .NET remoting work.

.NET Reflection

To better explain what .NET reflection offers you, let's first look at the following two ways to achieve the same result:

```
//The conventional way to call an object.
BusinessObject bo =new BusinessObject();
bo.DoWork();


//The .NET reflection way to call an object.
Assembly assm = Assembly.Load("TestApp");
Type objType = assm.GetType("TestApp.BusinessObject");
object objInstance = Activator.CreateInstance(objType);
objType.InvokeMember("DoWork",BindingFlags.InvokeMethod, null, objInstance,null);
```

The first block of code is something we have seen thousands of times. The second block of code achieves the exact same thing as the first block: create a BusinessObject instance and make a call on its DoWork() method.

You should always try to stay away from using reflection to create objects and making method calls unless you have some special reasons for it (I will show you a special reason next). Being able to show off your technical expertise to your colleagues by using more complex and fancier code than necessary is not one of those special reasons.

There are several drawbacks in using reflection. The biggest drawback besides making the program harder to read is that you remove the ability for the language compiler to type check the objects in your application. For example, if the method is named Dowork() instead of DoWork() and you are calling bo.DoWork(), the code compilation will fail. This allows you to identify bugs or problems at the earliest possible time. Had you used reflection to create the object and made method calls as shown in the previous example, the compiler would not be able to catch the error because the name of the object and method are of string type. The compiler would compile your program without a complaint even if you mistyped the class name or method name. You would learn of your problem until you received a nasty run-time error the first time you ran the application. Had you used Visual Studio.NET (and you should), you would also lose the Intellisense feature in the IDE when using reflection. Because you would no longer be referencing the strongly typed object in your application, you wouldn't get the dropdown list that shows the methods and data members of the object. You would end up typing in a lot more code by hand, which can be error-prone and unavoidably results in extra coding and debugging effort.

There are nonetheless special reasons for using reflection despite all these drawbacks. One of these benefits of using reflection is to provide a way of delaying specification of the concrete class until run time. Noticing that all the class names and method names in the second block of code are strings, you can replace those hard-coded strings with string variables whose values are assigned at run time. This prevents you from directly binding your application to specific concrete classes.

Before we talk about why the reflection code looks the way it does in the example just presented, let's examine what happens behind the scenes when an object is created in our .NET application. Figure 4-1 shows the AppDomain, assemblies, classes, and object instances and their relations to each other.

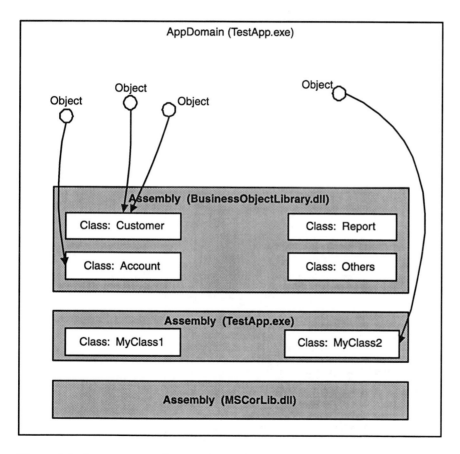

Figure 4-1. Components of an AppDomain

When we are running the application called TestApp.exe, .NET CLR will first create an AppDomain to host the TestApp.exe application. It will then start loading the assemblies that are referenced by the application into the AppDomain. MSCorLib.dll is an assembly that contains many of the classes in the System name space and its child name spaces, such as System, System.Text, and System.IO. It is an assembly that is loaded automatically in every AppDomain. CLR then loads the assembly to which the running application (TestApp.exe) belongs. Assemblies that we added to the application using the "Add Reference" feature in Visual Studio .NET are also loaded into the AppDomain. In the previous example, BusinessObject.dll is one such assembly that TestApp.exe uses. After the application is started, it may create many objects and call their methods. CLR will create objects of specified class types for the application. CLR determines what assemblies to load in order to run an application by looking into the application's manifest. You can view what's in an application's manifest using ildasm (Intermediate Language Disassembler), a tool that provides information on an application's classes, methods, and data member information as well as its application dependencies. Ildasm.exe comes with the .NET Framework SDK and is located in Program Files\Microsoft Visual Studio .NET\FrameworkSDK\Bin. Figure 4-2 shows the manifest information of TestApp.exe.

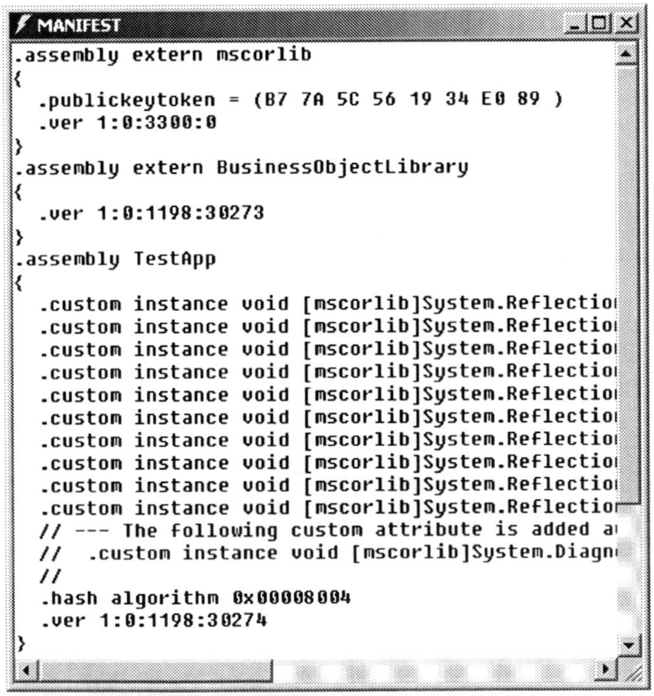

```
MANIFEST                                            _ □ ×
.assembly extern mscorlib
{
  .publickeytoken = (B7 7A 5C 56 19 34 E0 89 )
  .ver 1:0:3300:0
}
.assembly extern BusinessObjectLibrary
{
  .ver 1:0:1198:30273
}
.assembly TestApp
{
  .custom instance void [mscorlib]System.Reflectio
  .custom instance void [mscorlib]System.Reflectio
  .custom instance void [mscorlib]System.Reflectio
  .custom instance void [mscorlib]System.Reflectio
  .custom instance void [mscorlib]System.Reflectio
  .custom instance void [mscorlib]System.Reflectio
  .custom instance void [mscorlib]System.Reflectio
  .custom instance void [mscorlib]System.Reflectio
  .custom instance void [mscorlib]System.Reflectio
  .custom instance void [mscorlib]System.Reflectio
  // --- The following custom attribute is added a
  //     .custom instance void [mscorlib]System.Diagn
  //
  .hash algorithm 0x00008004
  .ver 1:0:1198:30274
}
```

Figure 4-2. The manifest data of TestApp.exe

By examining the application's manifest, CLR knows which additional assemblies used by the running application it needs to load. The text .assembly extern xxxxxxx in the manifest indicates the additional assemblies the application relies on. Notice that there is no file path for those assemblies. CLR will look for the assembly file at run time according to the predefined assembly probing rule, which you will see shortly. The other way to make CLR load the assemblies is through reflection. Let's return to the four lines of reflection code and take a closer look at what each one means.

There are four steps involved in making a method call through reflection:

- Load the assembly.

- Get the class type.

- Create an instance of the class type.

- Invoke a method call on the instance.

The System.Reflection.Assembly class has two static methods that are commonly used to load the assembly into the AppDomain: Assembly.Load(string assemblyname) and Assembly.LoadFrom(string filename).

You should use the Assembly.Load() method if you want CLR to locate the assembly with the given assembly name, which is the assembly's filename without the file extension. For example, the assembly names for TestApp.exe and BusinessObjectLibrary.dll are TestApp and BusinessObject, respectively. If the assembly is strongly named, you must provide the public key token along with the assembly name to indicate to the CLR that you want to try to load the assembly from the GAC first, followed by the application's based directory and the private path directories if not found in GAC.

> **NOTE** *If the CLR is unable to find the strongly named assembly in the GAC, it will attempt to locate the assembly in the location specified in the* /configuration/ runtime/asm:assemblyBinding:asm:dependentAssembly *element in the configuration file. If the assembly is not strongly named, you can instruct CLR to look into additional folders under the application directory by adding the additional folder name to the* /configuration/runtime/asm:assemblyBinding/asm:probing *element. By default, CLR looks only under the application-based directory and then the* \bin *folder of the application directory for the private assemblies.*

Another way to load an assembly is through `Assembly.LoadFrom(string filename)`. If the assembly you want to load is outside the CLR's probing range, you can use this method to load the assembly directly from a file location.

The first line of reflection code, `Assembly assm = Assembly.Load("TestApp");`, returns a reference to the existing `TestApp` assembly if the assembly has already been loaded. Otherwise, the CLR will load the assembly and then return the assembly reference to the caller.

The next line, `Type objType = assm.GetType("BusinessObjectLibrary.Business-Object");`, returns the class type information of a specific class in the assembly (`assm` in my case). The `GetType()` method takes quite a few overloads. In my example, I want to create a `Type` with a given type name that is Namespace + Classname (you need to provide the public key token and optional version number in addition if the class is in the GAC). You can get quite a lot of interesting information from `objType`, which is a `Type` instance that represents the `BusinessObject` class. For example, `objType.GetMethods()` returns information on all the methods in the `BusinessObject` class, and `objType.GetProperties()` returns all the property information.

You can ask CLR to create an object for a specific class type by calling the `Activator.GetInstance(Type type)` method. In our example, `objInstance = Activator.CreateInstance(objType);` is equivalent to `bo = new BusinessObject();`.

Now the last step is to invoke the `DoWork()` method. The `objType.InvokeMember()` method does the same work as `bo.DoWork()`. The `InvokeMember()` method allows you to pass in an object[] as an array of input parameters for the target method.

In relation to the class factory, `Activator.GetInstance()` and `Activator.GetObject()` are particularly interesting methods for us because they provide us a means to create objects of a specific type without knowing anything about the class at design time. Another interesting thing about these methods is that they also support creation of a remote object through .NET remoting, which we are about to look next. Using this feature, we can create a class factory service that produces remoting objects that are location-transparent to the developers who make calls to it.

.NET Remoting

One of the goals for the `SAF.ClassFactory` is the support of creation of remoting objects that are transparent to developers. In this section, I will talk about.NET remoting, which provides a mean for accessing .NET objects located remotely.

There are many reasons wanting to use a remoting call instead of a local call. One of them is to make the application more scalable. By separating the domain logic into different classes on different servers, we are able to allocate more resources to the parts of the application that need them. For example, we can move some classes that perform processing-intensive tasks onto separate servers and add extra processing power to those servers to handle the tasks, or deploy these classes onto multiple servers to create a server farm effect. We can also use remoting objects to reduce network load in our application. Many applications interact with a remote, centralized database server. If an application is interacting with the database directly, there may be a lot of data transferred back and forth across the network. However, if we deploy the classes that interact extensively with the database onto the database server or a system that has fast connections with the database server, we can reduce excessive network traffic by confining it to a fast and isolated network segment. However, in many other cases, we have to use remoting objects simply because we don't "own" the business objects and hence have no say as to where we can deploy them.

> **NOTE** *If we plan to use remoting calls to reduce traffic, we must first decide how much network traffic we are able to eliminate by adding the remoting objects to the application, since the act of adding the remoting objects themselves introduces a fixed amount of network traffic. Then we can figure out whether the remoting reduces the traffic or increases it.*

Calling remoting objects has been around for long time. Regardless of the technology, such calls all follow the same remoting model, which involves a client stub and a server proxy. The biggest difference between a local call and a remoting call is the way a method is invoked. When an object calls another object on the same machine, the caller object holds an object reference or pointer representing the memory location of the receiver object. In other words, the caller knows exactly where to find the receiver. However, this is not the case if the receiver object is located on a different machine. Because each machine allocates the objects in its memory differently, the caller has no way of finding out where to locate the receiver on another machine, since it doesn't have the "memory map" of the machine that hosts the receiver object.

General Remoting Model Overview

To solve this problem, a remoting model is developed that involves "middlemen" that convert the machine-specific information, such as the memory location of a certain object, to a predefined common protocol or rule that both caller and receiver agree upon. Figure 4-3 shows this remoting model at very high level.

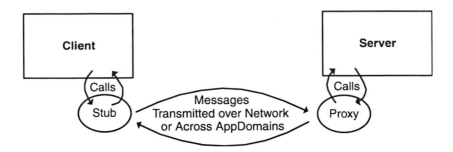

Figure 4-3. Object remoting model

Figure 4-3 show how the remoting model works. The client holds the stub, which is an object that stands in for the remote object. Because the stub has the same method signature as that of the remote object, the client can make a method call on the stub as if it were the remote object. The stub receives the calls and converts the method call to a message that is predefined and understood by the server application. The stub will send the message to the server across the network and wait for a response from the server.

On the other side, a proxy is listening on the network port for any "call" message. As soon as it hears the message sent by the stub, it will parse the message to find out who is sending it and what object and method the client wants to call. Although the stub just passes the request to the server on behalf of the client, the server proxy object has no knowledge of the actual client that made the method call. As far as the proxy object is concerned, the stub is the client.

Now, the proxy on the server side knows about which object and method the message wants to call, and it will load the requested class and create an instance of it and call its method. Because the proxy and server objects both reside on the same box, the proxy will invoke the server object via a local call. The server object will serve the method call and return a value if the method is not void. The server object treats the proxy as its client and has no knowledge of the real client and the stub on the other side of the network.

After the proxy receives the return value from the server object, it will perform a similar action to what the stub does. The proxy will convert the "method return" to a message and forward it to the stub on the other side of the network.

When the stub receives the return value in the message, it has to convert the message back to the type of the return value of the method call. At this point, the method call from the client has been blocked since the client first invoked the call, but as soon as the stub generates a "method return," it will pass it to the client, which will then continue on to the next line of code.

It is important to understand that the client object and server object do not interact with each other. Instead, they each act through their middlemen. This achieves the desired transparency when the client is making a call to the remote object. It also decouples the client from the server. Without a close tie, the underlying technology or implementation for transmitting the message and for how the message is formed can be replaced without affecting the existing application code.

.NET Remoting Model

Figure 4-3 shows a very high level overview of the remoting model. Let's go a little deeper and look at the components that are participating in a remote object invocation in the .NET world. Some of the terminology may be different, but the underlying concept of remoting is the same.

Figure 4-4 illustrates the possible participants in .NET remoting.

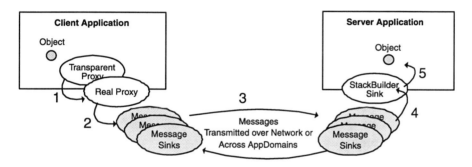

Figure 4-4. .NET remoting process flow

There are few new terminologies shown in Figure 4-4. Let's take a quick look at what they are:

Transparent proxy: As its name implies, the transparent proxy object achieves transparency in remoting calls. This means that it looks exactly like the remote object on the "surface" by possessing the same method signatures as the remote object. The client object will hold a reference to the transparent proxy and make method calls against it as if it were the real business object. When a client calls a method on a transparent proxy, the transparent proxy will create a message object (IMessage) that encapsulates the type, method name, and parameter information for the current call, and forward the message object to the real proxy.

Real proxy: The real proxy is the one that does the real "remoting" work. It will forward the message object passed in from the transparent proxy to a chain of message-processing units according to the remoting portion of the application configuration file. This chain of message-processing units, or message sinks, provides functionality such as serializing the method call request into a predefined format, applying certain user-defined actions on the message, and eventually establishing network communication with the server and sending the message out.

Message sink: These are the individual message-processing units. You can also create your own message sinks and plug them into the chain to customize the way messages are handled as they come in or go out. .NET comes with set of formatter sinks, such as the binary formatter and SOAP formatter, and transport sinks, such as the HTTP transport sink and the TCP transport sink. You can also create your own sink for remoting by modifying the remoting section of the configuration file.

StackBuilder sink: This is a special message sink that will convert the messages to method-call message on the target object's stack. Putting a "method-call" message onto an object's stack is the same as calling that object from another object located locally.

Figure 4-4 illustrates the process flow beginning with a transparent proxy, but how do you obtain a transparent proxy that stands in for the remote object in the first place? It turns out that there is another object, ObjRef, which participates in the .NET remoting process.

ObjRef is a serializable object that contains all the information the client needs to create a transparent proxy. Some of its properties, such as Url and TypeInfo, will eventually be used by the client to send a method invocation message to the remote server. ObjRef is created on the server side by either specifying a remoting object in the remoting section of the configuration file or by creating it programmatically. If you use the configuration file approach, ObjRef is automatically created for your remoting object and registered with the .NET remoting at run time. You can also create and register ObjRef manually by calling RemotingServices.Marshal(). For example:

```
BusinessObject bo = new BusinessObject();
ObjRef objRef = RemotingServices.Marshal(bo, someUrl);
```

ObjRef is created, serialized on the server side, and shipped to the client when the client is instantiating the remoting object by calling either new, Activator.GetObject(), or Activator.CreateInstance(). This process of converting an object reference to a serialized form is called *marshaling*. When the client receives the ObjRef object from the remote server, it can obtain the (transparent) proxy object by calling RemotingServices.Unmarshal(objRef). This process of converting from a serialized form to an object reference is called *unmarshaling*. Note that unmarshaling happens behind the scenes when you call the new keyword, Activator.GetObject(), or Activator.CreateInstance() to create a remote object on the client side, so you don't have to call the RemotingServices.Unmarshal() method directly from your code.

> **NOTE** *An object must extend a concrete class called* System.MarshalByRefObject *to be considered a remotable object. One of the methods of* MarshalByRefObject *is* CreateObjRef(), *which will be called by the CLR to generate an* ObjRef *object to ship to the client at run time. In other words, an object must know how to generate an* ObjRef *for itself to be considered remotable. If you forget to extend the* MarshalByRefObject *on your class, you will get an invalid cast exception when calling it from a remote client.*

After the client obtains a reference to a transparent proxy, it can continue its method calls on the transparent proxy object using the process shown in Figure 4-4.

With the .NET remoting model just described, we will now look at some examples on how to use .NET remoting in our applications.

.NET Remoting Sample

There are two flavors of .NET remoting object: *server activation* and *client activation*. The difference is that the lifetime of server-activated remote objects is managed by the server, whereas that of client-activated remote objects is managed by the client.

A good analogy for the difference between these two activation models is the two types of customer service model: customer service via telephone and customer service via on-line chat room. When you call the customer service line, you get a hold of a customer service representative. You take the time to ask whatever question you may have. Regardless of whether your questions are long or short, the customer service representative will not able to serve other customers while she or he is serving you. Customer service via on-line chat is different. One customer service representative can serve multiple clients simultaneously by replying to questions from many customers on-line. Client activation model is like that of customer service via phone. One client creates a remote object and holds that remote object until it is finished with it, and no other client may talk to that remote object in the meanwhile. In other words, that remote object is dedicated to a single client. The server activation model (singleton) is like that of customer service via on-line chat room. One remote object can server multiple clients at the same time.

There are two kinds of server activation: *singleton* and *single call*. Singleton, as implied by its name, ensures that only one instance of a class exists on the server at a given time. If a remote object is marked as "server activation through single-ton," then only one remote object is created on the server to serve all the requests for multiple clients. If a remote object is marked as "single call," then CLR will cre-ate one remote object for each method call from the client and destroy the remote object after the call finishes. If the same client is making another method call on the same transparent proxy it holds, the CLR on the remote server will create a brand new remote object to serve the call and destroy it afterward. Although the remote object serves only one client in this case (actually, it serves only one method call), the client is not able to maintain its state across the method calls, whereas this is possible in the client activation case, where a client can hold a proxy to a remote object and make multiple calls to that same object. There is no such concept as singleton or single-call client activation. In fact, there is only one kind of client activation: the kind by which the client holds the remote object as long as it wants.

Each remote object can be configured using either the configuration file or the `RemotingService` class to set up remoting objects programmatically. Let's take look at each of these options in detail.

Server Activation Using a Configuration File

Client-Side Application Code

The following code is on the client side, where a remote configuration is loaded and a new object is created using the new keyword:

```
RemotingConfiguration.Configure("RemotingClient.exe.config");
BusinessObject bo = new BusinessObject();
```

Client-Side Configuration File

When we are using the keyword new in our client code to instantiate a remote object, we must somehow inform the CLR that the object we are about to create is not a local object. The CLR needs to know about this because it needs to request the ObjRef object from the remote server and dynamically create the transparent proxy from it if the object being created is remote. We inform the CLR which types of objects are remote objects in the application configuration file's <system.runtime.remoting> section, as shown in the following code:

```
<configuration>
  <system.runtime.remoting>
    <application name="Client">
      <client>
        <wellknown url="http://localhost:8989/BusinessObjectA.rem"
          type="BusinessObjectLibrary.BusinessObject, BusinessObjectLibrary" />
      </client>
    </application>
  </system.runtime.remoting>
</configuration>
```

The wellknown objects are server-activated objects, and the <wellknown> element provides the CLR with enough information on where to request an ObjRef as well as which type of object is used by the client application. Now let's take a look at what the server needs to do to support its remoting objects.

Server-Side Application Code

On the server side, we need to create an application to host the remoting object. I use a simple console application in my example, but ideally, we should create a windows service application or use IIS to host the .NET remoting objects on the server:

```
RemotingConfiguration.Configure("RemotingServer.exe.config");
Console.WriteLine("Press enter to exit the application");
Console.ReadLine();
```

There is very little code for the server application. All it does is to load the configuration file and let the CLR register all the .NET remoting objects and transport channels automatically, such as the HTTP channel or TCP channel. A channel is responsible for transporting messages' data across different remoting boundaries. Note that you must use `Console.ReadLine()` in this case to keep the application running in order for the server application to serve its clients continuously.

Server Configuration File

The .NET remoting object is configured as Singleton in the following configuration example. It can easily be changed to SingleCall by specifying `mode="SingleCall"` in the `<wellknown>` element:

```
<configuration>
    <system.runtime.remoting>
        <application>
            <service>
                <wellknown
                    mode="Singleton"
                    type="BusinessObjectLibrary.BusinessObject,BusinessObjectLibrary"
                    objectUri="BusinessObject.rem" />
            </service>
            <channels>
                <channel ref="http" port="8989"/>
            </channels>
        </application>
    </system.runtime.remoting>
</configuration>
```

Client Activation Using a Configuration File

There are only about two lines in the configuration file that we need to change when we convert a .NET remoting object from server-activated to client-activated. The following comparison illustrates this difference.

The difference in configuration on the client side is as follows:

```
Server activation (client side)
<client>
    <wellknown url="http://localhost:8989/BusinessObjectA.rem"
    type="BusinessObjectLibrary.BusinessObject, BusinessObjectLibrary" />
</client>
```

```
Client activation (client side)
<client>
  <activated type="BusinessObjectLibrary.BusinessObject, BusinessObjectLibrary" />
</client>
```

The difference in configuration on the server side is as follows:

```
Server activation (server side)
<service>
  <wellknown
      mode="Singleton"
      type="BusinessObjectLibrary.BusinessObject,BusinessObjectLibrary"
      objectUri="BusinessObject.rem" />
</service>

Client activation (server side)
<service>
  <activated type="BusinessObjectLibrary.BusinessObject, BusinessObjectLibrary" />
</service>
```

To summarize the differences, the client activation uses the `<activated>` element to describe the remoting object, whereas server activation uses the `<wellknown>` element to describe the remoting object. Also, the client activation doesn't need a url or objectUri. Only server-activation objects need a url or objectUri attribute.

Putting the remoting object information into the configuration file enables us to change the behaviors of the remoting objects with no code change. However, there are times that we want to configure the .NET remoting dynamically according to some business rule. For example, we may want to change the object url for the purpose of load balancing, or register some new remoting objects without restarting the hosting application to refresh the configuration settings. Let's see how we can influence what the configuration file does programmatically.

Server Activation Without Configuration File

Client-Side Application Code

We can create a remote object by calling the Activator.GetObject() method. System.Activator is a class that contains methods that allow us to create objects either locally or remotely. The static method GetObject() takes the type and location of the target object as parameters. For example, the creation of a remote object BusinessObject without relying on the configuration file looks like the following:

```
BusinessObject bo= (BusinessObject)Activator.GetObject(
                              typeof(BusinessObject),
                              "http://localhost:8989/BusinessObject.rem");
bo.DoWork();
```

The GetObject() method is a very easy way to create a remote object, but it has drawbacks too. First, GetObject() only supports server-activated remote objects. Notice that you must provide a url for the remote object, a requirement of server-activated objects. Second, GetObject() will only cause the instantiation of the remote object through its default constructor. If you need to create a client-activated remote object or use a non-default constructor when creating the remote object, you need to use Activator.CreateInstance().

Server-Side Application Code

There is more code on the server side to setup the remoting objects. The code can be divided into two major parts: register channels and register remote object type, as shown in the followings.

```
//register the transport channel
HttpChannel channel = new HttpChannel(8989);
ChannelServices.RegisterChannel(channel);
//register the remote object type.
WellKnownServiceTypeEntry wste= new
    WellKnownServiceTypeEntry(typeof(BusinessObject),"BusinessObjectLibrary",
                        WellKnownObjectMode.SingleCall));
RemotingConfiguration.ApplicationName = "BusinessObject";
RemotingConfiguration.RegisterWellKnownServiceType(wste);
```

The previous code is for registering a server-activated object on the server. You can also register a client-activated object on the server using ActivatedServiceTypeEntry and RemotingConfiguration.RegisterActivatedServiceType(). It is helpful to overcome these confusing method names by keeping in mind the following mapping: "Activated = client activation"; "Wellknown = server activation"; "ServiceType = on the server side"; "ClientType = on the client side."

> **NOTE** *You don't have to register the remote object type (by calling* Remoting-Configuration.RegisterXXXXClientType()*) on the client side when you are calling* GetObject() *or* CreateInstance()*. However, if you want to use* new *to instantiate the remote object, you must either register the remote object on the client side by creating* XXXXClientTypeEntry *and register it using* RemotingConfiguration.RegisterXXXXClientType()*, or specify the remote object on the configuration file.*

We have just discussed .NET reflection and .NET remoting. We now have all the tools we need to create the SAF.ClassFactory service. For the rest of this chapter, we will look at SAF.ClassFactory in detail, walk though its code, and discuss the factory design pattern it uses to achieve its goals.

SAF Code Walkthrough

We want the class factory to do two things. First, the class factory should be able to provide developers with object instances without having developers directly instantiate the class. It should provide a way to "prepare" the object before it is sent out of the class factory. Second, the class factory should be able to make the instantiation of remote objects transparent to developers and reduce the amount of remoting configuration knowledge the developer has to possess to work with the remoting object.

The GOF's "abstract factory" pattern provides a good blueprint for our class factory service. Let's first find out what the abstract factory is all about and how we can leverage it in building a class factory service that achieves our two goals.

Design Pattern: Abstract Factory

Intend

To quote from the GOF's book, "Abstract Factory provides an interface for creating families of related or dependent objects without specifying their concrete classes." Figure 4-5 illustrates the structure of this pattern.

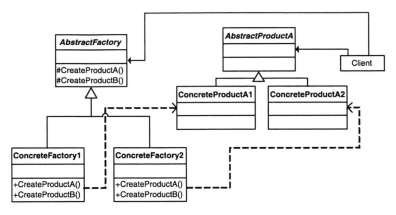

Figure 4-5. GOF's abstract factory structure

An abstract factory allows developers to use the concrete classes in their code without referencing the concrete classes. Instead, developers will reference the abstract base class of the concrete classes they want to use. The abstract factory removes the need for developers to call new ConcreteClassXX(). The following example shows the difference between the code without an abstract factory and code with an abstract factory.

```
// without abstract factory
ConcreteProductA1  cpa1 = new ConcreteProductA1();
cpa1.ShowPrice();
```

```
// with abstract factory
ProductA  pa = ClassfactoryService.Getfactory1().CreateProductA();
pa.ShowPrice();
```

In this first example, we must reference the concrete class inside our code; if we decided to create a different class to represent ProductA1, we would have to change our code to something like ConcreteNewProductA1 cnpa1 = new ConcreteNewProductA1(); and replace all the ConcreteProductA1 references throughout the code.

In the second example, we don't have to mention any concrete class. ProductA is an abstract base class that is inherited by all families of ProductA. When we want to obtain a concrete ProductA1 object, we just call the class factory and ask it to make it for us. The return type for CreateProductA is ProductA, even through the object is referencing a ConcreteProductA1 object internally. If we decide to create a different class to represent ProductA1, we only need to modify the CreateProductA1() method of the class factory. The client code needn't be changed, since the client code only deal with the abstract class ProductA. Following is the example for the CreateProductA1() method

```
public ProductA CreateProductA1()
{
    //ConcreteProductA1 p = new ConcreteProductA1();
    ConcreteNewProductA1 p = new ConcreteNewProductA1();
    return p;
}
```

The idea behind the abstract factory is the separation of the client code that uses business objects from the class that is creating these business objects. On the client side, we will try to access business objects through their parent abstract class or interface, hence eliminate the direct reference of the concrete child class. When the concrete child class happens to change, we would have to make only very few or no changes to our client code.

> **NOTE** *If you are using some concrete child-class-specific method or properties that are not part of its parent abstract class or interface in your code, you would have to cast the object to the concrete class before you could access such child-level resources. There is no way to get around of that kind of coupling. However, you should try to reference the object in its abstract parent type or interface when you are not dealing with such child-class-level-specific method or properties, so that when changes are necessary, only a minimum amount of code change is required.*

As we are developing our application framework, we want to ensure that developers will not mix object-creating code with concrete classes. The class factory service provides this feature for us. There is a difference between writing a class factory as part of a framework and writing a class factory as part of a customized application. In the latter case, we know exactly how many abstract class factories and how many types of concrete classes each factory is responsible for creating. However, when developing the class factory as a framework component, we have no knowledge about how many factories and classes developers will need when they are building the application. But with .NET reflection, we can create a class factory service that is flexible enough to absorb the new groups of classes added to the application. Figure 4-6 shows the structure of SAF.ClassFactory and its relation to application-specific class factories.

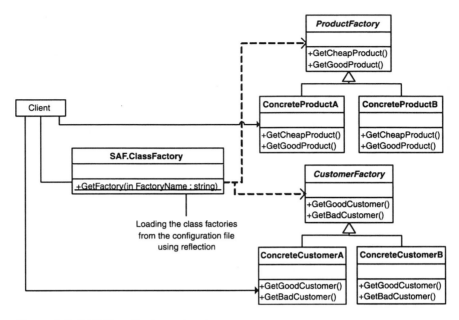

Figure 4-6. SAF.ClassFactory structure

There are three major components involved in SAF.ClassFactory. First is the ClassFactory class, a concrete class that has one static method called GetFactory(string factoryName). This method is responsible for loading the concrete application-specific class factories when requested and returning them to the caller. For the client side, the code that requests an application-specific class factory looks like the following:

```
ProductFactory pf;
//Assign application-specific factory class to abstract class type
pf = (ProductFactory)SAF.ClassFactory.GetFactory("ProductFactory-A");
//Assign concrete class to abstract class type
Product cheapProduct = pf.GetCheapProduct();
Product.RaisePrice();
```

In this example, ProductFactory and Product are abstract classes. Although we have not specifically defined anything as the concrete ConcreteProductA class and CheapProduct class, the CLR knows that when we call the RaisePrice() method, we are really calling on the Product A family's CheapProduct object obtained from an application-level class factory, which in turn is obtained from the SAF.ClassFactory service.

One of the goals we want to achieve is to use the strongly typed object as much as possible throughout our application, instead of references to the generic object type. When we are using strongly typed objects, the compiler can check for any type of mismatch error during compilation. Developers are more productive when dealing with strongly typed objects because they can get the Intellisense from IDE to help them identify the methods and properties they want to use. Had we chosen to define the object as Object type, developers would have to cast the object to a specific type before they could access the methods and properties inside the object. This would make the code hard to read and would sometimes require developers to know additional information about the class hierarchies of the objects that would otherwise be hidden from them. Therefore, we should try to use strongly typed objects as much as possible in our code. The following code is an example of using weakly typed (Object type) objects in code:

```
pf = (ProductFactory)SAF.ClassFactory.GetFactory("ProductFactory-A ");
```

The GetFactory() method returns a class factory as type object, so developers have to cast this into an application-specific abstract class type before they can use it. We can add some more methods in SAF.ClassFactory(), which returns strongly typed objects; for example, we can add GetProductFactory(), which returns a ProductFactory type, or GetCustomerFactory(), which returns a CustomerFactory type, but doing so would violate the rule to keep the application-specific knowledge away from the application framework. Adding such special methods in a framework component would cause the framework to change constantly when a new class factory arrives or an old class factory is removed. We would have to constantly add, remove, and modify the methods inside the SAF.ClassFactory class to accommodate such business-domain-level changes.

The application framework needs to be flexible enough to isolate itself from changes in the business domain. To achieve that goal, we sometime have to use weakly typed objects in the framework code to obtain an extra level of flexibility. However, if you really want to use strongly typed objects in the application and make life (work) easier for your developers, you could always write an extra layer on top of the application framework that uses application-specific strongly typed objects and make your developers code against the extra layer that sits on top of the framework instead of against the framework itself. Through this extra application-specific layer, you can isolate the framework from business-domain changes while providing a "strongly typed" environment for the developers to do their work. The testing sample accompanying this chapter demonstrates this approach. In the testing sample, the TestConcreteFactory project (which will call SAF.ClassFactory) represents such an extra application-specific layer containing the concrete factory for a specific business application.

Now, returning to the SAF.ClassFactory, this service uses a key such as ProductFactory-A in my case to identity which specific class factory to load. SAF.ClassFactory achieves this with the configuration file combined with the power of .NET reflection. There is one section inside the configuration file that contains information about all the application-specific class factories used by the application. The following shows what it looks like:

```
<SAF.ClassFactory>
    <Class  name="ProductFactory-A"
          type="TestConcreteFactory.ConcreteProductFactory,TestConcreteFactory"/>
    <Class name="ProductFactory-B"
         type="TestConcreteFactory.ConcreteNewProductFactory,TestConcreteFactory/>
    <Class name="CustomerFactory-A"
        type="TestConcreteFactory.ConcreteCustomerFactory, TestConcreteFactory" />
</SAF.ClassFactory>
```

Within each `Class` element, `SAF.ClassFactory` can obtain just enough information to load the class factory and create an instance of that class factory. In order to use reflection to create an object instance, we need at least one piece of information: the type information of the class for which we want to create the object instance. `GetFactory()` is the static method that uses such information in the configuration file to load class factories dynamically at each request. The following is the code in the `GetFactory()` method:

```
public static object GetFactory(string factoryName)
{
 object factory = null;
ConfigurationManager cm =
        (ConfigurationManager)ConfigurationSettings.GetConfig("Framework");
ClassFactoryConfiguration cf = cm.ClassFactoryConfig;
XmlNode classFactoryData = cf.GetFactoryData(factoryName);

//obtain the type information
string type = classFactoryData.Attributes["type"].Value;
Type t = System.Type.GetType(type);

factory = Activator.CreateInstance(t, null);
return factory;
}
```

I will explain how `ConfigurationManager` works in Chapter 6, when we talk about the `SAF.Configuration` service. Other than that, the code is quite self-explanatory if you haven't skipped the .NET reflection overview earlier in the chapter. By using reflection, we can add, modify, and remove class factories by modifying the information in the configuration file.

NOTE *There is probably no reason to re-create the class factory each time a client calls the* GetFactory() *method. You can perform some object-caching techniques so that the class factory is reused. You will learn more about object caching through* SAF.Cache *in Chapter 5.*

Imagine we have created a set of concrete product classes with different implementations or behaviors and a class factory to generate the new classes. We can simply modify the configuration file so that when the application reloads the next time, all requests to the old product classes will now go through the new set of product classes without any code change. The following comparison indicates the amount of changes needed in using the SAF.ClassFactory framework component:

```
Change from:
<Class name="ProductFactory-A" type="
        TestConcreteFactory.ConcreteProductFactory,TestConcreteFactory"/>
To:
<Class name="ProductFactory-A" type="
        TestConcreteFactory.ConcreteNewProductFactory,TestConcreteFactory"/>
```

It is easy to create a new application-specific class factory to be used with SAF.ClassFactory. The following is a skeleton of the ConcreteNewProductFactory class.

```
public class ConcreteNewProductFactory : ProductFactory
{
    //methods that return various concrete objects.
    public CheapProduct GetCheapProduct()
    {
        CheapProduct cp = new NewCheapProduct();
        //perform possible action on cp before returning it
        return cp;
    }

    public CheapProduct GetCheapProduct(string currency) {…};
    public GoodProduct GetGoodProduct() {…};
}
```

Within each method, you can simply create and return a object with the new keyword, as shown in the example, but you certainly don't have to stop there. You can perform an array of actions, from performing some type of object caching to setting properties of the newly created object according to some business rules. Indeed, the sky is the limit when it comes to the additional actions you can take within each method, as long as each returns an object reference to the caller.

As you can see, by using SAF.ClassFactory along with sets of application-specific class factories, you can separate the business logic of creating an object from the business logic of using such an object, thus minimizing the impact of changes to the underlying concrete classes. Having achieved the first goal of our class factory service, let's move on to make it support .NET remoting. There are two approaches to adding support for .NET remoting in the class factory: an easy one and a complicated one. Figure 4-7 shows the difference between these two approaches.

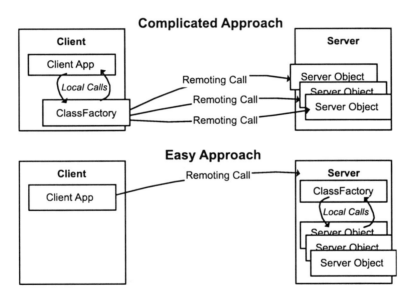

Figure 4-7. Comparison of two approaches to the class factory

The complicated approach requires you to use either the configuration file approach or the programmatic approach to register the remote objects on both the client side and the server side. In other words, you must perform a great deal of remoting object registration in each of the concrete class factories to produce the remoting objects on behalf of the clients. Because the class factory is a completely separate component from the client code, you can do whatever it takes to support the remoting objects in each of your concrete class factories without affecting the client code. This approach works, but it requires extra configuration and coding; an alternative is much simpler, and easier to implement.

Before we dive into the simple approach for supporting remoting objects in the class factory, let's forget about the class factory for a moment. If we just wanted to create a remoting object, we would either specify some configuration settings or register the remote object programmatically to inform the CLR that it should obtain a proxy for remote objects and make each call go through the proxy object. We could have used `Activator.GetObject()` or `Activator.CreateInstance()` to bypass such registration of remote objects on the client side, but we would still have to configure and register those remote objects on the server side to make the remoting work.

However, we can significantly reduce the amount of the work we have to do to support the remoting in our application by making the CLR do all the dirty work. The CLR has a rule that when an object is passed to a client that is at a remote location, it will automatically marshal the object and pass back the `ObjRef` object of the object instead. We talked about `ObjRef` earlier in the chapter. `ObjRef` is a serializable object that contains all the information the client needs to create a proxy that connects to the remote object. In other words, if we make made the application-specific class factory itself a remote object on the server, that remote class factory will return the `ObjRef` object to the client that requested the object. Figure 4-8 illustrates the idea behind the second approach.

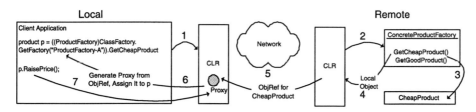

Figure 4-8. Process of .NET remoting call

The client application starts by requesting `CheapProduct` from the class factory `ConcreteProductFactory` (step 1). Because `ConcreteProductFactory` is located on the remote box, `ClassFactory` has to obtain the remote class factory by calling `Activator.GetObject()`. The CLR on the remote server will create a concrete class factory at the client's request (step 2). The `GetCheapProduct()` method is called, and a new `CheapProduct` object is returned (step 3). The `GetCheapProduct()` method returns the object (this is an object that is local to the remote server) to the CLR, which will forward the object to the client application sitting on another computer (step 4). The CLR understands that the client that has requested the object is on a remote box, so it automatically marshals the object to create an `ObjRef` object for the CheapProduct object, and it then returns the ObjRef object to the client machine (step 6). It is important that we not only make the factory class remotable, but also make the classes that are produced by the factory class remotable as well. To do so, we must make sure they all inherit from the MarshalByRefObject class. The CLR on the client side intercepts the ObjRef object and automatically unmarshals it into a proxy object (transparent proxy to be exact) and assigns the proxy object back to the variable p (step 7). The next time the client application accesses p, the client is actually talking to a proxy that knows how to convert the method calls to a message and forward it to the right location (the process I described earlier in the .NET remoting overview section).

The key to this approach is to deploy the concrete application-specific class factories to the remote location where the concrete business classes are and make the CLR on the remote box automatically return an ObjRef object for the business class that the client application requested.

To make SAF.ClassFactory support the remote concrete class factory, we must modify our GetFactory() method and the configuration file a little bit. The following is an example of the change we need to make to the configuration file:

```
Change from:
<Class name=" ProductFactory-A" type="
        TestConcreteFactory.ConcreteProductFactory,TestConcreteFactory" />
To:
<Factory name=" ProductFactory-A" type="
        TestConcreteFactory.ConcreteProductFactory,TestConcreteFactory "
        location="http://RemoteServer1/ClassFactory.rem" />
```

We also need to use Activator to obtain a proxy to the remote class factory. The following is the new implementation for the GetFactory() method:

```
public static object GetFactory(string factoryName)
{
        object factory = null;
        ConfigurationManager cm =

        (ConfigurationManager)ConfigurationSettings.GetConfig("Framework");
        ClassFactoryConfiguration cf= cm.ClassFactoryConfig;
        XmlNode classFactoryData = cf.GetFactoryData(factoryName);

        //obtain the type information
        string type = classFactoryData.Attributes["type"].Value;
        Type t = System.Type.GetType(type);
        //create an instance of concrete class factory
```

```
    if (classFactoryData.Attributes["location"] != null)
    {
        string location = classFactoryData.Attributes["location"].Value;
        factory = Activator.GetObject(t,location);
    }
    else
    {
        factory = Activator.CreateInstance(t,null);
    }
    return factory;
}
```

There is no need to set up an additional remoting configuration on the client side. However, we need to register each class factory on the remote server. Because there is no need to create more than one instance of each class factory, we should use Singleton as the server activation mode. The only remoting configuration settings on the server side would be the ones for the class factories, not the business classes. Using the CLR to automatically convert a local object reference to the marshaled ObjRef object eliminates the need for us to register each of the concrete business classes the factory produces as a remoting object.

> **NOTE** *The* SAF.ClassFactory *supports only client-activated remote objects. In other words, when the client receives a remoting object from the remote class factory, the remoting object is a client-activated remoting object, which means that the client can hold on to the same remoting object for multiple method calls.*

One more thing that is worth mentioning is the setup of class references on the client application during development. Because the class factories and concrete business classes are now at a remote location, developers must first obtain their type information in order to call them within their code. You can choose one of three options to make the type information available for the client application. The first option is to deploy the interface assembly for all the remoting objects to the client side. The second option is to deploy the actual concrete remoting objects to the client side. The third option is to deploy a new set of "empty" classes that have same type information and method signatures as those of remoting objects.

The first option is achieved by creating a set of remote interface classes that contain all the method signatures and implementing these interfaces in the remote concrete class factories and remote business classes. You can then compile this set of remote interfaces into an assembly file, send it to the developers, and ask them to add it into the project reference so that the client application has the type information it needs for calling the remoting factory objects and business objects. This option has two major drawbacks: First, you are not able to access the object's public fields, since public fields can't be put into the interface; hence they are not available for access from the client application. The second drawback it a bit more serious. When you try to call the remote method and pass it another remote interface object as one of its parameters, you will receive a run-time error. This error is raised when the CLR tries to marshal the parameter into an `ObjRef` object by calling the `CreateObjRef()` method on the base class of the parameter. Because the parameter object is just an interface for the remoting object, it doesn't extend `MarshalByRefObject` and doesn't have the `CreateObjRef()` method. The CLR will not be able to marshal the parameter successfully for the call.

The second option, which deploys the actual remoting classes to the client side, works and solves the problems in the interface option, but it really violates the principle of encapsulation or information hiding that we all try to achieve in object-oriented programming. There are some drawbacks to this option (besides it making you feel bad about yourself), but nothing that serious. In fact, Microsoft has been using this approach in numerous remoting examples in the .NET documentation. When shipping the implementation class or DLL files out, one can use `ildasm.exe` to figure out what is in the source code. There are also several tools available that reverse engineer the IL code into C# or VB.NET code, which makes your program vulnerable to security hacking, but most importantly, it makes the bugs in your program available for everyone else to see. Another risk is that you have to make sure your remoting configuration is correct, or your application may be calling the local version of the class implementation instead of the remote object across the network, and it could be very difficult to identify the problem.

Given the shortcomings of the previous two options, I recommend that you go with the third option, to deploy the type information for the remoting object to the client application. `SoapSuds.exe` is a tool that comes with .NET Framework SDK and is the tool for the job. This tool allows you to automatically generate an "empty" class that contains only the class definition of the remoting object. `SoapSuds.exe` will then put these empty classes into a DLL assembly or a source file that can be recompiled into an assembly later. Because `SoapSuds` creates a concrete "empty" class that extends `MarshalByRefObject`, we don't have the problem of the CLR raising run-time errors on interface type parameters, and the client application can now access all the possible public members of the class. With no method implementation code inside these classes, there is no risk of exposing your buggy code to strangers. `SoapSuds.exe` can be found in the `\Program Files\Microsoft Visual Studio .NET\FrameworkSDK\Bin` folder, and it is very simple to use. Here is an example:

```
c:\>soapsuds -nowp -url:http://RemoteServer1/ClassFactory.rem?wsdl
                                            -oa:ProductFactory.dll
```

ProductFactory.dll is the output file. You can add it to the reference of the client application using the "add reference" feature in Visual Studio.NET. It is important that we use the -nowp switch, which stands for "no wrapper proxy." Without this switch, SoapSuds will create a proxy class that performs the actual remoting calls using SOAP. It is not what we want. We want only the "empty" class definition so that our client-side code compiles. We will leave the job of creating a proxy object to the CLR when it receives an ObjRef from the remote server.

The Testing Project

The Test.SAF.ClassFactory project contains a demo application that you can run to test out the features in SAF.ClassFactory. The demo application demonstrates the usage of the SAF.ClassFactory service by creating a number of local and remote objects.

To run the demo, open the solution file Test.SAF.ClassFactory.sln and hit F5. There is no additional setup required to run the demo.

Summary

You have learned about the concept of the class factory through the abstract factory, a design pattern that allows us to use objects without referencing concrete classes. It also decouples the code for accessing such an object from the code that creates the object, thereby minimizing the impact in changing the underlying concrete classes that the client application is using. We have also looked at details of .NET remoting, its foundation and its implementation in application code. Using SAF.ClassFactory as an example, you learned about how to apply the abstract factory pattern in building a flexible class factory service as part of the application framework and how to reduce the configuration and managerial overhead associated with supporting remoting objects by leveraging .NET remoting techniques in the class factory service.

In the next chapter we will look at yet another SAF component, an object-caching service. You will learn about object-caching techniques in .NET and the design pattern that we can use to make the caching service more extensible.

CHAPTER 5

Caching Service

THIS CHAPTER IS ABOUT object caching. Caching can take many different forms and implementations. A database server is one example. As developers are coding their database access components, one of their major decisions is what kinds of SQL queries, stored procedures, and parameters the application uses to interact with the database server. Although it may appear that developers have no special object-caching code in their application, there are many objects or resources that are being cached behind the scenes. For instance, ADO.NET, by default, uses database connection pooling, or stores the database connection object for reuse. Database vendors also implement their own caching mechanisms to ensure that the least amount of computation is needed for certain requests. Database servers can store commonly accessed data in memory to avoid repetitive disk operations. The benefits of object caching are obvious. It is extremely useful to learn about some of the caching techniques to help you build more robust and scalable applications. I will talk about how we can develop a caching service that enables application developers to take advantage of object caching in their applications without writing a lot of code.

Motivation and Goals

In object-oriented applications, we create objects to model the business entities. A service in our application is achieved through creation and consumption of these business objects. Creating too many objects can require excessive computing resources. In many cases, creating an object is not as simple as writing `BusinessObject bo = new BusinessObject();`. We often have to obtain many additional parameters that are used to create the business objects. Obtaining these parameters is a whole different story and requires a whole set of computing resources by itself. One way to remove the need for re-creating an object, and hence to remove the overhead associated with object creation, is to create the object once and store it in a "location." The term "location" here can mean many different things. It can be private field, database, or Web service end point. The application can retrieve the object later from that location to access its service whenever the application needs it.

We will look at how we can build a caching service for the application framework. Before we start looking at the details, we should be clear about the goal for the caching service. The following are the high-level goals:

- It provides a mechanism for storing and retrieving the objects.

- It provides a simple and easy-to-use interface to application developers.

Because developers are the audiences for the application framework, understanding how to make their life easier when using the framework is an important factor for the success and usability of the framework.

In SAF, I implemented the caching service with an XML flavor. This helps to give a hierarchical structure to the objects being cached. XML is a technology that is well known and is relatively easy to work with. In the rest of the chapter, we'll explore how XML and some caching techniques are used in SAF, and what they bring to the table.

.NET Technology Overview

Before we dive into the actual implementation of the SAF caching service, we will first take a quick look at the major technologies that it uses. There are some key technical topics associated with object caching. Here is a list of the topics that I will talk about next:

- .NET garbage collector

- Static variables and hash table

- XML

- XPath

.NET Garbage Collector

Before we talk about how to store an object in the cache, we need first to understand object lifecycle management in the .NET framework. Objects are created and destroyed constantly within any application. We need to learn how to keep an object alive so that we can access it at a later time

First, let's look at the following example:

```
public void TestA()
{
    BusinessObject bo=new BusinessObject();
    bo.DoWork();
}
```

In this example, when `TestA()` is called, a `BusinessObject` instance is created and its `DoWork()` method is called. As the `TestA()` method completes, the local variable bo will go out of scope and become unreachable. At that moment, bo becomes eligible for garbage collection. If we call `TestA()` one more time, a new `BusinessObject` instance is created and becomes eligible and marked for garbage collection as the `TestA()` method finishes. We may not be able to say when exactly the `BusinessObject` instance created by the `TestA()` method is removed from system memory, but we know that it will eventually happen and no one will be able to access the `BusinessObject` instance that has been marked for garbage collection.

> **NOTE** *Although we can't determine exactly when garbage collection (GC) will occur in the application, we do have a means of forcing GC by using the* `GC.Collect()` *method. GC is a time-consuming process and is better left to the .NET run time to do the job. However, if you believe that the extra memory obtained by forcing GC more often than by default would benefit your application, you can certainly do so.*

Obviously, creating a `BusinessObject` instance each time `TestA()` is called is not very efficient, especially if it takes a significant amount of time to create `BusinessObject`. To make bo live longer, we must make bo ineligible for GC as the `TestA()` method exits. One way to achieve this is to assign bo or the `BusinessObject` instance to a class variable. The following example does just that:

```
class Class1
{
    private BusinessObject bo;
    public void Test()
    {
        bo=new BusinessObject();
        bo.DoWork();
    }
    public void TestB()
```

```
    {
        TestA();
        if (bo != null)
        {
            //bo is still accessible.
            bo.StillMoving();
        }
    }
}
```

In this example, bo is still accessible after the TestA() method has terminated. Because we have declared bo as a class instance variable, bo will live as long as the instance of Class1 lives. We are able to keep bo living a bit longer, but still, putting bo into a class instance variable doesn't make bo live long enough to be a vital solution for object caching. We must find a better vehicle that perpetuates bo.

A class static variable is a perfect vehicle for this goal. Static variables are instantiated when the class is loaded into the AppDomain. It will live as long as the AppDomain itself. Unlike a class instance variable, which is instantiated each time a class is created, a static variable is created only once. If we have created a static variable called ObjectCacheStore in a class and assign bo to it, then every piece of code inside our application can reach bo and call the bo.DoWork() method without creating a brand new BusinessObject instance!

> **NOTE** *An AppDomain is an isolated area for executing .NET code within one OS process. It achieves the same goal as an OS process, which protects the crash of one process from affecting other processes. An AppDomain is shut down when the application it hosts, such as an* .exe *application or a Web application, is shut down. Each OS process can have multiple AppDomains, and the crash of one will not affect other AppDomains in the same OS process. The .NET framework offers the AppDomain class (*System.AppDomain*), which contains a set of methods you can use to create and access a specific AppDomain at run time.*

Static Variables and Hash Tables

To develop a framework component, such as the caching service we have described, we shouldn't make any assumptions about how many objects and the types of objects developers might choose to cache. Instead of assigning objects to a static variable, we can add objects to a hash table (System.Collection.Hashtable), which doesn't put a limit on the number of objects as well as the types of objects you can put into it. A hash table consists of multiple key-value pairs, similar to a two-column data table.

> **NOTE** *The hash table requires the keys to be unique. If you are trying to add an object using a key that has already existed in the hash table, an exception will be thrown. The key in a hash table is the equivalent of the primary or unique key in a data table. If you want to store objects without such a unique key, you can used* ArrayList *or* object[].

Hashtable has two methods that enable you to add and retrieve objects to and from it. The following is a quick example:

```
class Cache
{
    private static Hashtable ObjectCacheStore = new Hashtable();

    public static void Add (object key,object bo)
    {
        ObjectCacheStore.Add(key,bo);
    }

    public static object Retrieve (object key)
    {
        return ObjectCacheStore[key];
    }
}
```

In this example, a simple Cache class contains two methods that add and retrieve object references to and from its static cache variable. A key is used to locate the correct object stored in the ObjectCacheStore hash table. Because this cache class doesn't keep or maintain its state for each caching request, we can make the methods static so that developers can access these methods without needing to instantiate the Cache object, and hence reduce the amount of code developers have to write to access the cached objects. One drawback of using static methods is that a method can't be static and abstract or virtual at the same time. This limitation restricts the extensibility of the Cache class because we cannot alter static method implementations without rewriting a new Cache class. We will look at how to overcome this shortcoming later this chapter, when we look at how we can make this Cache class extensible through the use of the virtual methods and strategy design pattern.

> **NOTE** *Although you can't override the static method in the inherited class, you can use the "new" modifier on the same static method in the derived class to provide a new implementation. However, doing so requires you always to specify what the derived class is when accessing its static methods. Hence, it doesn't really provide the "overriding" effect, as in dealing with an instance method.*

For now, our example provides a simple object caching solution. It is also rather easy to use. For developers, object caching is achieved through a few lines of code as follows:

```
static void Main(string[] args)
{
    BusinessObject bo = (Cache.Retrieve("MyBusinessObject")) as BusinessObject
    if (bo == null)
    {
        bo = new BusinessObject();
        Cache.Add("MyBusinessObject",bo);
    }
    bo.DoWork();
    // extra work goes here
}
```

In this example, the BusinessObject is created only for the very first time when Cache.Retrieve("MyBusinessObject") returns a null.

The caching service described earlier would work, but it could certainly use a couple of improvements. One of these improvements is to make the caching service more extensible. Using static methods prevents us from adapting certain OOP techniques such as abstract methods and method overriding, which give developers greater control over how object caching is performed. The second improvement is to give objects stored in the hash table a more manageable structure. The Cache class example we used earlier requires developers to access the cached object with a key. Because Hashtable has a flat structure, each object stored in the hash table is identified with a key that is on the same hierarchical level as other objects. There is no grouping among these objects. The ability to group items in a hierarchical structure may not seem beneficial when the number of cached objects is small, but as the number of entities grows larger, it will be much easier to have a broader view of these objects when you arrange them in a hierarchical structure. Hierarchical structures provide something that flat structures do not: the relationship of one entity to the others. Hashtable is like NT's domain model, in which each user is on the same level of others. Wouldn't it be great if we could create a caching service that had a structure like that of Active Directory, where each user belongs to an organizational unit, which can belong to another organizational unit, and so forth?

SAF.Cache is created to achieve these two improvements. Before we dive into the details of SAF.Cache, we need to understand some basic technology used in the SAF.Cache class, namely, XML and XPath.

Why XML?

The reason XML is used inside SAF.Cache is because of its hierarchical structure. Each XML document consists of two major components: elements and attributes. Although both components are holders for data, there are distinct differences between the way the two are used. The following is an example of an XML document:

```
<Movies>
    <Movie name="Yojimbo">
        <Actor age="42" gender="M">Toshiro Mifune</Actor>
        <Actor age="44" gender="M">Takashi Shimura</Actor>
        <Director age="52" gender="M">Akira Kurosawa</Director>
    </Movie>
    <Movie name="Memento" />
    <Movie name="Hidden Fortress">
        <Director age="52" gender="M">Akira Kurosawa</Director>
    </Movie>
</Movies>
```

<Movie>, <Actor>, and <Director> are elements. <Movies> is the root element. Each XML document can have only one root element. Each element can have multiple child elements. For example, there are two <Actor> elements and one <Directory> element under the <Movie> element; age and gender are attributes. One element can have multiple attributes, but each attribute must have a unique name. In other words, the following is not valid, because there are two attributes with the same name:

```
<Movie name="Yujimbo" actor="Toshiro Mifune" actor=" Takashi Shimura">
```

Aside from this limitation, you can use both attributes and elements as placeholders for data. It is up to your own personal preference when it comes to choosing either attributes or elements to store data. I prefer to put data that is uniquely associated with an element into an attribute. That makes it easier to search on specific elements by filtering on the attribute value when we use XPath. I will talk about XPath in the next section.

The .NET Framework offers very extensive features through several useful classes under the System.Xml name space. You can create an XML document using the XmlDocument class and load its content from a string or an XML file on the disk. The following is an example:

```
XmlDocument xml = new XmlDocument();
xml.Load(@"c:\temp\movies.xml");
// or
xml.LoadXml(@"<Movies><Movie name='Yujimbo'/></Movies>");
```

After you have created an XmlDocument object, you need to use XmlNode and XPath to retrieve the information from the XmlDocument object. XmlNode (System.Xml.XmlNode) represents an element in the XML document. XmlNode has a number of methods that let you squeeze out every bit of data. The following example demonstrates its features:

```
XmlElement movies = xml.DocumentElement;
foreach (XmlNode movie in movies.ChildNodes)
{
    Console.WriteLine("Movie name: {0}", movie.Attributes["name"].Value);
    foreach (XmlNode person in movie.ChildNodes)
    {
        Console.WriteLine("{0} -----{1}, {2}", person.InnerText, person.Name,
                                        person.Attributes["age"].Value);
    }
}
```

XmlNode represents an XML element, and it is the key to retrieving information from the XML document. XmlNode's ChildNodes property returns an XmlNodeList object. You can use a foreach statement to loop through each of the child elements and the child's child elements. When you get hold of one XmlNode object for a specific element in the XML document, you can use InnerXml to retrieve the value of the element, Attributes[key] to retrieve the value of a specific attribute of the element, and the Name property to retrieve the element's own tag name. The program that we just presented gives us the following output:

```
Movie name: Yojimbo
Toshiro Mifune -----Actor, 42
Takashi Shimura -----Actor, 44
Akira Kurosawa -----Director, 52
Movie name: Memento
Movie name: Hidden Fortress
Akira Kurosawa -----Director, 52
```

In practice, however, we rarely use a foreach loop to retrieve the information stored in an XML document. As with SQL, which allows developers to write a query to search on some specific data in a database, XPath provides a means to search on some specific element in an XML document. We must know about XPath to take full advantage of the power of XML. Let's have a quick overview of the XPath features provided by System.Xml.

XPath

Like XML, XPath is a W3C standard. XPath is a hierarchical expression of a certain element or elements in an XML document. For example, the XPath expression that represents the <Actor age="44" gender="M">Takashi Shimura</Actor> element is

```
/Movies/Movie/Actor[.='Takashi Shimura']
```

This expression represents an element that is under the <Actor> element, which is under a <Movie> element, which is under a <Movies> element, and the value of the <Actor> element is "Takashi Shimura."

The "/" represents the level of hierarchical structure. The "[…]" is the location where you can specify the condition of the element that must be met. It is the equivalent of the WHERE clause in SQL. In our case, the XPath expression just shown indicates that the condition for the <Actor> element is that its value must be "Takashi Shimura." The "dot" in "[.='Takashi Shimura']" represents the element value to which we want to compare.

Besides the element value, we can also search on an element's attribute by prefixing the attribute name with an @ sign, as shown in the following code. The following XPath example represents the actor who is 42 years old in the classic movie "Yojimbo":

```
/Movies/Movie[@name='Yojimbo']/Actor[@age='42']
```

XPath also allows you to express a parent-child relationship among elements. Sometimes you may want to obtain the parent element by specifying the condition on its child elements. For example, the following XPath expression represents the movie element whose director is the Japanese legendary film director Akira Kurosawa:

```
/Movies/Movie[Director = 'Akira Kurosawa']
```

The XPath expression shown earlier will represent multiple movie elements if the XML document contains several movies that are directed by Kurosawa. In dealing with multiple elements, it is useful to be able to pick out a particular element based on the order of the elements. XPath provides this cursor-like feature through the use of position(). For example, if you want to pick up the second movie listed in the XML document, you would use position() = 2 as the condition for the XPath expression, like the following:

```
/Movies/Movie[position() =2]
```

Here position() is one-based, so /Movies/Movie[position() =2] represents the movie element for "Memento."

Like the AND and OR operators in SQL, XPath also provides you with the ability to combine multiple conditions with "and" and "or." Based on our movie document, guess what you get from the following expressions:

```
/Movies/Movie[Director = 'Akira Kurosawa' and position() = 1]
/Movies/Movie[Director = 'Akira Kurosawa' or position() = 2]
```

The first expression results in the movie element for "Yojimbo," because it is the first movie on the list of Kurosawa movies. The second expression results in all three movie elements: Two Kurosawa movies resulted from the condition before "or" plus one movie that is the second movie on the movie list.

You can use XPath to locate an element without knowing its hierarchical position inside a document. /Movies/Movie/Actor shown in the previous examples indicates that you want the <Actor> elements whose parent element is <Movie>, which is under the root element <Movies>. You can simplify the expression if you want to get all <Actor> elements, regardless what the parent element is, by using //Actor.

You can combine the single slash and double slash to express the exact element you want to retrieve from the document. For example, //Movie/Director results in the <Director> elements that are beneath any <Movie> element in the document, whereas /Movies//Director results in all the <Director> elements that are beneath the <Movies> element, regardless whether the <Director> element is the child element of <Movies> or the great-grandchild element of <Movies>.

XPath is not something I can cover in less than two pages. It could well be the subject of another book. But the XPath knowledge in the past two pages should provide you with a good amount of ammunition to tackle most XPath problems. There have been many books on the subject of XPath, but if you want to figure it all out yourself by looking at some concrete example, you may want to search on "XPath, examples" on the Microsoft Visual Studio .NET Documentation that comes with VS.NET. It will show you the usage of many XPath expressions through concise examples.

With that, I am resting my case on XPath and the pertinent .NET technologies that I have discussed so far in this chapter. It is time to use these technologies to build a better object-caching service. We will now pay closer attention to SAF.Cache and how it can provide the two improvements over the very simple caching service we saw earlier in the chapter:

1. Gives a hierarchical structure to the cached objects.

2. Makes the caching service more extensible.

SAF Code Sample Walkthrough

We will now tackle the problems one at a time. A hash table is flat-structured by nature; XML is hierarchically structured. Can we use an XML document as the store for cached objects?

Unfortunately, XML documents are designed to hold text. When we retrieve attribute and element values from an XmlNode, we call the XmlNode.Attributes[] and XmlNode.InnerText properties, but both properties are of String type. We can't simply save the object to an XmlNode. Some readers may ask about using XmlSerialization to serialize the object to an XML string and store it inside an XmlNode. This may work, but it defeats the purpose of object caching altogether, since we have to go through the deserialization process later, which actually creates a new object behind the scenes.

Even through an XML document can't handle the object type, Hashtable supports the storage of object types natively. If we can merge these two technologies by borrowing the hierarchical structure from XML and the object reference storage support in Hashtable, we can create a caching service that achieves the first goal.

This is exactly how SAF.Cache does it. It provides an XML-friendly "interface" to developers who use this caching service and hides the lower-level calls to the hash table from developers. SAF.Cache also hides from developers the internal mapping between the hierarchical XML document and flat structured hash table. With the XML "interface," developers can easily assign a structure template for storing objects that best fits the logical structure of their application, and search on the specific cached object with the power of XPath.

There are three methods that allow developers to add, retrieve, and delete objects in the cache in the SAF.Cache.Cache class, namely, the AddObject(), RetrieveObject(), and RemoveObject() methods. The AddObject() method takes two parameters: a string for the XPath expression, and the object instance for the object that needs to be cached:

```
cache.AddObject("/Applications/EyeSurgeryCustomer/XinChen", bo);
cache.AddObject("/Applications/CountryZipCode", czc);
```

"/Applications/EyeSurgeryCustomer" is considered the group name. "XinChen" is the child element of that group. Because you use an XPath expression, you can create a variety of leveled structures that make the most sense to your application. Some of the group names are also be good candidates for constants, to reduce the amount of typing and typing errors.

> **NOTE** *You can avoid local objects thread-safe issues by ensuring that only one client is accessing the object. However, if you decide to pass the object reference to another client or another thread, you need to pay extra attention to the scenario in which multiple threads call the same object, which leads to a potential data consistency problem. You may want to add thread synchronization code such as locks or synchronization attributes to the methods of the objects that are cached.*

The RetrieveObject() method takes the string XPath expression and returns the cached object. You now may say that there is no difference between SAF.Cache and a hash table; after all, the XPath string itself can be considered the key and passed into the hash table as the identifier for the cached object. That is a very good observation. The next few methods will show the benefits of XML/XPath in the new caching service and things that you can't do using a simple hash table:

```
object[] customers = cache.RetrieveObjectList("/Applications/EyeSurgeryCustomer");
foreach (object customer in customers)
{
    //perform customer service
}
```

Because SAF.Cache relies on an internal XML document, we can group the cached objects in a way that is not possible in a flat structured environment. SAF.Cache makes it appear that objects are stored inside an XML document, but in fact, it merely provides a more user-friendly "interface" for developers to group, locate, and search on the cached objects more easily.

Another benefit of handling items in groups is revealed when we want to delete all cached objects when we end the application or session. The RemoveObject() method allows developers to remove all cached objects from system memory with one line of code. It alleviates the need for developers to track the cached objects one by one and reduces the possibility that certain cached objects might not be cleared after they are no longer needed. For example, the following line removes all the cached customer objects from the cache:

```
cache. RemoveObject("/Applications/EyeSurgeryCustomer");
```

We have just looked at some major features of SAF.Cache. There could be multiple implementations that produce the same result. We will spend the next few sections walking through my implementation of these features.

Code

Step 1: Declare Static Variables

We need to declare a pair of XML/Hashtable objects. The following two variables are storage for the XmlDocument and the cached objects:

```
private static Hashtable objectTable = new Hashtable();
private static XmlElement objectXmlMap=(new XmlDocument()).CreateElement("Cache");
```

Step 2: Create AddObject() and CreateNode() Methods

The real work is done in the AddObject() method. AddObject() works like this: It first identifies the group name in the xpath parameter. It then checks whether this group already exists in the objectXmlMap, which contains the XML "map" for the cached object. It calls the CreateNode() method to build the XML tree for the group dynamically if it does not already exist. The AddObject() method will then add an element to represent the object to objectXmlMap and add a new entry to objectTable:

```
private void AddObject(string xpath, object o,)
{
    //clear up the xpath expression
    string newXpath = PrepareXpath(xpath);
```

```
int separator = newXpath.LastIndexOf("/");
//find the group name
string group = newXpath.Substring(0,separator);
//find the item name
string element = newXpath.Substring(separator + 1);

XmlNode groupNode = objectXmlMap.SelectSingleNode(group);
//determine if group already exists. if not, create one.
if (groupNode == null)
{
   //allow only one thread to modify the xml tree at one time
   lock(this)
   {
      //build the xml tree for the group
      groupNode = CreateNode(group);
   }
}
//get a unique key to identity of object; it is used to map
//between xml and object key used in the cache strategy
string objectId = System.Guid.NewGuid().ToString();
//create a new element and new attribute for this particular object
XmlElement objectElement = objectXmlMap.OwnerDocument.CreateElement(element);
XmlAttribute objectAttribute =
                        objectXmlMap.OwnerDocument.CreateAttribute("objectId");
objectAttribute.Value = objectId;
objectElement.Attributes.Append(objectAttribute);
//Add the object element to the Xml document
groupNode.AppendChild(objectElement);
objectTable.Add(objectId,o);
}
```

The AddObject() method calls the XmlNode.AppendChild() and XmlAttribute-Collection.Append() methods to dynamically build the new elements in the XML document. The mapping between the XML document and hash table is achieved through a dynamically generated GUID, which is used as key in the hash table and an attribute value on the element representing the cached object. If the group name part of xpath doesn't exist in the XML document, we must first build an XML tree that represents the group and then attach the new element to the newly created group.

The CreateNode() method takes an XPath expression and builds the XML tree that matches it. CreateNode() contains a loop that iterates each level of xpath and creates the corresponding XML node in the objectXmlMap dynamically:

```
private XmlNode CreateNode(string xpath)
{
    string[] xpathArray = xpath.Split('/');
    string root = "";
    XmlNode parentNode = (XmlNode)objectXmlMap;
    //loop through array of levels and create corresponding node for each level
    //skip the root node.
    for (int i = 1; i < xpathArray.Length; i ++)
    {
        XmlNode node = objectXmlMap.SelectSingleNode(root + "/" + xpathArray[i]);
        // if the current location doesn't exist, build one
        //otherwise set the current location to the child location
        if (node == null)
        {
            XmlElement newElement =
                        objectXmlMap.OwnerDocument.CreateElement(xpathArray[i]);
            parentNode.AppendChild(newElement);
        }
        //set the new location to one level lower
        root = root + "/" + xpathArray[i];
        parentNode = objectXmlMap.SelectSingleNode(root);
    }
    return parentNode;
}
```

The method first converts the XPath expression into a string array of XML node names. It then checks for the existence of each node, starting from the top of the array, which contains the highest node of the XML tree. When it has found one node that doesn't exist in the XML tree, it will create one and append the new node to its parent node. When the loop finishes, all the necessary nodes will be present in the XML tree for the given XPath expression.

Step 3: Create Retrieve Methods

Believe it or not, all the heavy lifting code has already been done for this caching service. The retrieve methods are trivial and tiny; they merely perform a query on the XML document, identify the objectID stored in the element, and return the object that matches the objectID from the internal hash table. These methods are self-explanatory:

```
private object RetrieveObject(string xpath)
{
    object o = null;
    XmlNode node = objectXmlMap.SelectSingleNode(PrepareXpath(xpath));
    //if the hierarchical location existed in the xml, retrieve the object
    //otherwise, return the object as null
    if ( node != null)
    {
        string objectId = node.Attributes["objectId"].Value;
        //retrieve the object through cache strategy
        o = objectTable[objectId];
    }
    return o;
}
```

As mentioned earlier, you can also retrieve an array of cached objects that belong to a certain group using RetrieveObjectList(). The implementation of RetrieveObjectList() is very similar to that of RetrieveObject(), except that we want to use SelectNodes() to get a list of nodes that match the XPath expression. We will then loop through the list of nodes to create an object array dynamically to match the cached objects in the nodes:

```
private object[] RetrieveObjectList(string xpath)
{
    XmlNode group = objectXmlMap.SelectSingleNode(PrepareXpath(xpath));
    XmlNodeList results = group.SelectNodes(PrepareXpath(xpath) + "/*[@objectId]");
    ArrayList objects = new ArrayList();
    string objectId= null;
    //loop through each node and link the object in object[]
    //to objects stored via cache strategy
    foreach (XmlNode result in results)
    {
        objectId = result.Attributes["objectId"].Value;
        objects.Add(objectTable(objectId));
    }
```

```
    //convert the ArrayList to object[]
    return (object[])objects.ToArray(typeof(System.Object));
}
```

Step 4: Create Remove Methods

The remove methods are simple, too. When you call a remove method to remove a cached object, SAF.Cache will remove it from both the XML document and the hash table. The RemoveObject() method first identifies whether the xpath parameter is referring a group or an actual element. Because a group is only a container for the elements associated with cached objects, we want to remove only the group's child nodes and the cached object associated with each node in the hash table. This is exactly what RemoveObject() does:

```
private void RemoveObject(string xpath)
{
    XmlNode result = objectXmlMap.SelectSingleNode(PrepareXpath(xpath));
    //check if the xpath refers to a group(container) or
    //actual element for cached object
    if (result.HasChildNodes)
    {
        //remove all the cached objects in the hashtable
        //and remove all the child nodes
        XmlNodeList objects = result.SelectNodes("*[@objectId]");
        string objectId ="";
        foreach (XmlNode node in objects)
        {
            objectId = node.Attributes["objectId"].Value;
            node.ParentNode.RemoveChild(node);
            objectTable.Remove(objectId);
        }
    }
    else
    {
        //just remove the element node and the object associated with it
        string objectId = result.Attributes["objectId"].Value;
        result.ParentNode.RemoveChild(result);
        objectTable(objectId);
    }
}
```

The RemoveObject() method removes both the XML element and the item from the hash table when called. If the input parameter xpath references a group, the RemoveObject() method will then remove all the elements that contain the objectID attribute and items from the hash table whose keys match those objectIDs. The RemoveObject() method doesn't remove the group element, since the group element represent the logical layout of the cache objects and may potentially be reused by multiple instances of the clients.

After reviewing the add, retrieve, and remove methods, we know that the Cache class will enable developers to store and retrieve cached object through an XML-friendly interface, and to treat cached objects in logical groups. The next question on the improvement list is, How we can make this class more extensible? The cache service we have just seen would work, but how flexible is it really?

Strategy Pattern

Object inheritance is a powerful concept; it allows us to "program by difference." In other words, it allows us to code only methods that implement the business logic that is different from that of the base class. We can write a class to provide a certain service, such as SAF.Cache. This class provides a default implementation of object caching management and also can be used as the foundation class for any specialized caching service class in the future. We can achieve this in .NET by marking the method in the base class as "virtual," and marking the same method of the inherited class "override." Using our caching service example, we need to create a new class that extends SAF.Cache and overrides the selected methods if we want to use a different implementation for storing and retrieving the cached object:

```
public class Cache
{
    public virtual void AddObject(string xpath, object o){...}
    public virtual void RemoveObject(string xpath){...}
    //additional method omitted
}

public class SpecialCache : Cache
{
    public override void AddObject(string xpath, object o){...}
    public override void RemoveObject(string xpath){...}
    //additional method omitted
}
```

Figure 5-1 shows the relationship between `Cache` and `SpecialCache`.

Figure 5-1. Relationship between the `Cache` *and* `SpecialCache` *classes*

Inheritance saves us from duplicating the same code, yet at the same time provides a means for us to alter the behaviors for the child class. However, inheritance is not the only way to achieve code reuse. We can accomplish the same goal through delegation. Instead of owning the implementations for certain services, a class that uses delegation will forward the request to other external classes that provide the implementation for the service. In other words, instead of doing the work yourself, you would ask (or delegate) someone else to do the work. In the case of the delegation approach, a set of classes can act as service providers that are shared by a set of consumer classes and thereby reuse the code inside the service-provider classes. "Strategy," one of the GOF design patterns, uses the delegation approach to make your code extensible.

These are two completely different approaches to code reuse. How do we know when to use one or the other? Before we quickly jump to conclusions, let me tell you about some social observations that I found to resemble technical discussions about inheritance versus delegation.

Rich Son, Poor Son

There are always some names that come to mind when we think about the wealth that is passed down from one generation to the next: William Ford (heir of Henry Ford), Roberson Walton (Sam Walton's heir), and kings and princes around the world. They are the heirs of wealthy individuals who were extremely resourceful, and they are commonly portrayed as successful people and admired or envied by us. Those in this camp don't have to be extraordinary or exceptionally gifted. All they needed was a rich father who passed down his wealth to them.

Of course, the world would be a far less interesting place if the only way to become wealthy and successful were to have a wealthy father or mother. There is another camp of people, those who were brought up with little more than their own ambition. We can easily think of many individuals who built great things and possessed great wealth without inheriting money from their parents. While those in both camp may own a great quantity of resources, those from second camp have been an inspiration for generations of entrepreneurs. This group came into the world with very little, but they were able to learn from the people, events, and experiences surrounding them. The great things that such people accomplish are evidence of the extraordinary skills they have learned during their careers. Compared with this group of talented people, rich sons and daughters can be seen as ordinary people put into an extraordinary situation. Because their "success" came so easily, they don't have to work very hard.

The moral behind this rich son/poor son digression is that you don't have to have a rich father to be successful, and you don't have to be very talented to be "successful." Those who don't want to work hard can still be wealthy if they inherit their wealth from their parents. Similarly, a class doesn't have to be well thought out or well designed to do something well; it can simply inherit from a well-designed and resourceful parent class. As a developer, you can easily make a bare-bones class very useful by extending it from a resourceful base class and altering certain behaviors by overriding the parent method to satisfy particular business needs. Inheritance makes it easy for you to customize while having access to all the services in the base class without writing any code.

However, when you win something, you lose something too. In this case, you lose flexibility. You would have first to make your class a child class. This would couple your class tightly to the base class, which means that you will inherit from the base class whether you like it or not. When you have few child classes, things are not that bad, since through a good base class design we can put into the base class exactly the things that the child classes want. However, as you begin creating more child classes, you require more specialized behaviors for the child classes, and many things in the base class that were thought of as common features at beginning are common no longer. You then have to start to strip things out of the base class, since they are not common, and start implementing the specialized functionalities at each child class level. However, there may still be a considerable amount of common code among many of the specialized child classes, but because this code still doesn't qualify as being in the base class, you end up writing a great deal of duplicated code in the child classes. This is usually the sign that the class hierarchy needs improvement so that group common code can be effectively grouped among the classes. It is the same case as in inheritance of wealth. If you are the only child of a rich father, you are likely acquire considerable wealth from him. But if you have ten other siblings, you may get very little: The amount you stand to inherit becomes smaller, since there just isn't enough money (or the "common things" that each child needs) to spread around.

On the other hand, if you have chosen the delegation approach, you will need to identify the parts of your class that can be pulled out and shared by other classes. This approach provides you with maximum flexibility, because you can choose which common features your class wants to access. If you want the class to possess certain special features, you can add some special code for that particular class without affecting other classes, or better yet, you can put the special code into a new class if such code is considered common among similar classes. Through delegation, you are able to create a class by assembling existing functionalities of existing classes without creating tight coupling among classes. Of course, the cost of this flexibility is the extra work you have to invest up front to identify the code that can be considered reusable in your application. It is not always easy to spot the common themes in an application. Code that is considered unique to a class may turn out to be code that a family of classes can share. Creating a good application design involves striking a good balance between having to write too much duplicate code in classes and having to write too many "common functionality" classes that are rarely shared within an application.

To my mind, both approaches are equally important in promoting code reuse. Inheritance is the easier model to understand and implement, but if child classes are doing things beyond what the base class has anticipated, you will find yourself writing a lot of duplicated code across the child classes. Delegation is more flexible, and it allows you to assemble your class without restrictions, but the extra flexibility will do you no good if your application is unable to take advantage of it during its lifetime, especially when such extra flexibility is commonly associated with higher cost.

A well-known quotation from the GOF, "Favor object composition over class inheritance," stated in their design pattern bible (p. 20), should not be used as an excuse to choose delegation over inheritance blindly. Although we may despise those rich sons, don't we all secretly yearn to be rich without hard work? ;-)

Let's return to my caching service after this long-winded social commentary. The existing caching service works, but it is inflexible. Someone may want to store the object reference in something other than a hash table. Someone else may want to add certain special features to the caching service that make sense for their application; for example, they may use the caching service extensively and therefore decide to serialize and store some rarely used objects on the disk or remove the objects from memory completely. I want the developer to enjoy the flexibility of object grouping through the XML "interface," but that shouldn't stop them from choosing a different implementation for storing cached objects that makes the most sense to their own applications.

As part of the framework, the goal for the caching service is that it should be built in such a way that developers can easily plug in a different implementation of how objects are cached. Again, we have two choices before us: inheritance or delegation.

Inheritance is not a good choice for this particular problem, because each method in our caching service interacts with both an internal XmlDocument and an internal Hashtable. Had we chosen the inheritance path and replaced the hash table with some other object-storing mechanism, developers would have to extend our cache class and override every method and rewrite them from scratch with their own implementations. The end result is that there would be very little functionality that the child class could inherit, hence very little code reuse.

On the other hand, the strategy pattern, which uses the delegation approach, can provide us with the flexibility that SAF.Cache needs to meet our requirements.

Intent

We quote from GOF's book, which has this to say about the strategy pattern: "Define a family of algorithms, encapsulate each one, and make them interchangeable. Strategy lets the algorithm vary independently from the clients that use it." Figure 5-2 shows the structure of the strategy design pattern.

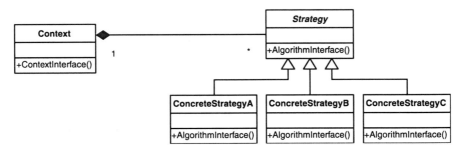

Figure 5-2. Structure of the strategy design pattern

My interpretation of strategy is this: When our application depends on certain parts of the code for its behavior, we can extract such code into a separate "strategy" class. We will then have the luxury of changing the behavior of our application without changing the application code by using separate plug-and-play strategy classes in certain spots in the application.

In the context of our caching service, we want to change the way objects are cached. We can extract the logic on how objects are cached into a separate CacheStrategy class. We can code our caching service in such a way that it depends on an external cache strategy class when it operates. Developers can then change the way our caching service operates by providing a different strategy class without having to touch a single line of code inside our caching service class. Figure 5-3 shows the new caching service which uses the strategy pattern. SAF.Cache.ICacheStragegy is an interface. It contains the method signature any concrete cache strategy class must implement before becoming pluggable strategy for our caching service.

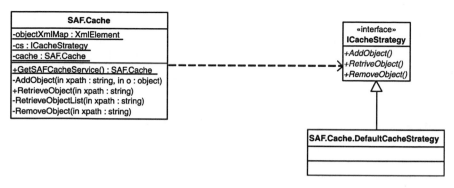

Figure 5-3. Class diagram for SAF.Cache

Notice the SAF.Cache.Cache class no long holds hash table variables; instead, it contains a new static variable cs of type ICacheStrategy. The variable cs is assigned to a concrete class that implements the ICacheStrategy interface in the class constructor of the Cache class. Figure 5-3 shows the one scenario in which SAF.Cache.Cache uses SAF.Cache.DefaultCacheStrategy for its object storage job. DefaultCacheStrategy can be easily replaced with another type of cache strategy class without the necessity of changes to the Cache class.

The following code fragment shows how the cache strategy class is dynamically selected and how the caching service delegates the object storage task to the cache strategy:

```
public class Cache
{
    private XmlElement objectXmlMap ;
    private SAF.Cache.ICacheStrategy cs;
    private static Cache cache;
    private XmlDocument rootXml = new XmlDocument();
    //making the constructor private forces developers to use the
    //singleton pattern to create the instance of this class.
    private Cache()
    {
        //retrieve setting from configuration file
        ConfigurationManager cm = (ConfigurationManager)
            ConfigurationSettings.GetConfig("Framework");
        //load the cache strategy object
        cs = (ICacheStrategy)cm.CacheConfig.GetCacheStrategy();
        //create an Xml used as a map between xml expression and object cached in
        //the physical storage.
```

```
        objectXmlMap = rootXml.CreateElement("Cache");
        rootXml.AppendChild(objectXmlMap);
    }
    public virtual void AddObject(string xpath, object o)
    {
        //code omitted
        //replace "objectTable.Add(objectId,o)" with the following
        cs.AddObject(objectId,o);
    }

    // code omitted.
    }
```

The new AddObject() method contains similar code. It adds the XML element
to the internal XmlDocument, and then, instead of storing the object to the internal
hash table, it delegates the object storing task out to the concrete strategy class by
calling cs.AddObject().

The reference of cs is assigned in the class constructor using the SAF.Configu-
ration service. The CacheConfiguration class will read the caching service section in
the configuration file and dynamically create and return the concrete strategy
object.

Because the Cache class doesn't treat each client request differently, we want to
make sure that there is only one instance of the Cache class created to provide the
caching service. We achieve this single instance of the Cache class through the singleton design pattern.

Design Pattern: Singleton

The singleton pattern is applied here for two reasons. First, the strategy class is
obtained from the configuration class, and it is assigned to the class variable. We
don't want to make calls to the configuration class for loading the strategy class a
frequent operation. Second, the cache service doesn't maintain any information
specific to a client to justify the separate instance for each client. Since the caching
service treats all object caching requests the same, one caching object instance
suffices to serve everyone. The following is the code that is responsible for creating
only once instance of the Cache class:

```
private static Cache cache;

private Cache()
{
   //code omitted
   private object lockObj = new object();
   cs = SAF.Configuration.CacheConfiguration.GetStrategy();
}
public static Cache GetSAFCacheService()
{
   if (cache == null)
   {
      //thread safety code to ensure only one Cache object is created.
      lock(lockObj)
      {
         if (cache == null)
         {
            cache = new Cache();
         }
      }
   }
   return cache;
}
```

The lock statement in the code ensures that the static method is thread safe, so that there is only one instance created even when multiple threads are calling this static method at the exact same time.

The Testing Project

The Test.SAF.Cache project contains a demo application that you can run to test the features in SAF.Cache. The demo application demonstrates how to store, retrieve, and remove objects from the cache using the SAF.Cache service.

To run the demo, open the solution file "Test.SAF.Cache.sln" and hit F5. There is no additional setup required to run the demo.

Summary

You have learned about some object-caching techniques through a number of caching programs. We started with a discussion of some of the .NET technology that empowers the SAF.Cache, such as XML, XPath, and Hashtable. Using XML as an "interface" gives developers a hierarchical mental map to where objects are stored logically, and allows them to search for and treat cached objects in groups. SAF.Cache implements this idea using the delegation approach with the singleton and strategy design patterns, which allow developers to use different caching algorithms for SAF.Cache without changing the framework code. As we went through the design of the caching service, we also looked at the pros and cons of two approaches in object-oriented programming, inheritance vs. delegation, along with an analogous social commentary on rich sons vs. poor sons.

In the next chapter we shall look at yet another SAF component, SAF.Configuration, which provides architecture for storing and retrieving configuration settings throughout the application.

The SAF.Configuration Service

APPLICATION CONFIGURATION IS a critical part of every application. We use configuration to make our applications more flexible. There are many types of data inside an application configuration. A user ID and password for a database server and a resource URL are some of the common types in application configuration. Application configuration can also take on multiple forms. It can be a simple flat file, an XML file, database records, or a Web service. This chapter is about developing a framework component that standardizes how the configuration data are handled throughout the application. Before the arrival of XML, it was common to use a registry key and flat file to store configuration data. Today, as XML has permeated every corner of software development, the power of XML has been recognized by developers. Many uses of XML have been found that take advantage of this wonderful technology. The .NET framework in particular has taken the XML approach in stride. From configuration files to object serialization, from ADO.NET to Web services, XML seems to pop up all over the place. The XML approach in application configuration under the .NET framework has made specifying and retrieving configuration information much simpler. You will learn about this brand new way to work with application configuration settings in this chapter. We will also look at the SAF.Configuration service, a framework component that is built on the basis of the .NET configuration approach and that adds additional features that simplify application configuration.

Motivation and Goal

Developers usually know several different ways of storing and retrieving the configuration data for their applications. This often results in multiple configuration mechanisms being implemented within an application as each team on the project tackles the application configuration problem in its own way. This leads to a management nightmare when it comes time to make different pieces of the application work together. The same set of configuration information may be used by multiple development teams and defined in multiple places. As configuration data change, developers have to make changes to all the configuration settings in different places and make sure that they are all properly synchronized. The goal for the SAF.Configuration service is to provide a consolidated and centralized approach to application configuration. Developers can define multiple configurations for different parts of an application, but they can also define a single configuration class from which all other scattered configurations are controlled through SAF.Configuration. SAF.Configuration also aims to reduce duplication of configuration data throughout the application.

The SAF.Configuration service also provides a foundation for creating strongly typed configurations. In other words, we can write a strongly typed configuration layer modeling SAF.Configuration that would make retrieval of the configuration data a much simpler task for developers.

.NET Technology Overview

SAF.Configuration is based on the .NET configuration architecture, so it makes sense that we must first understand how configuration files work in a .NET application before understanding how SAF.Configuration is implemented. We will take a closer look at the .NET configuration architecture next.

.NET Configuration

In .NET applications, configuration information is stored in the form of an XML document. There are two types of application configuration files: `web.config` and `*.exe.config`.

`Web.config` files are used to provide the configuration for ASP.NET applications (including Web service applications). They are located under the Web application folder. On the other hand, `*.exe.config` is used by executable applications, namely, console applications, windows applications, and Windows service applications. The `*` in the file represents the application assembly name. For example, the configuration file name for `TestApp.exe` must be `TestApp.exe.config`. The configuration file for the executable application is located in the same directory as the executable file. CLR would look for these configuration files at the predefined location described previously. Therefore, you must deploy the configuration file to those locations in order for CLR to be able to read it.

NOTE *When developing .exe applications in VS.NET, you can ask VS.NET to automatically copy the configuration file to the right location by adding an* app.config *file to the startup project. VS.NET will copy the content of* app.config *to a new file called* *.exe.config *and put it in the right location depending on whether it is debug build or release build during the compilation.*

After CLR has read the configuration file, it will configure your application based on the setting inside the configuration file. For example, CLR will configure a Web request to run under the user's account if one of the nodes in the web.config file is defined as follows:

```
<identity impersonate="true" />
```

By specifying the configuration file for your application, you not only provide information on the basis of which CLR will configure your application, but you also provide your application an easy way to access the information in the configuration file through various classes under the System.Configuration name space. For example, you can specify some application-specific information inside the configuration file and retrieve it from within your application code as follows:

```
string dbconnection - ConfigurationSettings.AppSettings["DatabaseConnection"];
```

The previous code will retrieve the database connection information stored in the AppSettings section of the configuration file as follows:

```
<appSettings>
    <add key="DatabaseConnection" value="Initial Catalog=
                                    Northwind;Data Source=localhost;" />
</appSettings>
```

Of course, one thing that is always true in software development is that there is no magic. As we can define what sort of information in the configuration file, someone has to read it, do something about it. The configuration settings wouldn't just magically appear when they are requested. In .NET, all the information in the configuration file "pass through" an special interface called IConfigurationSection-Handler.

This interface is very simple, it contains only one method.

```
object Create(
    object parent,
    object configContext,
    XmlNode section
);
```

The class that implements the System.Configuration.IConfigurationSection-
Handler is responsible for actual reading the Xml stored in the configuration file,
do something with it and make the information in such form that can be easily
consumed by your application. It is important we know about this method
because it is the method CLR will call at the runtime to retrieve the configuration
information and it is the foundation of .NET configuration architecture.

To better understand the .NET configuration architecture, we need to look at a
sample of configuration settings and see how IConfigurationSectionHandler plays
an important role to support the application configuration in .NET. Following is a
sample configuration file.

```
<configuration>
    <configSections>
        <section name="Lunch" Type="Life.Food,Life" />
        <section name="Dinner" Type="Life.Food,Life" />
    </configSections>
<!---------above is the section handler group----------->
<!---------below is the section group----------->
    <appSettings>
        <add key="Location" value="Close to work">
    </appSettings>
    <Lunch soup='eggdrop' soda='coke' dish='beef with broccoli' />
    <system.web>
        <identity impersonate="true" />
        <authentication mode="Forms">
            <forms name="LoginFrm" loginUrl="/ASPX/Login.aspx" />
        </authentication>
        ....
    </system.web>
</configuration>
```

This configuration is a simplified ASP.NET application's configuration file.
Everything defined inside the configuration file is wrapped in the <configuration>
tag, which is the root tag. The data can be broken into two groups: section handler
group and section group. In our case, the section handler group is defined inside

the <configSections> tag, and the section group is everything outside of the <configSections> tag. The comments in the previous example illustrate the boundary between these two groups.

The section handler group defines the classes that handle the data stored in different sections or tags in the section group. Notice that the type attribute under the <configSections> is actually the type information for the section handler class (class name followed by its assembly name, separated by a comma). The name attribute refers to the tag name under the section group. In our example, the configuration indicates that the Life.Food class in the Life assembly will be used to handle the information stored under the <Lunch> and <Dinner> tags defined in the section group. The relation between the section handler group and section group is a parent-child relationship. In other words, you can have a section handler for a nonexistent section tag, but you can't have a section tag if none of the handlers defined in the section handler group associates with it. You will get a run-time error when you try to run the application.

Now that we know the relation between the handlers and sections, we might ask how exactly the section handler handles the section tags it is associated with. Let's return to the IConfigurationSectionHandler interface. Each section handler defined in the configSections are classes that implement IConifgurationSection-Handler. When the application calls the following code at the run time, CLR will perform two tasks:

```
object lunchInfo = ConfigurationSettings.GetConfig("Lunch");
```

First, the CLR will locate the section handler whose "name" attribute is "Lunch" in the section handler group of the configuration file. It then creates the handler object based on the "type" attribute for the particular section handler through reflection. It will then call the "create" method on the newly created handler object and pass three parameters, the most important of which is the third parameter, which contains the actual XML (in XmlNode type) of a particular section content. In our example, the CLR will pass in the XmlNode, which contains <Lunch soup='eggdrop' soda='coke' dish='beef with broccoli' />, to the Create method as its third parameter. The handler is now in charge of extracting the useful information from the XmlNode object and returning an object that encapsulates the "lunch" information in a predefined form. For example, Life.Food's create method (of the handler class) can return a hash table as the return object. Developers can then figure out what I had for lunch by calling lunchInfo[key]. You can also make Life.Food's create method simply return the XmlNode so that developers have the freedom to parse the XML node themselves and extract whatever information they want. Another option is for the create method to return a strongly typed object so that developers can work with an object that contains multiple properties and methods instead of information in simple key-value pairs or an XML string. We will look at the strongly typed configuration later in this chapter.

It is important to know that CLR instantiates the handler class only once, when the application first calls the GetConfig method with a given section. CLR will cache the return object to serve any subsequent GetConfig calls on the same section. If you change the content of the Web application's configuration file (web.config) while the application is still running, CLR is smart enough to know that you have made a change to the configuration, and it will clear the cached configuration result so that it can reinstantiate the handler to obtain the updated configuration settings. However, CLR will not refresh the configuration when you are developing a non-Web application. You would have to implement such features yourself.

Now we know how CLR uses the section handlers, we can summarize the steps for creating and using your own customized configuration section handlers in three points:

- Create a handler class that implements the IConifgurationSectionHandler, and implement the create method so that it returns an object that encapsulates the configuration settings.

- Add the section handler under the <configSections> in the configuration file for the newly created handler class.

- Add the actual configuration settings that correspond to the handler classes to the configuration files. Make sure the tag name matches the name attribute of the handler in <configSections>.

These three steps apply to all the sections within the configuration file regardless of whether the section is defined by the user or comes as part of the .NET framework. You may ask why there are no section handlers defined for <system.web/>, <identity impersonate='true' /> that are commonly found in the configuration file. To answer that question, you need look no further than the machine.config file in the C:\WINDOWS\Microsoft.NET\Framework\v1.0.3705\CONFIG folder. A portion of machine.config is shown here:

```
<configuration>
    <configSections>
     <section name="appSettings" type="…NameValueFileSectionHandler.../>
     ...
     <sectionGroup name="system.web">
       <!-- security -->
```

```
        <section name="identity" type=
                        "System.Web.Configuration.IdentityConfigHandler.../>
        <section name="authorization" type="…AuthorizationConfigHandler.../>
        ...
      </sectionGroup>
    </configSections>
</configuration>
```

The file `machine.config` defines the .NET native configuration section. All the handlers in `machine.config` are automatically loaded, and therefore the entire configuration section can be used within each application configuration file without declaring those section handlers. Most of the section handlers defined in the `machine.config` file are used by .NET CLR to set up the run-time environment for your application. They are not intended to be used directly from your application code. In fact, VS.NET hides many of these handler classes as well as the configuration class they reference. Therefore, you wouldn't able to reference them inside your code even though you know they exist. However, you can use these handlers indirectly by specifying the configuration sections in your configuration file.

NOTE *The principle behind the configuration file for ASP.NET applications is exactly the same as for non-ASP.NET applications such as console applications.*

However, the .NET framework comes with four classes that developers can use to create customized configuration settings. Each of them implements the IConfigurationSectionHandler interface, so that they fit quite well into CLR's configuration architecture:

DictionarySectionHandler: Returns the configuration data as a `Dictionary` object. The key is specified in the "key" attribute, and the value is specified in the "value" attribute.

IgnoreSectionHandler: Always returns a null reference. Developers can use it to inform the CLR to bypass the information referenced by this type of handler.

NameValueSectionHandler: Returns the configuration data as a `NameValue-Collection` object, which is similar to a `Hashtable` object except that `NameValue-Collection` can store multiple strings for a single key.

SingleTagSectionHandler: Returns the data stored in the XML attributes as a `Hashtable` object.

Unlike appSettings, which force you to define information inside the `<appSettings>` tag, the four `*SectionHandler` classes don't impose such limitations on your configuration settings. In other words, you can define some settings like the following and still expect CLR to be able to read it:

```
<Lunch soup='eggdrop' soda='coke' dish='beef with broccoli' />
```

Now let's see how we can use the handler class that comes with the .NET framework to handle our Lunch data. First we must define the section handler inside the configSections as follows:

```
<configSections>
    <section name="Lunch"
        type="System.Configuration.SingleTagSectionHandler, System, Version..." />
</configSections>
```

This is all we need to do in the configuration file to set up the handler-section mapping. We will then need to retrieve what I had for lunch from the application code using the `GetConfig` method, as in the following sample code:

```
Hashtable lunch = (Hashtable)ConfigurationSettings.GetConfig("Lunch");
string soup = lunch["soup"].ToString();
string soda = lunch["soda"].ToString();
string dish = lunch["dish"].ToString();
```

Because we have used SingleTagSectionHandler to handle the Lunch element, the `GetConfig()` method will return a `Hashtable` object that contains each attribute with the attribute name as its key.

The four section handlers and AppSettings provide fairly good support for the customized configuration settings for our application, but off-the-shelf handlers lack the support of configuration data that are not in form of key-value pairs. The following is a kind of configuration setting that is not easily expressed in a key-value pair:

```
<MessageLogging>
    <Message type="error" enable="true">
        <Destination>
            <Email address="administrator@company.com"/>
            <Database connection="...."/>
            <Pager number="...."/>
```

```
            </Destination>
        </Message>
        <Message type="information" enable ="false">
            <Destination>
                <Database connection="..."/>
            </Destination>
        </Message>
</MessageLogging>
```

Developers need to provide more than a key to retrieve the database connection information used to store the error message in their code. Obviously, if your application configuration setting has a complicated hierarchical structure compared to the key-value pair, the .NET native configuration handler won't help you much. In such a case, you can develop your own configuration handler to read the settings. SAF.Configuration provides you with a generic handler that allows you to retrieve complex configuration settings. We will look at this in more detail later.

There is another problem associated with the application configuration in .NET. If you are following .NET's configuration architecture, you are required to put all the settings in a single configuration file. This poses no problem if your application consists of only a single executable file or one ASP.NET application; in such a case, a single configuration file is what you need in the application. This is hardly the case for most enterprise applications, where any single application relies on other applications or components to do part of its work. This leads to a problem, whereby the same piece of information is stored in multiple configuration files, leading to a maintenance nightmare when configuration changes occur. Let's look at a concrete example to understand better the effect of this configuration file restriction.

Suppose we want to develop an order-processing application in .NET. We develop an ASP.NET Web application, a Windows form application, and a Web service application. The Web application is used by customers who want to purchase an item on line. The Windows application is used by sales representatives to take orders when customers call in to place an order. The Web service application takes XML data from retail trading partners who submit orders in bulk. We also develop a back-end order-processing application as a Windows service application that processes the orders that come from any of those three channels. We want to make the order process asynchronous by adding a message queue between the three order receivers and the order back-end process application. Figure 6-1 illustrates its high-level design.

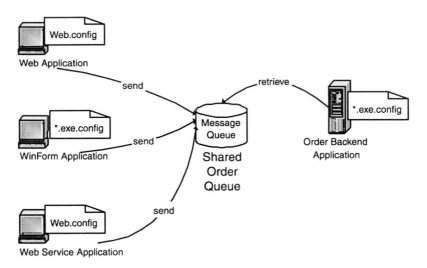

Figure 6-1. A sample application involving multiple configuration files

If we stored the location of the shared order queue in the configuration file, how many times would we need to specify the same information about the location of the queue to make this design work? The answer is four: one in each configuration file. When we need to change the location of the queue, we must remember to go back and change each of these configuration files. This is a common problem whenever there are settings shared by multiple applications. The .NET configuration architecture doesn't support a centralized configuration file that can be shared by multiple applications, but with the help of SAF.Configuration, we can create centralized configuration settings that are shared by multiple applications yet fit into the .NET configuration architecture.

We can summarize the benefits of using SAF.Configuration in two parts. First, it allows developers to specify more complicated configuration settings for the application. Second, it allows developers to use a centralized store for shared configuration settings. Let's take a closer look at how SAF.Configuration achieves these two benefits.

Using the MessageLogging example shown earlier in the chapter, let's think about how we can make the configuration settings of MessageLogging available to developers through configuration handler?

There are two options for transmitting complicated configuration settings from the configuration file to applications. The first option is to create a "barebones" handler class that simply returns the specific section as XML data, and rely on the developers to figure out what part of the data they need for their application. The second option is to create an object that encapsulates the information stored in the configuration file and makes such information easily accessible to developers through the object's properties or fields.

With the first option, the configuration handler would be very lightweight. But developers must have intimate knowledge of the configuration data and its XML structure in order to access the data in their application. The following handler class simply returns the XML data for a specific section:

```
public class GenericHandler: System.Configuration.IConfigurationSectionHandler
{
    public object Create(object parent, object context, XmlNode section)
    {
        return section;
    }
}
```

As you can see, the handler simply returns the XmlNode that contains configuration settings for a given section. Developers, however, wouldn't be able to write much lightweight code in their applications using this generic handler. The following code shows what the segment developer would have to write to get the database connection needed to store the error message:

```
XmlNode messageNode = (XmlNode)ConfigurationSettings.GetConfig("MessageLogging");
string xpathError =
            @"\\Message[@type='error' and @enable='true']\Destination\Database";
string xpathInfo =
            @"\\Message[@type='info' and @enable='true']\Destination\Database";
XmlNode databaseNode= messageNode.SelectSingleNode(xpathError);
string errorConnection = databaseNode.Attributes["connection"].Value;
databaseNode = messageNode.SelectSingleNode(xpathInfo);
string infoConnection = databaseNode.Attributes["connection"].Value;
```

You need seven lengthy lines of code to retrieve a couple of values. By passing the raw configuration data to the developers, you also pass the burden of understanding and parsing the configuration data to the developers in addition to the extra coding effort. The coding effort will duplicate itself many times if developers need to retrieve the same piece of configuration settings at multiple places inside the application. The headache will intensify if the structure of the configuration data is subject to change.

The second option solves this problem by putting the configuration retrieval logic into a separate configuration class and exposing the configuration settings through the class properties or fields. With an additional class, not only do you just need to write the XML parsing logic once, but you also hide the complexity of the hierarchical structure of the configuration data from the developers. One additional benefit for developers who refuse to use Notepad to develop their applications is that they can see exactly what settings are available on the configuration classes through the IntelliSense feature of the VS.NET IDE, since all the settings are expressed as properties, fields, or even methods.

The following is an example of how we can create a configuration object to encapsulate the hierarchical configuration data and allow developers to access the configuration data in an object-oriented way:

```
public class ConfigurationManager
{
    public ErrorMessageConfiguration ErrorMessageConfig;
    public InfoMessageConfiguration InfoMessageConfig;

    //constructor to instantiate the class for specific message types
    public ConfigurationManager(XmlNode messageNode)
    {
        errorMessageConfig = new ErrorMessageConfig(messageNode);
        infoMessageConfig = new InfoMessageConfig(messageNode);
    }
}

//class that holds the config data of error message
public class ErrorMessageConfiguration
{
    public string EmailAddress;
    public string DatabaseConnection;
    public string Pager;
    public ErrorMessageConfiguration(XmlNode messageNode)
    {
        EmailAddress = ...//your XML parsing code here
        ...
    }
}
//class that holds the config data of info message
public class InfoMessageConfiguration
{
    public string DatabaseConnection;
    public InfoMessageConfiguration(XmlNode messageNode)
    {
        DatabaseConnection = ...//your XML parsing code here.
    }
}
```

The ConfigurationManager class is responsible for converting the XML-based information stored in the configuration file into the object-oriented information stored in object method and fields. The following sample code illustrates the use of configuration objects from the developer's perspective:

```
ConfigurationManager cm = (ConfigurationManager)
                          ConfigurationSettings.GetConfig("Framework");
string errorConnection = cm.ErrorMessageConfig.DatabaseConnection;
string errorPager = cm.ErrorMessageConfig.Pager;
string infoConnection = cm.InfoMessageConfig.DatabaseConnection;
```

Compared with the XML code that developers have to code in their applications, the strongly typed configuration object is much easier to understand, and moreover, it eliminates the need for developers to interpret the XML data in the configuration file.

Figure 6-2 shows how we can combine the .NET configuration architecture and strongly typed configuration object approach to create a comprehensive application-configuration mechanism.

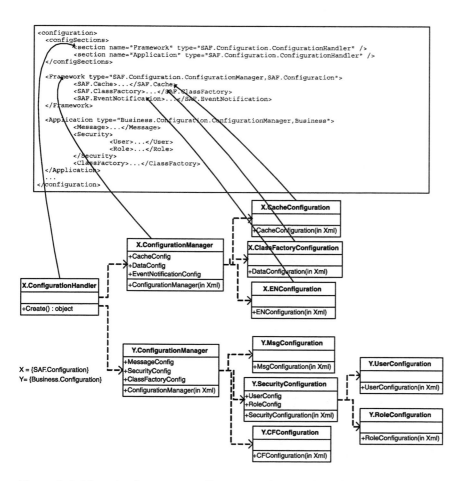

Figure 6-2. Mapping between configuration data and configuration object

There are quite few classes in the figure, but they are all very lightweight. We can categorize the classes into three groups: the handler class, configuration manager class and configuration class.

On the left side of class diagram is the `SAF.ConfigurationHandler` object. It is a class that implements the `System.Configuration.IConfigurationSectionHandler` interface and is called by CLR when the client calls `ConfigurationSettings.GetConfig(sectionName)`. SAF.ConfigurationHandler will initiate the loading of all the configuration objects in the diagram. However, the SAF.ConfigurationHandler doesn't actually load all the configuration objects by itself. Instead, it will load only the "root" configuration object or the configuration manager object; in my case, these would be `SAF.Configuration.ConfigurationManager`, which comes with the SAF framework and is responsible for loading all the configuration objects used by the framework components, and `Business.Configuration.ConfigurationManager`, which needs to be created by the application developers for loading all the configuration objects for their business components. Each of these "root" configuration objects is responsible for loading all the rest of the configuration objects, such as `CacheConfiguration` and `SecurityConfiguration`. From the physical point of view, the "root" configuration object is no different from all these configuration objects. They all follow a simple rule: They all have a constructor that takes XML string parameters, and they set the value for the public fields or properties when their constructors are called. However, there is a difference from the logical point of view. Developers will use the "root" configuration as the entry point to all the configuration information under such a root. The following sample code shows how a developer can use these configuration objects:

```
SAF.Configuration.ConfigurationManager scm =
                ConfigurationSettings.GetConfig("Framework");
Business.Configuration.ConfigurationManager bcm =
                ConfigurationSettings.GetConfig("Application");
SAF.CacheStrategy cacheStrategy = scm.CacheConfig.GetStrategyObject();
string eventServer = scm.EventNotificationConfig.EventServer;
string userName = bcm.SecurityConfig.UserConfig.UserName;
```

As you can see in the sample code, the first two lines of code generate the "root" configuration objects that are the entry points for all other configurations. Developers can retrieve the configuration information by selecting the data fields or "child" configuration objects from the dropdown menu of the IntelliSense of the "root" configuration object. By replacing the lengthy XML parsing code with the strongly typed configuration object, developers can work with application configuration data in a more productive and standardized way.

> **NOTE** *For simplicity, I used the public fields to hold the configuration object reference and configuration data. You can also mark the pubic fields as "read only" and set their value in the configuration object's constructor if you don't want the fields to be overridden. You can replace the public fields with properties if necessary.*

You can create configuration objects that logically represent your application's partitions. For instance, you can create a WebConfiguration object to represent your front-end application, and a BackendConfiguration object to represent your back-end trade-processing application. Because SAF's approach to application configuration goes through configuration components, you can reuse some of the configuration components in multiple applications. For example, you can create one SharedJobQueue configuration object that is shared by many applications that need to send and retrieve messages to and from a centralized queue.

SAF Code Sample Walkthrough

In this section, we will look at some of the code in the SAF.Configuration service, which includes SAF.Configuration.ConfigurationHandler, SAF.Configuration.ConfigurationManager, and a number of configuration classes for the individual framework components, such as CacheConfiguration and ENConfiguration (for event notification). Although SAF.Configuration provides configuration for the framework components exclusively, you can use it as a model to develop your own strongly typed application-level configuration object, because the principle behind these strongly typed configuration objects is the same.

SAF.Configuration.ConfigurationHandler provides a linkage between the .NET configuration file and the strongly typed configuration objects you develop. The following code is for the ConfigurationHandler class:

```
public class ConfigurationHandler  :
                System.Configuration.IConfigurationSectionHandler
{
    public object Create(Object parent, object configContext, XmlNode section)
    {
        Type type = System.Type.GetType(section.Attributes["type"].Value);
        object[] parameters = {section};
        //call the configuration object's constructor
        object configObject = Activator.CreateInstance(type, parameters);
        return configObject;
    }
}
```

The Create method is responsible for creating the "root" configuration object by calling its constructor and passing in the XmlNode that the configuration object needs to interpret. To create an object instance using other than the default constructor, you need to use the CreateInstance method and pass in the object array that contains the matching parameters for the constructor you want to call.

We also need to create the "root" configuration object, the one that is created by the ConfigurationHandler. I will use the SAF.Configuration.ConfigurationManager class as an example. SAF.Configuration.ConfigurationManager is responsible for loading all the configuration data into its public fields and making its "child" configuration objects load the data into their public fields, too. The following sample code exemplifies this approach:

```
public class ConfigurationManager
{
    public SAF.CacheConfiguration CacheConfig;
    public SAF.ClassFactoryConfiguration EventNotificationConfig;
    public ConfigurationManager (XmlNode section)
    {
        CacheConfig = new CacheConfiguration(section.SelectSingleNode("SAF.Cache"));
        ClassFactoryConfig = new
ClassFactoryConfiguration(section.SelectSingleNode("SAF.ClassFactory"));

        ...

    }
}
```

ConfigurationHandler creates the ConfigurationManager object by calling its constructor and passing it the "<Framework>" XmlNode. ConfigurationManager will then create the configuration objects for each of the framework components by calling their constructors and passing in the specific child node under the "<Framework>" node to the corresponding constructor. The "child" configuration objects have a constructor that takes the XML node for which they are responsible and populates the public fields or properties with the data in the XML node. As you can see, when SAF.Configuration.ConfigurationHandler creates the SAF.Configuration.ConfigurationManager, this sets off a chain reaction that creates all the "child" configuration objects and populates the public fields within them. Because CLR will cache the objects returned by all IConfigurationSectionHandler classes registered in the configuration file, this chain reaction happens only once, at the start of the application. Since the root configuration object is cached by CLR and the root configuration object holds the references of all the "child" configuration objects directly or indirectly, all the configuration objects under the root are unavoidably cached also. Beside of the initial chain reaction that creates all the configuration objects, there is no overhead of accessing the data stored in these objects repeatedly throughout the application.

Accessing Centralized Configurations

The second goal for SAF.Configuration is to allow applications to use centralized configuration data to reduce duplicated settings among different applications. To achieve this, we need to be able to retrieve the configuration data from a centralized location, and we need to create some configuration agents whose sole job is to query a location for configuration data.

SAF.Configuration.IConfigurationAgent is an interface that has two methods: Initialize and GetConfigurationSettings. The ConfigurationManager class will call them at run time to retrieve the configuration data from other locations. The following is the definition of IConfigurationAgent:

```
public interface IConfigurationAgent
{
    void Initialize(XmlNode xml);
    string GetConfigurationSettings(string key);
}
```

TestConfigurationAgent.ConfigurationWSAgent is a concrete class that implements IConfigurationAgent and is capable of retrieving configuration data from a Web service. Its source code is located under SAF\Test.SAF.Configuration\ TestConfigurationAgent\TestConfigurationAgent.cs. Let's first look at how ConfigurationWSAgent works. We will look later at how it fits into the SAF.Configuration.

The configuration for the agent class is also described as part of "<Framework>." The following is the configuration for the ConfigurationWSAgent class:

```
<Framework>
    ...
     <SAF.Configuration>
     <ConfigurationAgent>
       <Agent name = "
TestConfigurationAgent.ConfigurationWSAgent,TestConfigurationAgent">
           <Parameters>
               <Section>SAF.ClassFactory</Section>
               <Environment>QAEnvironment</Environment>
               </Parameters>

<Url>http://localhost/ConfigurationData/ConfigurationService.asmx</Url>
        </Agent>
     </ConfigurationAgent>
     </SAF.Configuration>
     ...
    <SAF.ClassFactory ConfigurationAgent="WSAgent1" />
  ...
</Framework>
```

ConfigurationWSAgent is a generic class that is able to retrieve data of type string through a Web service with Url, method, and parameter information. In the example shown, the SAF.ClassFactory component relies on WSAgent1 to retrieve the configuration data. ConfigurationWSAgent uses the information defined under SAF.Configuration/ConfigurationAgent to retrieve the data from the Web service at run time. WSAgent will make a Web service call to http://localhost/ConfigurationData/ConfigurationService.asmx and invoke the GetConfiguration Web method and pass in two string parameters: SAF.ClassFactory that indicate that the configuration data are related to the <SAF.ClassFactory> section and QAEnvironment to indicate that the information is for the QA environment only. The following code shows its implementation:

```
public class ConfigurationWSAgent : IConfigurationAgent
{
    private string section;
    private string environment;
    private string url;
    public ConfigurationWSAgent(){}
    /// this method sets up the agent with parameter information
    /// defined in the configuration file.
    public void Initialize(XmlNode configData)
    {
        section= configData.SelectSingleNode("Parameters/Section").InnerText;
        environment =
            configData.SelectSingleNode("Parameters/Environment").InnerText;
        url = configData.SelectSingleNode("Url").InnerText;
    }
/// this method calls the Web service and retrieves the actual configuration data
    public string GetConfigurationSetting()
    {
        localhost.ConfigurationService cs = new localhost.ConfigurationService();
        cs.Url = url;
        return cs.GetConfiguration(section,environment);
    }
}
```

The boldface code in the previous example represents the Web service call made to http://localhost/ConfigurationData/ConfigurationService.asmx. ConfigurationWSAgent implements the IConfigurationAgent, interface, which provides the entry point for the framework to call at run time. We must change the ConfigurationManager class a bit to incorporate the scenario in which a certain section of the configuration file relies on the external data resource for its content.

Instead of simply passing XmlNode to the "child" configuration object's constructor, we need to make SAF.Configuration check whether certain sections rely on the configuration agents and load the agents accordingly:

```
public class ConfigurationManager
{
    public ENConfiguration EventNotificationConfig;
    public ClassFactoryConfiguration  ClassFactoryConfig;
    private XmlNode configurationData;
    public ConfigurationManager (XmlNode sections)
    {
        configurationData = sections;
        //ConfigurationAgentManager is responsible for loading the necessary
        //ConfigurationAgent object to retrieve the configuration data
        // from external sources.
            ConfigurationAgentManager cam = new
        ConfigurationAgentManager(configurationData);
        ....
        ClassFactoryConfig = new
ClassFactoryConfiguration(cam.GetData("SAF.ClassFactory"));
    }
}
```

ConfigurationAgentManager, shown in the boldface code in the previous example, represents the class that is responsible for retrieving the configuration setting either by reading from the local configuration file or by calling the configuration agent to retrieve the data from the external resources:

```
public class ConfigurationAgentManager
{
    private XmlNode configurationData;
    public ConfigurationAgentManager(XmlNode configData)
    {
        configurationData = configData;
    }
    /// it returns the XML containing the configuration settings for a given key
    public XmlNode GetData(string key)
    {
        XmlNode result=null;
        XmlAttribute agentAttribute =null;
        if (configurationData.SelectSingleNode(key) != null)
        {
```

```
            //check whether there is an agent defined for a particular
            //section or key.
            //If there is, load the agent and make it retrieve the data;
            //otherwise, just load the data from the configuration file
                agentAttribute =
        configurationData.SelectSingleNode(key).Attributes["ConfigurationAgent"];
                if ( agentAttribute == null)
                {
                    result = configurationData.SelectSingleNode(key);
                }
                else
                {
                    //retrieve the data using the agent
                    string data =
                        GetAgent(agentAttribute.Value).GetConfigurationSetting();
                    XmlDocument xml = new XmlDocument();
                    xml.LoadXml(data);
                    result = (XmlNode)xml.DocumentElement;
                }
            }
            return result;
        }
        /// the method loads the agent using reflection and returns
        /// an instance of the agent to the caller
        private IConfigurationAgent GetAgent(string agentName)
        {
            XmlNode agentNode = configurationData.SelectSingleNode("//Agent[@name =
                '" + agentName +  "']");
            Type type = Type.GetType(agentNode.Attributes["type"].Value);
            IConfigurationAgent agent =
                    (IConfigurationAgent)Activator.CreateInstance(type,null);
            //Initialize method sets up the agent object with the
            //parameter information specified
            //in the file that is needed for the agent to do its job
            agent.Initialize(agentNode);
            return agent;
        }
    }
```

> **NOTE** *Because the configuration agent is loaded through reflection at runtime,*
> *you want to make sure that you put the* dll *file containing the agent class in the*
> *application's* \bin *directory. You can do this either through the "add reference"*
> *feature in VS.NET (recommended) or by physically copying the* dll *file to the* \bin
> *folder. This is the rule not only for the configuration agent classes, but for all the*
> *classes that are loaded through reflection. You must make sure that when your*
> *application is loading these classes (or the assembly they belong to) at run time,*
> *it knows where to find them.*

With pluggable configuration agents, developers can create their own configuration agents to extract data from other external resources, such as database or flat file. The configuration agent is an example of enabling a hot spot through composition. The SAF.Configuration service is responsible for loading the custom agent object into the framework to fill in those hot spots for retrieving data from the external resources. With the SAF.Configuration service and custom configuration agents, you can start consolidating your configuration data for applications by storing the configuration settings that are shared by multiple applications in a centralized location.

Testing the Project

Test.SAF.Configuration project contains a demo application that you can run to test the features in SAF.Configuration. The demo application shows you how to create configuration objects, a configuration manager, and a configuration agent in the application. It also shows you how to use SAF.Configuration to access the application configuration settings in the client code.

Because the demo contains a Web service project, you must first set up the Web virtual directory before you can run the demo. Setting up the Web service project involves two steps: First, copy the ConfigurationData folder from the Test.SAF.Configuration folder to c:\inetpub\wwwroot. Second, set up a virtual web directory called ConfigurationData for the c:\inetpub\wwwroot\ConfigurationData folder.

After you perform the previous steps, you can open the solution file under the Test.SAF.Configuration folder and run it by hitting F5.

Summary

In this chapter you learned about how the .NET application uses a configuration handler to access the information stored in the configuration file. You also learned how to create your own customized handler that provides configuration settings through a strongly typed configuration, which simplifies the retrieval of the configuration settings in an application and decouples an application from the tasks of retrieving and parsing configuration settings from different resources.

In the next chapter, we will look at the SAF.EventNotification service, a framework component that provides a centralized event notification service for local and remote .NET applications.

CHAPTER 7

SAF.EventNotification

YOU WILL LEARN to create an event-notification service in this chapter. So what is event notification? Actually, event notification is common in our everyday life. We can spot it almost everywhere. For example, you can register for a news alert, having CNN e-mail breaking news. You want to be notified when some breaking "event" occurs. It is a much more effective way of receiving breaking news than watching CNN on TV and waiting for breaking news to appear. Breaking news does not occur very often. If you have set up a news alert, you can work on other things during a slow news day. If you had no other choice than to catch the breaking news as it is being broadcast on TV, you would have to sit in front of your TV set all day and achieve nothing. The efficiency of event notification can be easily transferred to application development. In every application, regardless size, you can always identify clients and servers, or service consumers and service providers, for whom event notification would be of benefit.

The most common way for a client to request some service from a server is through a synchronous process in which the client creates an instance of the server and calls its method. This process is easy to understand, but if the server takes a long time to complete its work (or finish the method call), the client will be blocked on method calls and be unable to do anything else. The other way for a client to request services from a server is through event notification, which follows an asynchronous process. In this case, the client requests the service by registering an "event" on the server, and the server can start processing the request. Because clients in this model aren't waiting idly for a response from the server, it is free to perform other tasks and fully utilize the "wait" time that is wasted in the synchronous model. Asynchronous processes are not as straightforward as synchronous processes, since you can't be sure when the server will complete your request, and you have to reconstruct your normal workflow so that your application can perform some additional tasks during the time the server is processing the client requests.

The event-notification model, which has an asynchronous process at its core, is widely used in application development to increase the application's responsiveness and decouple the client from the server, which we will see later in this chapter. SAF.EventNotification is a framework component that allows application developers to take advantage of the event-notification model to build decoupled asynchronous .NET applications. We will spend the rest of this chapter discussing

.NET technologies that enable asynchronous processes in applications and how to build an event-notification service using the example of SAF.EventNotification.

Motivation and Goal

We often need to develop an application that interacts with other applications. We can do this through either a synchronous process or an asynchronous process. For a service that takes a very long time to complete or about which we are not sure when it will complete, asynchronous processes provide the most efficient way for multiple applications to communicate. When multiple applications are involved in completing certain tasks, one goal we want to achieve is for each application to have very little knowledge of the other participating applications. Without an intimate knowledge of other applications, we can decouple the application that provides the service and the applications that consume the service. This will reduce the effect on our applications if one application suddenly changes its operating procedures.

SAF.EventNotification is a framework component that achieves three goals. First, it offers developers an easy way to achieve asynchronous processes in their applications. Second, it decouples the event client and event server so that they can change independently. Third, it will enable .NET applications from different process domains or systems to communicate with each other through event notification.

SAF.EventNotification achieves the first goal through .NET's "delegate" feature, the second goal through the event subscribing and publishing model or event-notification model. And the third goal is met through the use of .NET remoting. To further understand how SAF.EventNotification achieves these goals, we need first to understand how the .NET framework supports asynchronous processes as well as the concept of the event-notification model and its architecture. We will look at both of these in the following section.

.NET Technology Overview

There are some key .NET technologies used in the EventNotification service, namely delegation, asynchronous programming calls, and remoting. We have talked about .NET remoting in Chapter 4, so we will focus on the former two in this chapter.

Delegation

Delegation is a bit difficult to absorb at first glance. This is because it runs against conventional thinking on how a method should be called. In short, delegation is an object-oriented way to call a method. Figure 7-1 illustrates the difference between a conventional method invocation and delegation.

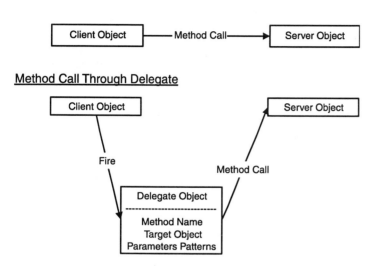

Figure 7-1. Comparison between a conventional method call and a method call through delegation

During a conventional method call, you create an object that contains the methods you want to call, then invoke the method, passing the required parameters. Everything happens in one shot, including defining what object and method to call and invoking the call. However, the method call through delegation takes a different approach. It splits up the definition of the method call and the actual invocation of the call into two parts. Look carefully at Figure 7-1; there is a delegate instance that encapsulates the method information that is necessary for invoking a method call. When using delegation, invoking a method involves three steps: defining a delegate object, creating an instance of the delegate, and firing the delegate instance. As you can see, a delegate is eventually an object for a "method," which is quite different from what is perceived as a "method" in most of our code.

As always, having indirection between two objects promotes decoupling, as we have seen time and time again. Putting a delegate or "method" object between the client and server enables us to define certain actions without invoking them. We can also pass the delegate object around to different applications and have it invoked at different locations. We can also dynamically define the target of the method calls without hard coding it into a conventional method call, in which we have to prefix the method name with the actual target object, such as result = ObjectA.DoWork(). A delegate's ability to delay the invocation of the method and dynamically assign the target of the method calls makes it an excellent underlying technique for asynchronous processes. Let's take a closer look at how delegation is used in .NET.

The information encapsulated inside a delegate about a "method" can be categorized into two groups: method signature and method target. Method signature includes information about the number and type of the method parameters as well as the return type. Method target includes the name of the method and the object in which the method resides.

When we create a delegate object that encapsulates a method call, we must provide these two sets of information. The following is an example of how to create a delegate object in C#:

```
class Test
{
    //define a delegate class
    public delegate int CalculationHandler (int x, int y);
    static void Main(string[] args)
    {
        Math math = new Math();
        //create a new instance of the delegate class
        CalculationHandler sumHandler = new CalculationHandler(math.Sum);
        //Invoke the delegate
        int result = sumHandler(3,4);
        Console.Write("result is: " + result);
    }

}

public class Math
{
    public int Sum(int x, int y)
    {
        return x + y;
    }
}
```

The first thing we need to do to use delegation in our program is to define a delegate class by specifying the signature of the method the delegate class is capable of handling. In our example, I defined a delegate class called CalculationHandler that is capable of handling a method with two integer parameters and an integer return value. If the method doesn't have a return value, then use "void" instead. This rule is the same as that for defining the regular method. After we have defined CalculationHandler, it effectively becomes the inner class of the existing class (in our case, it would be an inner class of the Test class)

After we have defined a delegate class, the next step is to create an instance of the class and bind it to a specific target. In my case, I create a CalculationHandler object called ch and bind it to the math.Sum method. There are two things that require extra attention. First, the delegate class has only one constructor, which takes the "method target" as its only parameter. This effectively binds the delegate object to a physical target. This newly created delegate object now has everything it needs to invoke a method. Second, the method target specified in the constructor must match the method signature defined in the delegate class. In other words, we must make sure that the Sum method matches with the definition of CalculationHandler, which says that the target method must take two integer parameters and have an integer return value. Taking a step further, if you have multiple overloaded methods, you would have to create multiple delegate classes, each matching a specific method signature pattern.

The last step is to fire the delegate. You fire the delegate object by treating it as a method and passing it the actual parameter values. In my example, sumHandler(3,4) returns the value 7. You can also create a delegate that binds to a different target of the same method signature. For example, you can write the following code to get the product of two integers using the same CalculationHandler delegate:

```
CalculationHandler multiplyHandler = new CalculationHandler(Math.Mutiply);
int result = multiplyHandler(3,4);
```

Because we are now treating the method call as an object, we can create a set of such objects and invoke them at once. When we define a class using the keyword "delegate," we are actually creating a class of System.MulticastDelegate type. The definition of MulticastDelegate is shown here:

```
public abstract class MulticastDelegate : Delegate
```

As you can see, Delegate is the base class of MulticastDelegate. In our example, CalculationHandler is of type MulticastDelegate. The term "multicast" in the name indicates that it is capable of invoking method calls on multiple targets. Although most of the time we want to create a delegate object that points to a single "method target," the MulticastDelegate object is in fact one that is created behind the scenes. In other words, when we create a delegate object in our application, we are actually creating a MulticastDelegate object, even though we never declare everything as MulticastDelegate in our application. It is very easy to create a delegate that invokes multiple targets. Here is an example:

```
CalculationHandler allTargets = null;
CalculationHandler sumHandler = new CalculationHandler(math.Sum);
CalculationHandler mutiplyHandler = new CalculationHandler(math.Multiply);
CalculationHandler subtractHandler = new CalculationHandler(math.Subtract);
//chain the delegates together
allTargets += sumHandler;
allTargets += multiplyHandler;
allTargets += subtractHandler;
//fire the multiple targets with one shot
int  result = allTargets (4,3)
```

As you can see in this example, "+=" is used to chain multiple delegates together. If you have written ASP.NET applications or Windows forms applications, you will find this operation very familiar. ASP.NET and Windows forms use the very same operator to hook up events, such as click events, with its handling method. The "–=" operator (not shown in the program) does the opposite. It removes a particular delegate from the chain. When the delegate object has multiple targets, such as allTargets in our example, CLR invokes each individual target one at a time in the order in which the delegates were added to the chain when we fire the delegate. Using the allTargets delegate as an example, CLR will call the Sum method first, then the Multiply method, and the Subtract method last. Delegate invocation in this example follows a synchronous process, but we will see later in the chapter how to invoke a delegate asynchronously, and also how asynchronous programming relies on the concept of delegation for its features.

There are two things about a delegate consisting of multiple targets that we need to keep in mind. First, the return value of the delegate reflects only the return value of the very last target. Result is equal to 1 in the previous example, because the Subtract method is the last target for the allTargets delegate. Due to this restriction, delegation is designed to contain multiple targets that normally don't have a return value, since it would be of little use if you were able to retrieve the value of only the last target. However, there is a way to get around this problem, which we will see next. Second, if one of the target methods throws an exception, the delegate will also stop invoking any further targets. For example, if the math.Multiply method throws an exception, math.Subtract will never get called. This presents a problem in many cases, especially when a delegate is used for some kind of event-notification system. You certainly don't want to stop notification if one of the event subscribers is causing some type of error.

To solve these problems, we need to invoke each of the targets inside the delegate manually by using the GetInvocationList and DynamicInvoke methods.

GetInvocationList is an instance method for MulticastDelegate, which is the class type for all the delegates you define in your code. This method returns delegate[]. Each item in delegate[] is a delegate object that contains a single target. In fact, the GetInvocationList method converts a delegate consisting of multiple targets into multiple delegates each consisting of a single target. The following sample code shows the use of the GetInvocationList method and how we can invoke a delegate manually. The code is a continuation of the previous sample code:

```
Delegate[] delegates = allTargets.GetInvocationList();
object[] parameters = {4,3};
foreach (Delegate dg in delegates)
{
    try
    {
        int result = (int)dg.DynamicInvoke(parameters);
        Console.WriteLine("result is {0}", result);
    }
    catch(Exception ex)
    {
        //ignore the exception.
    }
}
Output on the console:
result is 7
result is 12
result is 1
```

In this example, we use the GetInvocationList method to obtain an array of delegates and then call the DynamicInvoke method to invoke each individual delegate. The DynamicInvoke method takes an object[] as its parameter, which represents the input parameters of the target method. The return value is an object type, which can be cast back to the original return type of the target method. Notice the try-catch block inside the foreach loop. We need a try-catch to ensure the continuity of the loop as the DynamicInvoke method is tried on each of the delegates. As you can see in the result, using GetInvocationList() allows us to retrieve the return value for each of the targets, which is not possible had we invoked the delegate by calling allTarget(4,3).

GetInvocationList and DynamicInvoke are very useful methods, The SAF.Event-Notification service relies on them to call the event subscribers, as you will see later in this chapter.

When we use a delegate to encapsulate method calls, our mindset must shift from the conventional view of method calls to an object-oriented view. Of course, we need to have a compelling reason to adopt an "unconventional way" of invoking method calls. The example we have just seen is nice, but we can get along with calculating sums and products without using delegation. Like e-mail to the Internet, we need to find a killer app for delegation before it can become popular.

Asynchronous programming is the killer app for delegation. In the next section, we will look at how asynchronous programming works in .NET.

Asynchronous Programming

We apply asynchronous techniques in our programs for the same reason we apply them in our daily life. The next time you are waiting in the checkout line at the supermarket, you can think about the process you are engaging in. When the line is short and fast, you will probably just wait in line holding your groceries without doing anything. But if the line is long or someone in front of you has a full cart of groceries, you will probably not just wait there for the next twenty minutes. Instead, you will probably pick up a magazine and try to make the most of the idle time spent in line.

As we are developing business applications, we also try to avoid making the application wait idly for certain tasks. Let's continue using the calculation application as an example. This time, we introduce a SlowAdd method. As the name implies, it takes a long time to add two numbers. This method is useful when you want to demonstrate that the human brain is quicker than a computer:

```
CalculationHandler slowAddHandler= new CalculationHandler(Math.SlowAdd);
int result = slowAddHandler(3,4);
```

As I mentioned earlier, invoking delegates is not asynchronous by default, so it would take SlowAddHandler long time to return the result. The code works, but it blocks the running thread for a long time during the SlowAdd method, because the thread can't continue to the next line of code until the SlowAdd method returns. If we are using a Windows application and calling the SlowAdd method on the main thread, the Windows application would appear to hang for a moment while the thread is blocked. If we are developing a server application, each of the clients will be blocked for the duration of the method call. As a result, the client application's performance will appear sluggish, and the server would have to maintain a large number of blocking threads on the server side, which would drain system resources. Had the client application requested the service asynchronously and the server application served the request asynchronously, the performance and responsiveness on both sides would have been much better.

We can improve the application by adding an asynchronous flavor to the delegate. In the .NET framework, the CLR invokes an "asynchronous" delegate by putting the delegate object into an internal work queue. Threads from an internal thread pool are responsible for watching the internal work queue, retrieving the delegate object from the queue and actually invoking them. As you can see, when an asynchronous delegate is invoked, it is not really invoking in the sense that the target method of the delegate is called as in the "synchronous" delegate scenario, but instead, it been put into a queue where the delegates are processed at a later time. The idea of "storing the delegate and invoking it later" is the central theme of "asynchronous delegation." The following code shows how we call methods asynchronously:

```
CalculationHandler slowAddHandler= new CalculationHandler(math.SlowAdd);
//invoke method asynchronously
IAsyncResult ar =slowAddHandler.BeginInvoke(4,3,null,null);
//check whether the calculation is complete
while (!ar.IsCompleted)
{
    System.Threading.Thread.Sleep(1000);
}
//collecting the result of the method call
object slowResult = slowAddHandler.EndInvoke(ar);
Console.Write ("SlowAdd returns " + (int)slowResult);
```

There is lot of code and new objects in this new sample and may seem to be confusing, but we can summarize everything new about this code into three words: BeginInvoke, IAsyncResult and EndInvoke. Let's take a look at them one at a time.

BeginInvoke and EndInvoke are compiler-generated methods for a specific delegate class. In other words, they are created during the code compilation. Because they don't exist on the CalculationHandler class before compilation, you wouldn't see these two methods in the IntelliSense if you typed a dot right after slowAddHandler. After you compile the program, you can use ildasm.exe to check the newly created methods. Figure 7-2 shows the class structure of the compiled application.

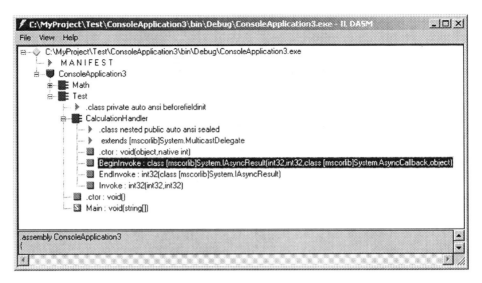

Figure 7-2. The ildasm *tool shows the application's IL code.*

Note that the first two parameters for the BeginInvoke method are of integer type, which matches the method signature for the SlowAdd method, proving that the method has been especially created for the CalculationHandler delegate by the compiler. The last two parameters are used for the callback, which I will talk about very soon.

The difference between a BeginInvoke and the regular way of invoking a delegate object is shown in the following code fragment:

```
//synchronous call
int sum = slowAddHandler(4,3);
//asynchronous call
IAsyncResult ar = slowAddHandler.BeginInvoke(4,3,null,null)
```

When the BeginInvoke method is called, CLR will put the delegate object being invoked into an internal queue, where it will get picked up by a free thread from the internal thread pool. A thread pool is a collection of free threads. A free thread can be taken out of the pool to process some tasks such as method calls, and then returned to the pool when the work is done. The BeginInvoke method returns very quickly because it doesn't take much processing power to drop the delegate object into the internal queue. It is important to remember that the actual target method is not necessarily started when the BeginInvoke method returns. The only thing we know is that the target method will be invoked at some time in the future. The return object of the BeginInvoke method is also significant. The BeginInvoke method returns an AsyncResult object, which encapsulates everything about the result of the delegate method and the state of the method call. For example, AsyncResult.IsComplete tells us whether the delegate method call has been completed. We can write a loop to check it periodically, as the code does in the previous example. Of course, there is a better way than using a loop to obtain notification when the method call is complete. We will see how to achieve that using the AsyncWaitHandler later in this chapter.

> **NOTE** *Each app domain has one thread pool with a default of 25 threads. CLR will use this pool to process the delegates when they are invoked using* BeginInvoke. *If more asynchronous delegates than there are available free threads in the thread pool arrive, CLR will queue the delegates internally and process them as more threads are freed up from the pool.*

If the AsyncResult.IsComplete property returns true, this tells us that the invocation on the method is finished, and we can now query for the return value of the target method. To obtain the return value, we must call EndInvoke and pass in the AsyncResult object returned from BeginInvoke:

```
object slowResult = slowAddHandler.EndInvoke(ar);
```

The return value of the EndInvoke method is the return value of the target method. In this case, it is the sum of two integers. Because the EndInvoke method always returns an object type, we need to perform a type cast to the original return type of the target method. The AsyncResult object stands in a one-to-one relationship to each BeginInvoke call, so we can use AsyncResult to locate the specific result of the method call among multiple asynchronous invocations, as following example shows:

```
IAsyncResult ar1 = slowAddHandler.BeginInvoke(4,3,null,null)
IAsyncResult ar2 = slowAddHandler.BeginInvoke(40,30,null,null)
IAsyncResult ar3 = slowAddHandler.BeginInvoke(400,300,null,null)
...//do some more work with the current thread.
int result1 = (int)slowAddHandler.EndInvoke(ar1);
int result2 = (int)slowAddHandler.EndInvoke(ar2);
int result3 = (int)slowAddHandler.EndInvoke(ar3);
```

By using the asynchronous approach, delegate objects are fired and forgotten. While the target methods are being called, the current thread can perform additional tasks or start a loop to check whether the target method is complete. We can put the current thread to sleep for some time so that it can surrender its time slice to other threads in the system while the target method hasn't yet completed. This approach eliminates some thread blockage in the synchronous delegate example. As a result, more tasks get started at once, but putting a thread through an infinite loop is not by itself an efficient use of system resources. Furthermore, we have to estimate how long we want the thread to sleep between each check for the method completion status. Setting the sleep time too long will make the application sluggish, since the EndInvoke method is called at a much later time. Setting the sleep time too short will demand more system resources than required, since the loop will run more frequently than necessary and produce overhead during the process.

We can improve the second example if we can remove its need to constantly query the IsComplete property in a loop. It would be great if we could add some type of callback mechanism so that instead of having to check constantly for the completion, I get notified when the method completes. It works just like telephone callback. My friend is busy when I call him for a chat. I can call him every two minutes to check whether he is not busy and ready to chat, or I can ask him to call me back when he is not busy. Obviously, the first option is very annoying to both my friend and me (I am the one who is dialing the 16+ digits of the international number and paying the costs). So, how do we implement the callback in .NET? Once again, delegation provides us with an elegant solution.

The .NET framework provides us with a class called AsyncCallback that solves all our problems. Here is its definition:

```
public delegate void AsyncCallback(IAsyncResult asyncResult)
```

Notice that this class is of delegate type. There are two steps invoked in setting up the callback. First, we need to create a "result-catching" method that CLR will call after the original target method completes. This method is responsible for extracting the return value using EndInvoke. The second step is to create a delegate object and make it point to the "result-catching" method. It will be helpful to see how AsyncCallback works by presenting an example. First we need to create the callback or result-catching method that handles the result from the delegates:

```
public void OnSlowAddComplete(IAsyncResult result)
{
    AsyncResult resultObject = (AsyncResult)result;
    //retrieve the delegate object for the result object
    CalculationHandler completedDelegate =
            (CalculationHandler)resultObject.AsyncDelegate;
    //get the return value
    int sum = (int)completedDelegate.EndInvoke(result);
    Console.Write("the result is " + sum);
}
```

This method must take the AsyncResult as its only parameter, as mandated by the AsyncCallBack delegate. It first extracts the delegate from the AsyncResult object, and it will call EndInvoke on that delegate to retrieve the return value and do something with it.

After we create this "result-catching" method, we must inform the CLR to use it when the target method completes. The second-to-last parameter of the BeginInvoke method is there for exactly this purpose:

```
AsyncCallback callback = new AsyncCallback(this.OnSlowAddComplete);
IAsyncResult ar = slowAddHandler.BeginInvoke(4,3,callback,null);
```

As you can see, the callback is pointed to the OnSlowAddComplete method, which gives CLR enough information about what to do after the target method completes.

The very last parameter of BeginInvoke is of object type. It can be used for anything. Most commonly, it is used to provide additional information about what to do with the result. The following code shows one of its uses:

```
//delegate invoking side
string wsUrl = "http://company/ResultCollection.asxm"
...
IAsyncResult ar =slowAddHandler.BeginInvoke(4,3,callback,wsUrl);

//delegate result-handling side
public void OnSlowAddComplete(IAsyncResult result)
{
    ...
    string wsUrl = (string)result.AsyncState;
    //calling web service using the url...
}
```

In my example, the code that invokes the delegate and that invoking the callback method are within the same class. In reality, however, you can put them in separate classes. For example, you can put all the callback methods into one class so that you can change how the results are processed independent from the client code that invokes the delegate. In this case, many variables or instructions on how the results should be processed are invisible to the callback methods in another class. The AsyncState object is the vehicle for transmitting such variable/instruction or other type of information to the callback method.

NOTE *You need to be very careful about issues of thread safety when making the* BeginInvoke *call. One way to avoid such problems is to make sure that each* BeginInvoke *call uses a different callback object from other* BeginInvoke *calls. Otherwise, the same method of the same object that handles the callback may be called by multiple threads at the same time, and any instance members inside the callback method will be subject to data corruption.*

Asynchronous delegate invocation combined with the callback methods is a good approach when the application's flow does not depend heavily on the results of the delegates. For example, you may just want the results of the delegates to be processed at some point, and the outcome of the results does not have a great effect on how the rest of the application proceeds. In that case, such an approach is the best choice for you. However, in many other cases, your application relies on the result of the delegates to do its work. For example, your application dispatches several lengthy method calls through delegates and will make some decision based on the results of those methods. In such a situation, the application flow can't continue until all the results are back, so it depends on the results of the invoked delegates. Here .NET provides you with a much simpler solution through WaitHandle to solve exactly this type of problem. Let's continue with the calculation example, but now with a little twist. We want to add all the results of the delegates and print out "+" if the sum is positive and "−" if it is negative:

```
IAsyncResult ar1= sum.BeginInvoke(4,3,null,null);
IAsyncResult ar2 = multiply.BeginInvoke(4,-3,null,null);
IAsyncResult ar3 = subtract.BeginInvoke(-4,-3,null,null);
WaitHandle[] waitArray =
{ar1.AsyncWaitHandle,ar2.AsyncWaitHandle,ar3.AsyncWaitHandle};
//do some other work
WaitHandle.WaitAll(waitArray);
//at this point all the results of delegates are available.
int result1 = sum.EndInvoke(ar1);
int result2 = multiply.EndInvoke(ar2);
int result3 = subtract.EndInvoke(ar3);
if ((result1 + result2 + result3) > 0)
{
    Console.Write("+");
}
else
{
    Console.Write("-");
}
```

WaitHandler.WaitAll(WaitHandle[]) is a static method that will block the current thread until all the delegate invocations associated with WaitHandler[] have completed. For example, if the delegate invocations for the sum and subtract methods each take 1 second to complete the call, and the invocation for the multiply method takes 5 seconds to complete the call, then the WaitAll method will block the thread for 5 seconds before it returns, so that the current thread can continue to the next line of code. Therefore, by using the WaitAll method, you can ensure that no further process can happen until all the delegate invocations have completed.

There is one more thing I want to mention before we close the discussion on .NET's asynchronous programming. The way exceptions are handled in asynchronous calls is slightly different from that of synchronous calls. In the synchronous call scenario, we are immediately notified when an exception in the method is thrown. However, in the asynchronous call scenario, the client doesn't know about the exception of the target method when it happens, since the client never knows when exactly the target method is invoked. So what happens to the exception if it is thrown inside the target method? It turns out the CLR will catch such exceptions and "suppress" them until the client is ready to retrieve the result of the target method. The client will encounter such an exception when it calls the EndInvoke method on the failed method. Let's look at an example to see how to handle an exception in the asynchronous scenario:

```
IAsyncResult ar = divideHandler.BeginInvoke(3,0,null,null);
WaitHandle.WaitAll(new WaitHandle[1]{ar.AsyncWaitHandle});
//catch the possible exception
try
{
    int result = divideHandler.EndInvoke(ar);
}
catch (Exception ex)
{
    Console.Write(ex.Message);
}
```

Instead of putting the try-catch block around BeginInvoke, we need to put it around the EndInvoke method. In the previous example, the console will print out "Attempting to divide by zero."

With that, we are done with our discussion of delegation and asynchronous programming in .NET. Although there are many aspects of these topics that we haven't covered in this chapter, such as asynchronous support in many .NET framework classes and synchronization issues associated with asynchronous programming, we now have a good enough understanding of these technologies to continue on to the event-notification service. We will look at the architecture of the event-notification service and how it is implemented using the .NET technologies about which you have just learned.

SAF Code Sample Walkthrough

Before we dive into the SAF.EventNotification code, let's have a quick high-level look at the architecture of event notification. The event-notification model consists of at least two parties: the event subscriber and the event publisher. One or more event subscribers register certain events on the event publisher. When an event occurs, the event publisher is responsible for sending notification to each of the subscribers who have registered for such an event. Figure 7-3 illustrates this idea.

AppDomain

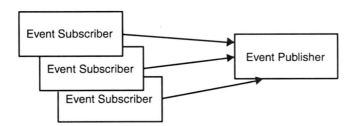

Figure 7-3. Simple event-notification service

As simple as this model appears, it implies a very important application design approach: "Don't call us; we will call you." A rather more technical term for this is the "observer" design pattern. It is the foundation of asynchronous programming.

Design Pattern: Observer

Intent

We quote from the GOF's book: "Observer: Define a one-to-many dependency between objects so that when one object changes state, all its dependents are notified and updated automatically." Figure 7-4 illustrates the observer design pattern.

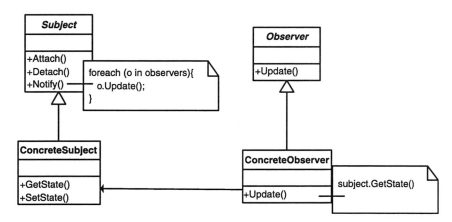

Figure 7-4 GOF's "observer" design pattern

The observers (event subscribers) will receive an "update" when the subject (event publisher) decides to notify each observer. As described in the diagram, attach and detach methods are responsible for registering and unregistering observers who want to participate in the notification. As the event that observers are interested in knowing about occurs, the subject will call the notify method, which in turn will loop through each of the registered observers and notify them by calling its update method.

This approach is identical to that of delegation. You can add an additional delegate or remove a delegate from an existing delegate chain by calling the += or -= operation. For example:

```
delegate chain = new EventHandler(observer0.Update);
EventHandler obs1 = new EventHandler(observer1.Update);
EventHandler obs2 = new EventHandler(observer2.Update);
chain += obs1;
chain += obs2;
//...fire the delegates
chain(this,arg);
```

Here `observer1` and `observer2` are like the observer object in the diagram, while `obs1` and `obs2` are the delegate objects (or the method entry points) for the subject to feed the information to each observer. When the subject, which would be the program that contains the code just presented, is ready to notify each registered observer, it will fire the chain object, which contains a list of registered observers. The CLR will loop through each delegate in the chain and call the `DynamicInvoke` method just as the `Notify` method in the diagram does.

As you can see by comparing the observer pattern and the techniques of delegation, they are based on the same approach when it comes to notifying the registered clients that are interested in certain types of information. When we are using delegation (multicast, to be exact) as the means of invoking multiple methods to respond to certain predefined events, we are unavoidably implementing the observer design pattern.

Given the approach of the observer design pattern, it is obvious that it will provide us an excellent foundation for an event-notification service. However, in taking a close look at the observer pattern, we see that there is always room for improvement.

Figure 7-4 illustrates a shortcoming in the observer pattern. In the diagram, observers need to register themselves by calling the `Attach` method on the subject. The subject, on the other hand, notifies each observer by explicitly calling the method on the observers. Observers and subject must have explicit knowledge of each other to work together. Because the observer holds references of the subject, the observer is being forced not just to subscribe to an "event," but to subscribe an "event" on a particular event publisher. As we introduce additional publishers into the picture, subscribers have to be changed to accommodate the new publishers. With the direct reference between publisher and subscriber, the publisher would also be subjected to constant changes as more subscribers are introduced into the picture. Suppose we added some subscribers that are written in different language, such as Java. The publishers will no longer be able to deliver the event through the invocation of delegates, since a Java program doesn't understand .NET delegation. To talk to the Java subscriber, we would have to add some special communication feature such as a Web service to each potential publisher. As you can see, we would be unable to isolate either publisher or subscriber from the other if we made them reference each other directly as in the observer design pattern.

Fortunately, another GOF design pattern helps to decouple subscribers and publishers, hence allowing subscriber and publisher changes independently.

Mediator Design Pattern

Intent

We quote from GOF's book: "Mediator: Define an object that encapsulates how a set of objects interact. Mediator promotes loose coupling by keeping objects from referring to each other explicitly, and it lets you vary their interaction independently." Figure 7-5 illustrates the mediator design pattern.

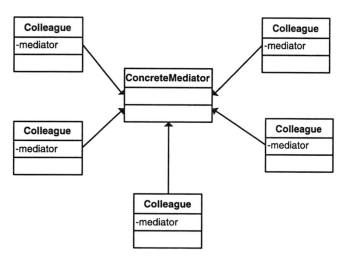

Figure 7-5. GOF's "mediator" design pattern

The mediator design pattern is fairly straightforward. "Colleague" represents the different parties who need to talk to one another. Instead of having a direct linkage between different colleagues, each colleague will communicate directly with a centralized mediator, who will channel the communication among the various colleagues. In the case of event notification, the colleagues can represent event subscribers and event publishers. We can easily convert Figure 7-5 to a blueprint for building our event-notification service, as shown in Figure 7-6.

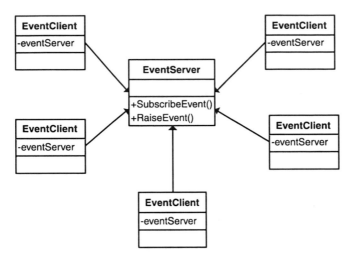

Figure 7-6. Architecture of the event-notification service

Figure 7-6 shows what the SAF.EventNotification service looks like at a high level. Each event client can act as both event subscriber and event publisher. By positioning an event server in the middle, event subscribers and publishers are no longer required to know about each other. All they need to know about is a centralized event server that will automatically route the event notification to the correct parties. Hence it decouples the subscribers and publishers. For the rest of the chapter, we will look at how the event-notification server is actually implemented.

SAF Code Sample Walkthrough

Before we implement the event-notification service, we still have to make one more decision: What kind of communication mechanism will there be between the subscriber and publisher?

We talked about delegation earlier in this chapter. The .NET delegation seems to offer a fairly good mechanism to register and unregister subscribers through the operators "+=" and "-=" and to deliver events through the invocation of delegates. It is a perfect vehicle for delivering event notification between subscribers and publishers in a single app domain. However, there is a problem with delegation when subscribers and publishers are located in different app domains. Figure 7-7 illustrates this problem.

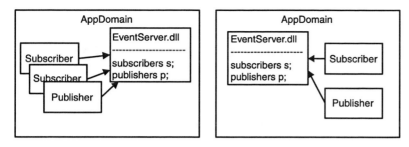

Figure 7-7. Event server in different app domains

If both event subscribers and publishers are within the same app domain, everything seems to work fine. Multiple subscribers and publishers can communicate freely with one another through delegates. This is possible, since all the subscribers and publishers within the same app domain hold the same EventServer object. This is not the case in a multi-app-domain environment, in which the publisher of one app domain tries to push the events to the subscribers located in another app domain. Because each app domain will load a separate EventServer.dll, it doesn't share the same list of subscribers and publishers, and it is impossible for subscriber and publisher to communicate across the app domain boundary. This is a big drawback, since communication fails if two applications that need to communicate with each other are located on different machines or different app domains.

To solve this problem, we must make sure that only one EventServer.dll is loaded for all the applications that want to participate in the event-notification service. We need to have a single centralized event server that every subscriber and publisher from every app domain can easily talk to. Figure 7-8 illustrates this new approach to event notification among separate applications.

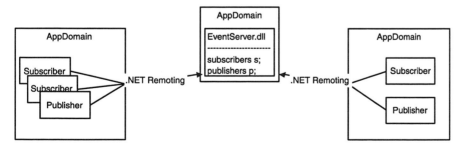

Figure 7-8. The event-notification service with a single event server

The design in Figure 7-8 has one and only one centralized event server, and therefore all the subscribers from separate app domains can register themselves on a single event server. When publishers from separate app domains want to push the event, they will simply send the event to the centralized event server, where it will be propagated to subscribers in several app domains.

We need to rely on remoting technology to support this centralized event server. In the case of the SAF.EventNotification service, I chose .NET remoting for communication between observers and mediator, or subscribers/publishers and event server.

SAF.EventNotification consists of two classes: EventClient and EventServer. EventClient is used by each subscriber or publisher that wants to participate in the event-notification service. The event server is used by the centralized server that hosts the actual event-notification service.

Event Client

Let's first take a look at the EventClient class. It has three major tasks: Establish a connection to a remote event server, allow clients to subscribe or unsubscribe to an event, and publish an event to the remote event server.

EventClient's constructor will get a remote instance of the event server using the GetObject method, as shown in the following code:

```
private EventServer es;
public EventClient(string url)
{
    ChannelServices.RegisterChannel(new TcpChannel(0));
    es = (EventServer)Activator.GetObject(typeof(EventServer),url);
}
```

The SAF.EventNotification.EventServer will be hosted as a well-known server object, since an event client doesn't need to maintain its state across multiple remoting calls. Normally, the client doesn't need to register a channel for the remoting call, but EventClient is different. EventClient not only has to make remote calls to the remote event server, but also must accept notification calls from the remote server when events are published. Registering a TCP channel with port 0 allows the remote event server to push the event back to the clients through .NET remoting.

After a client creates an EventClient object that will hold an internal reference to the remote event server, the client can register, unregister, and publish the event through the remote event server, as shown in the following code:

```
private Hashtable repeatDelegateTable = new Hashtable();
public void SubscribeEvent(string name, EventProcessingHandler s)
{
    //check if the event has already subscribed by the client
    Delegate handler =(Delegate)repeatDelegate[name];
    //if already subscribed, chain up the delegates
    //otherwise, create a new delegate and add it to the repeatDelegate
hashtable
    if (handler != null)
    {
        //chain up the delegates together
        handler = Delegate.Combine(handler, s);
        //reset the delegate object in the hashtable
        repeatDelegate[name] = handler;
    }
    else
    {
        repeatDelegate.Add(name,s);
        EventClient.EventProcessingHandler repeat = new
                    EventClient.EventProcessingHandler(Repeat);
        //subscribe the "repeat" delegate to the event server.
        es.SubscribeEvent(name,repeat);
    }
}
//the method that dispatches the invocation to
//client's delegate objects for a given
//event
public void Repeat(string eventName, object content)
{
    EventProcessingHandler eph = (EventProcessingHandler)repeatDelegate[eventName];
    if (eph !=null)
    {
        eph(eventName, content);
    }
}
```

The `SubscribeEvent` method on the client side works as follows: When a client calls this method and passes in the event name and a client-side delegate object for the callback method, `SubscribeEvent` will first add the event name and the delegate to an internal hash table. It will then create another delegate that points to the `EventClient.Repeat` method and register this newly created delegate to the remote event server. Now, you may ask why not simply register the client's delegate directly to the event server. Why add an extra step in between? This is very good question. The answer lies in the fact that the event server wouldn't have the type information for every client that registers the event. The delegate object contains the target method on a certain target object. Without the type information, the event server wouldn't know how to interpret the delegate objects that are sent to it through the remoting calls. Since we don't know at design time how many different types of clients will be using the event server, we can't fix the problem by adding the type information of potential clients to the event server. To solve this problem, we must add a middleman or object whose type information is known by both client and server. This middleman is the `EventClient.Repeat` method.

As far as the event server is concerned, it only knows how to invoke a delegate that is pointing to the `EventClient.Repeat` method. The `Repeat` method is called by the remote event server when it pushes the event to the subscribers. As you can see in the sample code, the `Repeat` method simply retrieves the delegate chain stored in the hash table earlier and relays the invocation on the delegate chain. The `Repeat` method acts like the dispatcher who redirects the event to each of the client's delegates. Without this middleman to relay the calls, you would be getting a run-time `System.IO.FileNotFound` exception complaining that CLR is unable to find the file containing the type information of your client class. Another benefit of using a "middleman" to dispatch the calls is to reduce network traffic. If a client registers multiple handlers to the same event, instead of registering every handler for the event on the event server, `SubscribeEvent` on the client registers the "middleman" only once for the event on the event server. Because the client registers only one handler for the event, the client gets only one notification from the event server when the event occurs, as opposed to many notifications if multiple client handlers were registered for the same event. The middleman is responsible for dispatching the notification to the multiple client handlers it tracks locally, hence significantly reducing the network traffic needed to subscribe an event and receive its notifications.

> **NOTE** *There is one thing you need to watch out for when you are using hash tables or arrays to store the delegate object: You must be careful when modifying the delegate using "+="or "-=" or* Delegate.Combine(...) *or* Delegate.Remove(...). *Because using these operators and method results in a new instance of the delegate object, you must reset the object reference stored in the hash table or arrays. Otherwise, the hash table or arrays would still hold the delegate object prior to delegate modification.*

EventProcessHandler is a delegate that the event server will invoke when it is ready to push out certain events to the subscribers. In other words, EventProcess-Handler is the callback entry point on the client side to which the event information is fed. Here is the definition of this delegate:

```
public delegate void EventProcessingHandler(string eventName, object content);
```

The following sample code demonstrates how EventProcessHandler and EventClient are used on the client side:

```
public class TestApp
{
static void Main(string[] args)
{
string remoteEventServer ="http://localhost:4000/EventServer/EventURI";
//get the event client object
EventClient ee = new EventClient(remoteEventServer);
//create a delegate object for the callback
EventProcessingHandler eph =
             new EventProcessingHandler(TestApp.ProcessEventContent);

ee.SubscribeEvent("Test_Event",eph);
ee.RaiseEvent("Test_Event", "This is a test");
Console.ReadLine();
}
//process the event from the event server
public static void ProcessEventContent(string eventName, object content)
{
Console.WriteLine((string)content);
}
}
```

The sample code shows that a client subscribes to an event and raises the event within a single method, which is rare in the real world, but it does get the point across on how the EventProcessHandler works. In the real world, however, you will have a client calling the SubscribeEvent method in one application, and the publisher calling the RaiseEvent method in another. To subscribe to an event, a client has first to create an EventProcessingHandler delegate object (Event-Client.EventProcessingHandler) that points to a callback method for handling the event notification. The client then calls the SubscribeEvent method on the Event-Client class, which intercepts the client delegate and instead informs the event server to use a "dispatch repeat" delegate object for delivering the event to the client side.

The UnSubscribeEvent and RaiseEvent methods are much simpler than the subscribe method:

```
public void UnSubscribeEvent(string eventName, EventProcessingHandler s)
{
    Delegate handler =(Delegate)repeatDelegate[eventName];
    //check if the handler is null
    //if not null, remove the event processing handler from the chain
    if (handler != null)
    {
        handler = Delegate.Remove(handler, s);
        //reassign the chain back to the hashtable.
        repeatDelegate[eventName] = handler;
    }
}

public void RaiseEvent(string eventName, object content)
{
    es.RaiseEvent(eventName,content);
}
```

Event Server

Let's take a look at the event server implementation. The subscribe method will take the event name and delegate object as input parameters and put them into the internal hashtable. When multiple clients subscribe to the same event, the subscribe method will use "+=" operation to chain up the multiple delegate objects. Following is the subscribe method in the EventServer class:

```
public void SubscribeEvent(string eventName, EventClient.EventProcessingHandler
handler)
{
    //ensure that only one thread modifies the delegate chain at a time.
    lock(this)
    {
        Delegate delegateChain = (Delegate)delegateMap[eventName];
        //check if the delegate chain is null. if null, add the
        //client side delegate as the initial handler. Otherwise,
        //add delegate to the chain.
        if (delegateChain == null)
        {
            delegateMap.Add(eventName,handler);
        }
        else
        {
            //add the delegate to the chain
            delegateChain = Delegate.Combine(delegateChain,handler);
            //reset the delegate chain in the hashtable
            delegateMap[eventName] = delegateChain;
        }
    }
}
```

The SubscribeEvent method first checks whether there is already a delegate object for the event name. If the event name already exists, it will pull the delegate chain associated with that event and append the client's delegate object to it using the Delegate.Combine method. Otherwise, it will create an event and associate the client's delegate object with it as the first delegate in the chain. The SubscribeEvent method uses a hash table to store the delegate references.

UnSubscribeEvent is much simpler than the SubscribeEvent method. It uses Delegate.Remove to remove a specific client's delegate object:

```
public void UnSubscribeEvent(string eventName,EventClient.EventProcessingHandler
                      handler)
{
    //ensure that only one thread modifies the delegate chain at a time.
    lock(this)
    {
        Delegate delegateChain = (Delegate)delegateMap[eventName];
        //check if the delegate chain is null. if not null, remove the
        //client side delegate from the delegate chain.
        if (delegateChain != null)
        {
```

```
                    //remove the delegate from the chain
                    delegateChain = Delegate.Remove(delegateChain,handler);
                    //reset the delegate chain in the hash table
                    delegateMap[eventName] = delegateChain;
                }
        }
}
```

The RaiseEvent method is the one that invokes a delegate chain to signal the occurrence of certain events. It is used by the publishers to push the events to the subscribers:

```
public void RaiseEvent(string eventName, object content)
{
    Delegate delegateChain = (Delegate)delegateMap[eventName];
    //retrieve the list of individual delegates from the chain
    IEnumerator invocationEnumerator =
                delegateChain.GetInvocationList().GetEnumerator();
    //loop through each delegate and invoke it.
    while(invocationEnumerator.MoveNext())
    {
        Delegate handler = (Delegate)invocationEnumerator.Current;
        try
        {
            handler.DynamicInvoke(new object[]{eventName,content});
        }
        catch (Exception ex)
        {
            //if the client that receives the event notification is no longer
            //available, remove its delegate
            delegateChain = Delegate.Remove(delegateChain, handler);
            delegateMap[eventName] = delegateChain;
        }
    }
}
```

The RaiseEvent method retrieves the delegate chain that matches the event name and invokes each individual delegate in the chain using the DynamicInvoke method. As discussed earlier in the chapter, using DynamicInvoke combined with a try-catch block allows us to keep processing the delegate even when some of the delegates throw exceptions. For example, if one client is disconnected from the network, we still want the event notification to continue for other clients that subscribe to the events. In the RaiseEvent method, the delegate that caused a problem is removed from the chain in the catch block. You can also add some retry logic so that the client still receives the event when the connection is only temporarily down for very short period of time.

It is important to know that the "handler" stored in the delegate chain on the event server is the transparent proxy to the delegate on the client side. When a client registers an event by calling the SubscribeEvent (string eventName, EventProcessingHandler handler) method on the remote event server, CLR automatically creates a proxy object that stands in for the "handler" parameter. You can verify this by putting a breakpoint at the DynamicInvoke call and adding the "handler" to the watch window. Figure 7-9 shows the watch window containing the "handler" object.

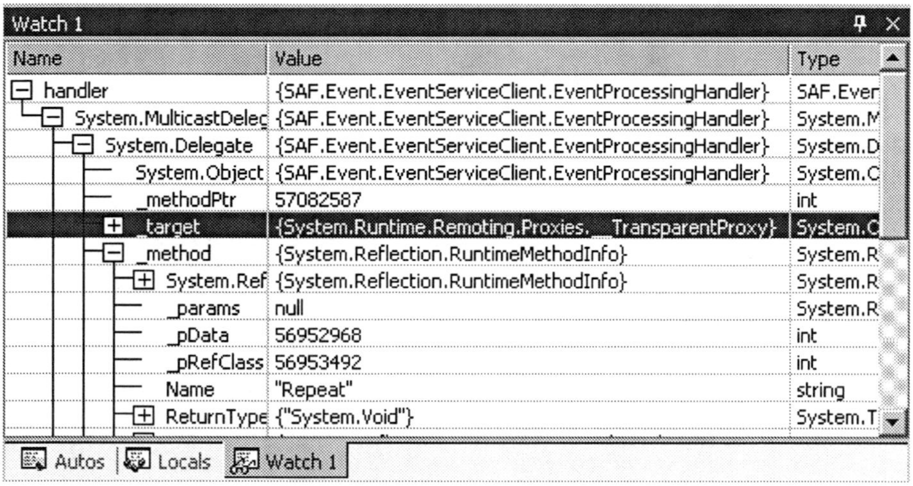

Name	Value	Type
⊟ handler	{SAF.Event.EventServiceClient.EventProcessingHandler}	SAF.Ever
└⊟ System.MulticastDeleg	{SAF.Event.EventServiceClient.EventProcessingHandler}	System.M
├⊟ System.Delegate	{SAF.Event.EventServiceClient.EventProcessingHandler}	System.D
├── System.Object	{SAF.Event.EventServiceClient.EventProcessingHandler}	System.C
├── _methodPtr	57082587	int
├ ⊞ _target	{System.Runtime.Remoting.Proxies.__TransparentProxy}	System.C
├⊟ _method	{System.Reflection.RuntimeMethodInfo}	System.R
├⊞ System.Ref	{System.Reflection.RuntimeMethodInfo}	System.R
├── _params	null	System.R
├── _pData	56952968	int
├── _pRefClass	56953492	int
├── Name	"Repeat"	string
└⊞ ReturnType	{"System.Void"}	System.T

🔲 Autos 🔲 Locals 🔲 Watch 1

Figure 7-9. Watch window for the delegate object in debug mode

The "_target" of the handler is pointing to a transparent proxy of the remote client's delegate object, which in turn points to the dispatching "repeat" method on the client side (also shown in Figure 7-9). As you can see, CLR automatically performs the marshaling on the client's delegate objects as they are sent across different app domains. You may recall that SAF.ClassFactory service uses the same technique to eliminate the .NET remoting configuration for the remote classes.

As the loop invokes each of the client delegate objects in the delegate chain, the remote client will receive the remoting call messages from the event server, and CLR on each client will automatically unmarshal the message and forward the call request to the target method defined in the original delegate.

Now that we have considered each piece in the event-notification service in detail, it is time to put all the pieces together into a complete picture. The process flow for the event-notification service is illustrated in Figure 7-10.

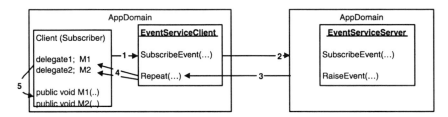

Figure 7-10. Process flow of the event-notification service

Before the client application can begin to participate in event notification, it first needs to create an entry point in the program for accepting the notification. Here delegate1 and delegate2 are delegates to such entry points, (M1, M2). Suppose that now the client wants to register a certain event. It will first call the SubscribeEvent method on the EventClient object and pass in the event name and delegate object. EventClient.SubscribeEvent will store the delegate objects (in my case, delegate1 and delegate2) in an internal hash table and invoke the EventServer.SubscribeEvent method on the remote event server, passing in the event name and the dispatcher delegate (which points to the repeat method on the EventClient object). When the event occurs, the event server will invoke the dispatcher delegate, which in turn will invoke all the client's delegate objects associated with the specific event name through a lookup on the internal hash table. Each client's delegate object will in tern trigger the underlying method, M1,M2 in my case. And that is the end of the event-notification process flow and discussion of SAF.EventNotification.

A Word About Deployment

I would like to say a few words about deployment of the event-notification service. For simplicity, I put EventClient and EventServer into a single assembly. If we stick with the distributed computing principle, we should separate these two classes into two separate assemblies so that the event client will reference only EventClient and the event server will reference only EventServer. Because we are using .NET remoting to link between the client and the server, we should also not forget to deploy the type information to the application that needs to reference it. In Chapter 4, you learned how to use soapsuds.exe to extract the type information into an assembly, which can be added to other applications as reference. We would need to do something similar for the event server for the event client application, since it needs to reference a remoting proxy of the EventServer class.

Since I put two classes into the same assembly, you don't have to do anything except add the SAF.EventNotification.dll reference to the client application. The same is true on the server side. You need to add the SAF.EventNotification.dll reference to the server application that hosts the event server for remoting. During development, a simple console application will suffice, but you should host it in either a window service or IIS in the production environment. The following is a sample configuration file for hosting the EventServer class on the server side:

```
<configuration>
    <system.runtime.remoting>
    <application name="EventServer">
        <service>
            <wellknown mode="Singleton"
type="SAF.EventNotification.EventServer,SAF.EventNotification"
                   objectUri="EventURI" />
        </service>
        <channels>
            <channel ref="http" port ="4000" />
        </channels>
    </application>
    </system.runtime.remoting>
</configuration>
```

You don't need a special .NET remoting configuration setting on the client side. However, you do need to store the URL information for the remote event server somewhere. The URL information is used in Activator.GetObject(type,url) on the client side to create a proxy object for the remote EventServer object.

Testing the Project

The demo for SAF.EventNotification requires you run the client project (Test.Client.SAF.EventNotification) and the server project (Test.Server.SAF.Event-Notification) at the same time in order to demonstrate how the event is registered on the server and how the server notifies to the client. Running the demo requires two steps.

First, open the solution in the Test.Server.SAF.EventNotification folder and hit F5 to start it and wait until the server console application is blocked at Console.ReadLine().

Second, open the solution in the `Test.Client.SAF.EventNotification` folder and hit F5 to run the client console application.

After performing these steps, you should have two instances of VS.NET running side by side. As you step through the code on the client console application, you will notice that the debugging cursor jumps to the server console application as the remoting call is invoked.

Summary

In this chapter, you have learned about developing an event-notification service through the example of SAF.EventNotification. You learned about the important concept of .NET delegation and how it facilitates asynchronous programming in .NET. Using delegation as an example, you also learned about the observer design pattern and the mediator pattern and how these two patterns provide a good blueprint for building an event-notification service. Finally, we looked through the code of the SAF.EventNotification service and saw how ideas of observer and mediator patterns are implemented in .NET using delegation and .NET remoting. In the next chapter, you will learn about window service, which allows us to host many applications that need to be in continuous running mode, such as an event-notification service.

CHAPTER 8

Windows Services

RECALL THE EARLIER EXAMPLE on .NET remoting, in which we created a console application that hosts the remoting objects. To make the remoting objects available to access from clients, we must first start the console application. This is perfectly all right during development. It is no trouble at all to take the extra step to start the hosting application for the remoting objects. That is not the case when we deploy the application in a production environment. Users expect your remoting objects to be up and running after they turn on the machine. If you used the same console applications to host your remoting object, the system administrator would have to log on the machine and start each console application one by one in order for the remoting object to work, and they would have to repeat this process each time the machine reboots. Even after the console applications are started, they can be accidentally turned off by closing the console window. Running your application on the console also has security implications. When the administrator logs on the machine and starts your applications, you application will be running under the identity of the administrator. Some administrators prefer to use the local administrator account, while others prefer the domain administrator account. So your application may have either too little or too much privilege with respect to what it actually needs.

As the old saying goes, there are at least three ways to the do everything in Windows. A console application allows you to start your application, but due to the fact that a console application requires interactive user logon, it is neither the best nor the easiest way to start a "service" or an application that starts automatically without human intervention and continues running until explicit termination. In .NET you can create a Windows service application that achieves the same goal as that of an NT service on an NT platform. Using a Windows service, you can configure your application to start when the operating system starts. You can also specify a user account that your application uses regardless of whether anyone has logged on the system or who is currently logging on the system. You can also manage the Windows services through the service console, an administrative tool that allow you perform start, stop, pause, and other managerial duties on a specific Windows service, so your application cannot be easily shut down with a simple mouse click.

Given the benefits of Windows services over regular console applications, there are arrays of application that make use of this advantage, such as "server" applications and "listener" applications. In this chapter you will learn in depth about the Windows service in .NET and its development and deployment. Later in the chapter, we will also look at a Windows service example through SAF.WindowsService, which is built on top of a Windows service and provides some features that ease the development and deployment of Windows services.

Motivation and Goals

Developing a Windows service application is not without its share of overhead. First, you must create a special "service" class as part of your Windows service application. Second, unlike the regular console application and Windows application, installing a Windows service application requires you to develop a special installation project. Although these extra development efforts are small, as you will see later in this chapter, it could add a fair amount of coding and maintenance effort in creating and installing multiple Windows service applications.

Because each Windows service application has to include the special service class and installation project, we can remove the developer's need to replicate such tedious plumbing work by extracting such work into a framework component so that one set of the special service class and installation project is shared by multiple business objects that want to take advantage of the Windows service application.

SAF.WindowsService is a such a component that will take the responsibility of providing the Windows service plumbing work away from developers so that they can focus on the business logic that is performed when the service starts. With SAF.WindowsService, developers can make their business objects participate as part of a Windows service with a simple configuration file change. We will look at how this is done later in the chapter.

.NET Technology Overview

Before we start looking into the SAF.WindowsService, we need first to understand the Windows service application, since the SAF.WindowsService component itself is a Windows service. We will also need to understand some basic concepts about threading, which provides SAF.WindowsService's ability to serve multiple applications simultaneously. The following are the topics we will discuss next:

- .NET threading

- .NET Windows service application

.NET Threading

A thread represents a slot of a CPU's availability to process tasks. You can think of a CPU as a versatile developer, and each task assigned to it is a thread. To make the developer work on something new, the project manager needs to create a task and assign it to the developer. On a given day, a developer may work on multiple tasks. He or she might work on the coding of new application features in the morning, iron out the bugs issued by the QA team in the afternoon, and go to numerous meetings the rest of the time. However, the developer can't work on multiple tasks at any given moment. After all, even if (s)he has only has more than one pair of monitor and keyboard to deal with, (s)he still has only one brain. Some tasks are more important than others, so the developer has to look at each task and its priority and decide how much time to spend on each task on any given day. A critical bug may require the developer to work the whole day to resolve it. On the other hand, documentation can wait almost indefinitely ;-).

When you want your computer to do something for you, you need to first create a task or thread. For example, when we create a console application and run it, CLR will automatically create a thread and register it with the operating system so that computer's CPU knows that it has to take care of this console application's Main() method. If you want to create additional tasks for the CPU, you need to create additional threads yourself.

Just as assigning more tasks to a developer doesn't make him get the project done any faster, creating more threads in your application doesn't automatically make it run faster either. The CPU can take care of one thread only at every single moment, just as a developer can take care of only one task at a single moment. However, there are situations in which you can make multiple independent tasks perform in a parallel fashion, as opposed to a serialized fashion, through multiple threading. In such a case, the total time it takes to complete multiple independent tasks in parallel fashion is shorter than that in a serialized fashion.

.NET offers us a comprehensive model for working with threads. System.Threading is the name space that contains all threading-related classes. The most commonly used one is the System.Threading.Thread class. The following is an example of creating multiple threads within an application:

```
namespace ThreadTest
{
    class Class1
    {
        static void Main(string[] args)
        {
            BusinessObject bo = new BusinessObject();
            //set up the delegates object
            ThreadStart ts1 = new ThreadStart(bo.DoWork);
```

```
            ThreadStart ts2 = new ThreadStart(bo.DoMoreWork);
            //creating new threads
            Thread t1 = new Thread(ts1);
            Thread t2 = new Thread(ts2);
            t1.Name = "DoWork thread";
            t2.Name = "DoMoreWork thread";
            //Start the new threads.
            t1.Start();
            t2.Start();
            Console.ReadLine();
        }
    }
    public class BusinessObject
    {
        public void DoWork(){…}
        public void DoMoreWork(){…}
    }
}
```

I hope you got a good grasp on delegation from the previous chapter. In order to create a new thread, you need first to create a ThreadStart delegate. ThreadStart specifies what program code thread needs to call when the thread is started; in other words, it binds the actual thread with a physical method call. The definition of ThreadStart class is as follows:

```
public delegate void ThreadStart();
```

ThreadStart can take only methods that have no return value and take no input parameters, such as the DoWork and DoMoreWork methods.

After the ThreadStart delegate is created, we must bind it to a thread. The following two lines create two thread objects, and each is associated with a ThreadStart object:

```
Thread t1 = new Thread(ts1);
Thread t2 = new Thread(ts2);
```

Creating a thread object doesn't automatically start the thread. There are many properties and methods on the thread objects, and we will look at some of them later. Starting a thread is a simple as calling the Start method on the thread object. The Start method returns control to the caller right away so that it won't block the main thread from continuing to the next line of code. We can monitor the status of the threads within the application through the Threads window in VS.NET. (select Debug➤Windows➤Threads on the menu bar of VS.NET during debugging). Figure 8-1 shows the threads window in running the sample code just given.

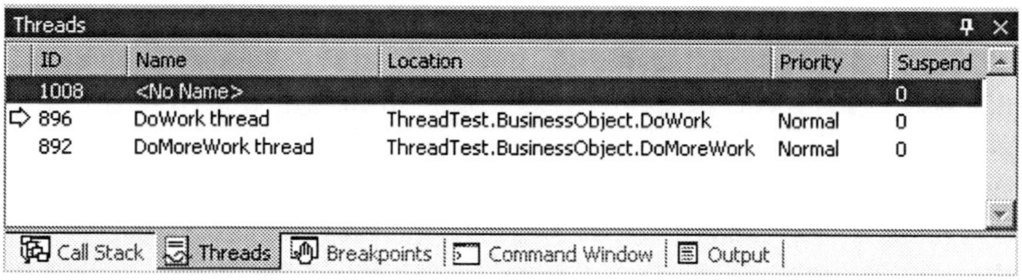

ID	Name	Location	Priority	Suspend
1008	<No Name>			0
⇨ 896	DoWork thread	ThreadTest.BusinessObject.DoWork	Normal	0
892	DoMoreWork thread	ThreadTest.BusinessObject.DoMoreWork	Normal	0

Call Stack Threads Breakpoints Command Window Output

Figure 8-1. The Threads *window in VS.NET*

The threads with IDs 896 and 892 are the two threads we created programmatically. The location column indicates the method to which the thread is assigned. Because we explicitly create these threads, we can control the thread directly through methods such as Sleep and Join. There is also a way to create threads inexplicitly through the use of a thread pool. We can't control such threads, since the CLR will create and manage the threads for us.

Imagine that the DoWork and DoMoreWork call some web methods which each take five minutes to complete. Without multiple threading, you would have to call the two methods one after the other. It would take a total of 10 minutes to complete them. However, when you assign each method to a separate thread, as shown in the code sample, it takes only a total of 5 minutes, since the two methods are invoked at the exact same time.

Let's also take a look at some commonly used operations on the thread object after it has been started.

Sleep is a static method that will put the current thread to sleep for a certain amount of time. The operating system will not allocate a CPU time slot to the sleeping thread for the duration of sleep. The Sleep method is commonly used in the looping process when you want the thread to work periodically. The following is an example of using the Sleep method:

```
public bool canContiune = true;
public void DoWork()
{
    while (canContinue)
    {
        Thread.Sleep(1000);
        Console.WriteLine("some serious work");
    }
}
```

The Sleep method blocks the thread for a certain amount of time. Thread.Sleep(1000) indicates that the thread that is calling the DoWork method will be blocked for one second (1000 milliseconds). Thread.Sleep(-1) indicates that the thread will be blocked indefinitely. Thread.Sleep(0) will cause the thread to give up its right to execute for a time to give other threads an opportunity to execute. You can "wake up" a sleeping thread with the Thread.Interrupt method. This method causes the sleeping thread to throw a ThreadInterrupted exception. The following sample shows the relationship between the Sleep and Interrupt methods:

```
static void Main(string[] args)
{
    ThreadStart ts1 = new ThreadStart(bo.DoWork);
    Thread t1 = new Thread(ts1);
    t1.Start()
    //do some work, now wake up t1
    t1.Interrupt();
}
public void DoWork()
{
    public bool canContiune = true;
    while (canContinue)
    {
        try
        {
            Console.WriteLine("Do some work");
            //block the call until interrupted
            Thread.Sleep(-1);
        }
        catch (ThreadInterruptedException tie)
        {
            Console.WriteLine("Don't be lazy");
        }
        finally {…}
    }
}
```

A thread starts when the Start method is called on the Thread object. A thread finishes when the target method that it binds to returns. If you want to keep the thread running, you need to make sure that the method the thread binds to does not return. For example, a loop inside the DoWork method can keep the thread alive indefinitely.

Not every thread needs to live indefinitely. Most of them simply need to call a method and then die after the method returns. Sometimes you need to ensure that all the threads complete their methods before any further calls can be processed. In such a situation, you can use the Join method to block the calling thread until certain threads complete. Using the earlier example, assume that DoWork and DoMoreWork take a long time to complete, and we want to ensure that threads on both methods complete before we exit the application. The following code demonstrates this goal:

```
Thread t1 = new Thread(ts1);
Thread t2 = new Thread(ts2);
t1.Start();
t2.Start();
//do some work
t1.Join();
t2.Join();
Console.WriteLine("Both threads have finished");
```

Because Join is a blocking call, the main thread will wait at t1.Join until the t1 thread is finished. Then it will move on to t2.Join and wait there until the t2 thread is finished. So when the main thread is ready to call Console.WriteLine, both threads have finished and been destroyed. Calling IsAlive on t2 after the t2.Join call would return false, indicating that the thread is gone. You can also specify the timeout period for the Join method using the overload method Join(int millisecondsTimeout) or Join(TimeSpan timeout). If timeout is reached and the thread has still not yet finished, a value of false is returned, which indicates that the thread is still running; otherwise, a value of true is returned to indicate that the thread is finished.

You can also shut down a thread at any time through the Abort method. Calling the Abort method will cause the method to which the thread binds to throw a ThreadAbort exception. If the method involves a lengthy task or an infinite loop, a ThreadAbort exception can effectively jump out of whatever the thread is doing and exit the method. You should have a try–catch–finally block to perform some cleanup work for the aborted thread, such as releasing unmanaged resources. The following is an example using the Abort method:

```
static void Main(string[] args)
{
    ThreadStart ts1 = new ThreadStart(bo.DoWork);
    Thread t1 = new Thread(ts1);
    t1.Start()
    t1.Abort();
    t1.Join() ;
}
public void DoWork()
{
```

```
public bool canContinue = true;
try
{
    while (canContinue)
    {
        Console.WriteLine("Do some work");
        Thread.Sleep(1000);
    }
}
catch (ThreadAbortException tae)
{
    Console.WriteLine("Being aborted");
}
    finally {...}
}
```

Abort is not a blocking call, which means that the thread may still be in the middle of aborting after the Abort method returns; for example, the finally block can take some time to clean up resources. To ensure that the thread has enough time for cleanup, you should add a Join method to ensure that no further calls can proceed until the thread is indeed completely aborted.

We will take a look at some applications of these thread methods later in the chapter when we dive into some code of SAF.WindowsService.

.NET Windows Service

Creating a Windows service using .NET involves two major steps. First, we need to create a service class that inherits System.ServiceProcess.ServiceBase. Second, we need to create an installation project for the service class. Let's first take a look at how to create a service class.

Open VS.NET, and then select "new project." A project window comes up in which you specify the name of the project and the type of the project, as shown in Figure 8-2.

Selecting Windows service as template makes VS.NET create the template code for developing a Windows service application. The template code is nothing more than some C# (or VB.NET) code generated by VS.NET; for example, the generated code contains a class that extends ServiceBase, which is required for a Windows service and lays out a number of methods you need to implement. It makes development much easier.

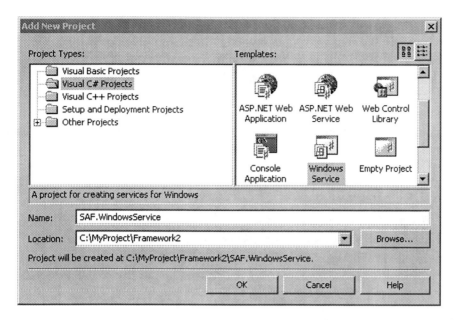

Figure 8-2. Creating a Windows service project

In a nutshell, we need to override some of the virtual methods of the Service-Base class, which provides most of the functionality as a service. At the least, you need to override the OnStart method to provide the business logic that you want to run as a service. The OnStart method is called when you start the service through either the service console or the command "net start…." It is an opportunity for you to create a business object to handle any future requests.

One important aspect of the OnStart method is that it is the place to start your business logic, but not the place to execute it. The OnStart method must return very quickly; otherwise, a timeout error "system cannot start the service in a timely manner" will be generated when you click on the start button using the service control. Obviously, you can't put the business logic code inside the OnStart method if you want to provide a continuous service. The following is an example of what we can do with the OnStart method:

```
BusinessObject bo = new BusinessObject();
protected override void OnStart(string[] args)
{
    ThreadStart ts = new ThreadStart(bo.DoWork);
    Thread t = new Thread(ts);
    t.Start();
}
```

In this example, we create an additional thread that will process the business logic continuously. Because we spun a separate thread for the business logic, the OnStart method returns right away. After we start a thread in the OnStart method, we must keep the thread alive for a long period time so that it can provide continuous service. We saw earlier in this chapter how to keep the thread alive through looping and thread blockage. We can deploy the same techniques to ensure that the BusinessObject object continues to provide service to its clients.

Another method that we want to override is the OnStop method, which CLR calls when you click on the "Stop" button in the service console. This is where you can clean up what the OnStart method created.

A Windows service also needs a name, so that user can identify it in the service console. You can name your service by setting the value of the ServiceName property.

After creating the Windows service class, we also need to create an installation project to install the Windows service. To create the installation project, go to the property page for the service class and click on AddInstaller, as shown in Figure 8-3.

Figure 8-3. Property page of the service class

VS.NET will create a ProjectInstall.cs file, which contains the code with instructions on how to install the service. You really don't have to write any code as far as the installer is concerned. You can replace the name shown in the service console with a friendlier name by setting the DisplayName property of the serviceProcessInstaller. In my case, I set it to MyTestService Demo.

> **NOTE** *There are several interesting properties you can set on the installer object. For example, you can specify the user account used to run the service, whether the service is automatically started when the operating system starts, and what other dependencies the service has. Many of those properties can also be overridden through the service console using administrative tools.*

After compiling the Windows service project, you will have an `*.exe` file. The next step is to install the Windows service application on the system. The .NET framework comes with a tool called `InstallUtil.exe` (under `%SystemRoot%\Microsoft.NET\Framework\[version]\`), which you can use to install the service. `%SystemRoot%` represents the location where you install the Windows operating system on the computer, such as `C:\Windows`. At the command prompt, type the following:

```
C:\InstallUtil SAF.WindowsService.exe
```

If installation is successful, you will see "The Commit phase completed successfully," and you should find that your Windows service is also shown in the service console, as in Figure 8-4.

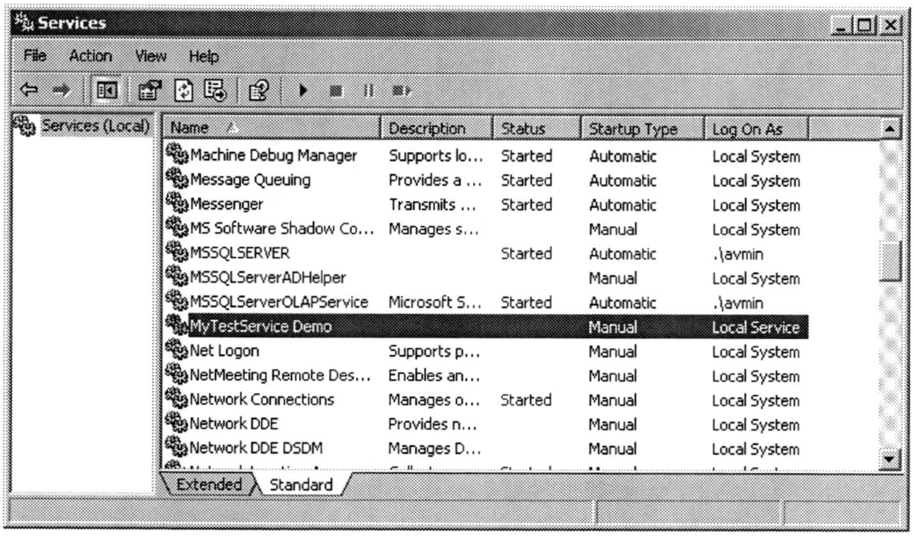

Figure 8-4. The service console

I would like to say a few words about debugging the Windows service application. Because you can't start a Windows service application directly from VS.NET, you can't debug it as you do the console application with F5 (shortcut for Debug ➤ Start from the menu bar). We need to use the debug process feature in VS.NET to debug a running Windows service. After the Windows service application that you want to debug is running, open the project that contains the source code for the Windows service application and put some breakpoints at a location that you know will be reached soon, such as the entry point of some "while" loop. Then click on the Debug ➤ Processes on the menu bar of VS.NET. A new window will appear, as shown in Figure 8-4b.

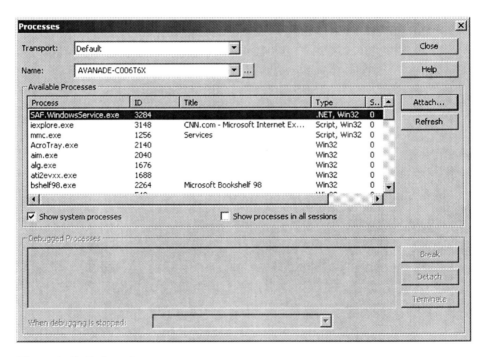

Figure 8-4b. Debugging a process

In the middle of the screen, a list box shows the available applications that are running on the system. You must check the check box labeled "Show system process" in order for the Windows service application to appear. Sorting on the "Type" column will bring the .NET application to the top of the list. In this example, I want to debug SAF.WindowsService.exe. Highlight the application and then click on "Attach." A new window, called "Attach to process," should appear. Choose the "Common Language Runtime" check box and click the "OK" button to close. Now you are ready to debug the Windows service. The next time the CLR is executing the line of code marked with the breakpoint, it will stop at that breakpoint, and you can use F10 or F11 to step into the code.

We have just looked at threading and Windows services, and we now have all the knowledge necessary to build an actual Windows service. For the rest of the chapter we will look at the implementation of SAF.WindowsService.

SAF Code Sample Walkthrough

SAF.WindowsService enables developers to start their business logic as part of a Windows service without having to create a Windows service application and installer. To achieve this goal, we must create a Windows service application that initializes and starts all customized business logics. Figure 8-5 illustrates the high-level design of the SAF.WindowsService component.

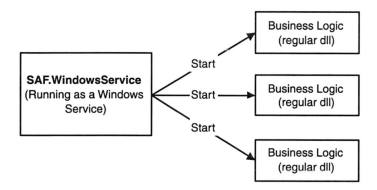

Figure 8-5. High-level design of SAF.WindowsService

In Figure 8-5, SAF.WindowsService is running as a Windows service. When the service starts, it will have an opportunity to load regular DLLs that contain business logic that will participate as part of the Windows service. Because each business DLL operates independently from other business DLLs, SAF.WindowsService allocates one thread for each individual DLL and starts the execution of each DLL in parallel. To achieve this, we must first ask developers to specify which business DLLs they want to start when SAF.WindowsService starts. The following is a section of the configuration file for SAF.WindowsService:

```
<configuration>
  <configSections>
    <section name="Framework"
            type="SAF.Configuration.ConfigurationHandler,SAF.Configuration" />
    <section name="MyApplication"
            type="SAF.Configuration.ConfigurationHandler,SAF.Configuration" />
  </configSections>
```

```
<Framework type="SAF.Configuration.ConfigurationManager,SAF.Configuration">
  <SAF.WindowsService>
  <Service name="service1" type = "Business.OrderListener,Business" />
  <Service name="service2" type = "Business.RequestListener,Business" />
  </SAF.WindowsService>

  ...

</Framework>
...
</configuration>
```

As you can see, you can easily add more business components to participate as part of the Windows service. SAF.WindowsService will use reflection to load these business components when SAF.WindowsService is started. Of course, we have to make sure that all the business components that are called by SAF.WindowsService have certain common characteristics, so that SAF.WindowsService can start all of them at run time without any knowledge of what the components actually do.

> **NOTE** *The current implementation of SAF.WindowsService starts and stops all the participating business components at once and doesn't allow you to start or stop individual business components. You can, however, create a file listener to watch the content changes in the configuration file and turn on or off individual services separately.*

The SAF.Library.WindowsService.IService interface provides such common characteristics for the business components. Each business component must implement the IService if it needs to participate as part of the Windows service through SAF.WindowsService. IService contains three interface methods defined as follows:

```
public interface IService
{
    void Start();
    void Stop();
    void Initialize(XmlNode configXml);
}
```

The Initialize method takes some XML configuration data and prepares the business component. The Start and Stop methods do what their names imply: start and stop whatever services the component provides. SAF.WindowsService.Empty-Service is a sample business component that implements the IService interface and shows an example of how these interface methods can be implemented. (Empty-Service can be found under the SAF.WindowsService project.) You can implement the Start method to do whatever you want, but under most scenarios, you would employ a while loop in the Start method to provide continuous service. Please refer to the source code of EmptyService for more detail on the Start method.

With each service class implementing the IService interface, we can easily use the reflection techniques we have learned in earlier chapters to load each service defined in the configuration. We can then use .NET's multithreading feature to invoke the IService.Start method on each of the service objects that have been created so that each service can run on its own thread.

Now let's look at code that will start each service class (or business component participating in the Windows service) on a separate thread during the start of the Windows service and stop these service classes during the shut-down of the Windows service. The implementations of "startup" and "shutdown" of a Windows service are defined in OnStart and OnStop, the two virtual methods of System.ServiceProcess.ServiceBase that SAF.WindowsService has overridden to carry out its customized logic:

```
protected override void OnStart(string[] args)
{
    //obtain the configuration information for SAF.Service
    ConfigurationManager cm =
            (ConfigurationManager)ConfigurationSettings.GetConfig("Framework");
    SAF.Configuration.ServiceConfiguration serviceConfig = cm.ServiceConfig;
    XmlNode servicesXml = serviceConfig.ServicesXml;
    //loop through service nodes and start them one by one
    foreach (XmlNode node in servicesXml.ChildNodes)
    {
        try
        {
            string typeInfo;
            //obtain the type information from the XML data
            typeInfo =node.Attributes["type"].Value;
            Type type = Type.GetType(typeInfo);
            IService instance = (IService)Activator.CreateInstance(type);
            //initialize the service
            instance.Initialize(node);

            //create a new thread to process the service
            ThreadStart ts = new ThreadStart(instance.Start);
            Thread t = new Thread(ts);
```

```
            t.Start();
            threadArray.Add(t);
        }
        catch (Exception ex)
        {
            //write to the event log
        }
    }
}
```

The OnStart method first retrieves the configuration data related to the SAF.WidnowsService section and creates an instance of the business component for each node under the SAF.WindowsService section through reflection. The method then calls the IService.Initialize method on each newly created instance object and passes in the configuration information that is specific to a particular business component. Next, the OnStart method creates a new thread for each instance of the business component and starts the threads by calling their IService.Start methods. Within the for-each loop, the OnStart method also adds thread objects to the hash table called threadArray. The hash table is used to keep track of the different threads that we have created so that we can terminate running business components and perform the cleanup when the Windows service is shut down, as you will see shortly. Using the sample configuration file shown earlier as an example, there will be two extra threads created by the OnStart method. One thread is used to run the IService.Start method on an instance of the Business.OrderListener class, and the other is used to run the IService.Start method on an instance of the Business.RequestListener class. Because there is no thread blockage during the OnStart method, the method returns quickly, and the Windows service (SAF.WindowsService) starts successfully.

At some point, you will want to shut down the Windows service along with all the business components the service has started. The OnStop method is called by CLR when you shut down the Windows service through the command prompt or Windows service console. We want to make sure that all the business components are properly shut down before the Windows service shuts down. The following code shows what we can do to terminate the running business components and the threads allocated to them during the service shutdown:

```
public delegate void OnStopDelegate();
protected  void OnStop()
{
    foreach (object o in instanceArray)
    {
        try
        {
```

```
            IService service = (IService)o;
            if (service !=null)
            {
                //call the stop method asynchronously to avoid thread block
                OnStopDelegate osd = new OnStopDelegate(service.Stop);
                osd.BeginInvoke(null,null);
            }
        }
        catch (Exception ex)
        {
            //write to the event log
        }
    }
    //give some time for each instance to shut down gracefully
    Thread.Sleep(5000);
    foreach (object o in threadArray)
    {
        try
        {
            Thread t = (Thread)o;
            if (t !=null)
            {
                if (t.IsAlive == true)
                {
                    //force the thread to shut down if it is still alive
                    t.Abort();
                }
            }
        }
        catch (Exception ex)
        {
            //write to the event log
        }
    }
}
```

The OnStop method contains two major code blocks. The first block loops through each instance object in the hash table and calls the ISerivce.Stop method on each instance. This give the instance object an opportunity to perform some cleanup and release of resources. Observe that calls to the Stop method are invoked through BeginInvoke. We use asynchronous calls here to make sure that the current thread is not blocked due to the implementation of the Stop method in certain business components. If the thread that is running the instance object is in the waiting or blockage state and doesn't terminate in a timely fashion (in our case, five seconds), we have a couple of ways to focus on a thread to terminate it, such as `Thread.Interrupt()` and `Thread.Abort()`, as we have seen in an earlier discussion.

After the `Stop` method has been called on each instance, the thread is put to sleep for five seconds so that each instance will have enough time to clean itself up. The second block of code will loop through each thread object in the hash table to check whether every thread that was created earlier is still alive. The `OnStop` method will call the `Thread.Abort` method on each thread to shut down the thread forcefully if it is still alive at that moment.

SAF.WindowsService is a very simple framework component. It significantly reduces the amount of code that developers have to write and configure to set up a component that runs like a Windows service application. However, the `OnStart` method shown previously has security-related shortcomings. When we develop a regular Windows service application, we have an option to specify what user account we want the service to run as. We often need to specify different user accounts for different services according to their security requirements. This becomes a problem for SAF.WindowsService, since all the business components that it triggers have to run under one user account, since there is only one real Windows service application. Because having different services running under different user accounts is such a common requirement for many applications, I want to make sure that SAF.WindowsService supports running different business components under different user accounts.

There are two parts to enabling this very nice security feature. First, we need to find a way to switch a thread's security context to a new user account. Second, we need to modify SAF.WindowsService so that its `OnStart` method will perform this thread security switch before it starts invoking on each business component defined in the configuration file.

To complete the first part, we need to rely on the `LogonUser` method in `advapi32.dll` to perform the thread security switch. Because `advapi32.dll` contains unmanaged code, we have to use P/Invoke, or platform invoke, to call its methods from managed .NET code.

> **NOTE** *In order for your code to perform P/Invoke on native APIs, the code must have UnmanagedCode permission. This permission is granted to your code by default when the code is fully trusted. You can find out whether your code has this permission by checking the Runtime Security Policy in the .NET Framework Configuration console under Administrative Tools.*

Platform invoke allows us to call unmanaged code from managed code. To call an unmanaged method through P/Invoke, we need to first identify which unmanaged DLL to call, then create a method definition in the managed code that matches that method in the unmanaged code. We can then use the method in our code as if it were a managed method. The following code shows how to declare a method to match an unmanaged method in the DLLs:

```
[DllImport(@"advapi32.dll")]
public static extern bool LogonUser(String lpszUsername, String lpszDomain,
        String lpszPassword, int dwLogonType,
        int dwLogonProvider, out IntPtr phToken);
```

The DllImport attribute indicates which DLL contains the unmanaged method you want to call. You also need to use static extern as the modifier of the method. After you have declared the matching managed method, you can call it as a regular method in your .NET app. For example, the following code calls the LogonUser method:

```
bool loggedOn  = LogonUser("xin","mydomain","password",
            LOGON32_LOGON_NETWORK_CLEARTEXT   LOGON32_PROVIDER_DEFAULT, phToken)
```

The last parameter represents the empty security handler, which will be filled with the real value that represents a specific user if the call succeeds. LOGON32_LOGON_NETWORK_CLEARTEXT has a constant value of 3, which indicates that the logon type. LOGON32_PROVIDER_DEFAULT holds a constant value of 0, which indicates that a default security provider is used to validate the user logon. Now let's return to SAF.WindowsService We need to find a way to run the business component with a specific user account. SAF.Utility.SecurityUtility provides a method that will switch the running thread's security context to that of a specific user account. To accommodate the new security requirement, we need to indicate the user account as part of the configuration data associated with the participating business component, as follows:

```
<SAF.WindowsService>
    <Service name="service1" type = " Business.OrderListener,Business">
            <RunAs InheritIdentity="false">
                <Domain>mydomain</Domain>
                <User>user1</User>
                <Password>password</Password>
            </RunAs>
      </Service>
    <Service name="service2" type = " Business.RequestListener,Business">
```

```
            <RunAs InheritIdentity="true" />
        </Service>
</SAF.WindowsService>
```

The user name, password, and domain are three local variables whose values
are assigned during the IService.Initialize method. The SecurityUtility.Switch
method performs the actual user account switch for the current thread. After the
Switch method returns, all the rest of the code in the Start method will be executed under the new user account. If you call WindowsIdentity.CurrentUser.Name,
you should get a user name that matches the user name passed into the Switch
method.

> **NOTE** *The password is shown in clear text in the preceding configuration data.*
> *This, of course, is not secure. One way to hide such sensitive information is*
> *through data encryption. So instead of storing the password in clear text, we*
> *should store the encrypted password and decrypt it inside the application before*
> *using it to log onto the user account. We will look at more on data encryption in*
> *Chapter 12.*

Let's take a look at the Switch method, which does all the hard work to switch
the security account of the running thread:

```
//declare for p/invoke
[DllImport(@"advapi32.dll",SetLastError=true)]
public static extern bool LogonUser(String lpszUsername, String lpszDomain,
                        String lpszPassword,
    int dwLogonType, int dwLogonProvider, out int phToken);


[DllImport(@"advapi32.dll", CharSet= CharSet.Auto, SetLastError=true)]
public extern static bool DuplicateToken(IntPtr hToken,
    int impersonationLevel,
    ref IntPtr hNewToken);
private WindowsImpersonationContext impersonationContext = null;
public void Switch (string userName, string password, string domain)
{
    IntPtr token = IntPtr.Zero;
    WindowsImpersonationContext impersonationContext = null;
    //log on as the give user account
    bool loggedOn - LogonUser(
        userName,
```

```
            domain,
            password,
            LOGON32_LOGON_NETWORK_CLEARTEXT,
            LOGON32_PROVIDER_DEFAULT,
            // The user token for the specified user is returned here.
            out token);
    if (loggedOn == false)
    {
        throw new System.Security.SecurityException(userName + " logon failed" );
    }
    IntPtr tokenDuplicate = IntPtr.Zero;
    WindowsIdentity tempWindowsIdentity =null;
    //duplicate the security token
    if(DuplicateToken(token, SecurityImpersonation, ref tokenDuplicate) != false)
    {
        tempWindowsIdentity = new WindowsIdentity(tokenDuplicate);
        //change the current thread's run-as to the new window identity.
        impersonationContext = tempWindowsIdentity.Impersonate();
    }
    else
    {
        throw new System.Security.SecurityException("Logon use failed");
    }
}
```

LogonUser and DuplicateToken are unmanaged functions, and therefore, we must first declare these methods with DllImport before use them in the Switch method.

The Switch method first tries to log onto the user account using the information stored in the configuration file. If loggedOn returns true, it means that the logon was successful. The next step is to create an impersonation token using the new user token generated by the LogonUser method. The Switch method then creates a WindowsIdentity object using the impersonation token. Calling WindowsIdentity.Impersonate will cause the current calling thread to switch to the new user account. Any further calls from that thread would appear as calls made by the new user. To switch the thread back to the original user account, we need to call the UndoSwitch method, which in term calls the WindowsImpersonationContext.Undo() method, as follows:

```
public void UndoSwitch()
{
    impersonationContext.Undo();
}
```

> **NOTE** *Impersonation is a special privilege, and not every user account is allowed to perform the security switch on the thread. In order for SAF.WindowsService to work properly, you need to make sure that the Windows service (*SAF.Windows-Service.exe*) is running as either local administrator or system account; otherwise, you must go to the Local Security Policy console under Administrative Tools and grant the user account you want to use to run* SAF.WindowsService.exe *the "Act as part of operating system" privilege.*

With the SAF.Utility.SecurityUtility class you can specify a different user account for each participating "service" inside a single service application (SAF.WindowsService).

Now let's modify the OnStart method of SAF.WindowsService so that it creates different threads under different security contexts. At first glance, this may seem to be a straightforward task. We can simply call the SecurityUtility.Switch method just before we start each newly created thread. However, it is not as simple as you may expect. Calling the SecurityUitlity.Switch method (which in turn calls LogonUser) would in fact switch the current running thread's security context; in other words, it will switch the main thread that runs the Windows service application. You would have to call the UnSwitch method to restore the main thread's security context before creating the next new thread. This approach would work, but it involves unnecessary context switching of the main thread. A better and more flexible solution is to create a thread wrapper class that allows you to perform custom services such as thread security switching before the thread starts doing its work.

If you have worked with the System.Thread class, you will know that when you are creating a thread, you must first create a ThreadStart delegate that you want to invoke when the new thread is started. The ThreadStart delegate represents a target method that takes no parameters and returns void:

```
public delegate void ThreadStart();
```

The fact that the target method can't take a parameter makes it harder to pass into the target method some data that would customize its behavior. A thread wrapper class offers a very good solution to this problem. In our case, we want to perform the security switch on the newly created thread before it invokes the target method. The following code shows such a wrapper class:

```
public class SecuritySwitchThread
{
    private ThreadStart serviceDelegate;
    private XmlNode runAs;
    private Thread newT;
```

```csharp
    //constructor that accesses more than one parameter
    public SecuritySwitchThread (ThreadStart start, XmlNode xml)
    {
        serviceDelegate = start;
        runAs = xml;
        //create a new thread that calls WrappingMethod
        newT = new Thread(new ThreadStart(WrappingMethod));
    }
    //method that starts the thread
    public void Start()
    {
        //start the thread.
        newT.Start();
    }
    // WrappingMethod wraps performs the security
    // switch and then invokes the ThreadStart delegate.
    private void WrappingMethod()
    {
        //retrieve the user account information to which thread is
        //switched.
        bool inheritIdentity =
                    Boolean.Parse(runAs.Attributes["InheritIdentity"].Value);
        if (inheritIdentity == false)
        {
            string userid = runAs.SelectSingleNode("User").InnerText;
            string password= runAs.SelectSingleNode("Password").InnerText;
            string domain = runAs.SelectSingleNode("Domain").InnerText;
            //call the utility class to switch
            //the current thread's security context.
            SecurityUtility su = new SecurityUtility();
            su.Switch(userid, password,domain);
        }
        //invoke the ThreadStart delegate object passed in
        //on the class constructor
        serviceDelegate();
    }
    // BaseThread property provides access to the
    // underlying thread, which allows an external program
    // to control the thread.
    public Thread BaseThread
    {
        get
        {
            return newT;
        }
    }
}
```

The key to the thread wrapper class is its construction. Notice that the SecuritySwitchThread constructor contains the target method delegate or ThreadStart object and XML that contains some configuration data that will be used to switch the thread's security context to that of another account. Within the constructor, the wrapper class will store the ThreadStart object and XML in internal variables and then create a real brand new thread, which is also stored in an internal variable. When SecuritySwitchThread.Start is called by SAF.Windows-Service, the original ThreadStart object is not invoked immediately; instead, the internal method WrappingMethod is called. Inside WrappingMethod, we can perform a series of tasks to customize how the thread will invoke the ThreadStart delegate. In my case, it will call the SecurityUtility.Switch method on the thread, which is a new thread created in the constructor. After the security context is switched, WrappingMethod will invoke the ThreadStart object via a standard invocation of the delegate.

With the thread wrapper class, you can control when and how the ThreadStart object is invoked by the new thread. You can also control what goes before and after the invocation of the ThreadStart object. Of course, the best way to understand the thread wrapper class is to load the testing project that comes with this chapter into VS.NET and going through the code in debug mode.

We now need to modify our earlier version of the OnStart method so that it takes advantage of this thread wrapper class. The following code shows a segment of the OnStart method. The modification is highlighted in boldface to illustrate the changes:

```
protected override void OnStart(string[] args)
{
    //...more code here...
    foreach (XmlNode node in servicesXml.ChildNodes)
    {
        try
        {
            string typeInfo;
            //obtain the type information from the XML data
            typeInfo =node.Attributes["type"].Value;
            Type type = Type.GetType(typeInfo);
            IService instance = (IService)Activator.CreateInstance(type);
            //initialize the service
            instance.Initialize(node);
            XmlNode runAs = node.SelectSingleNode("RunAs");
            instanceArray.Add(instance);
            //create SecuritySwitchThread object to process the service
            ThreadStart ts = new ThreadStart(instance.Start);
            SecuritySwitchThread sst = new SecuritySwitchThread(ts,runAs);
            //start the SecuritySwitchThread's thread.
```

```
            sst.Start();
            threadArray.Add(sst.BaseThread);
        }
        catch (Exception ex)
        {
            //write to the event log
        }
    }
    //...more code here...
}
```

It is easy to deploy SAF.WindowsService. It involves three steps. First, you install SAF.WindowsService by calling `installutil SAF.WindowsService.exe` at the command prompt. Second, make sure you have a `<SAF.WindowsService>` section defined in the `SAF.WindowsService.exe.config` file. Third, type `net start SAF.WindowsService` or start `SAF.WindowsService` from the Service Control.

The Testing Project

Unlike other SAF components, SAF.WindowsService doesn't have its own testing project, since SAF.WindowsService is an executable and is tested by installing `SAF.WindowsService.exe` using `installutil.exe`.

The source code for SAF.WindowsService also includes a service component called `EmptyService`. You can use it as a sample to create more service components, which can be plugged into SAF.WindowsService. After you create your own service component, you can test it out with the Windows service in three steps.

The first step is to add the type information into the `app.config` file, which is located in the SAF.WindowsService folder, and modify the user account information used to start the service in the `app.config` file so that it matches that of your computer. You also need to recompile the code so that `SAF.Windows-Service.exe.config` reflects the modifications in `app.config`.

The second step is to copy the DLL file that contains your service component to the `bin` folder, so that SAF.WindowsService can load the DLL.

The third step is to restart the Windows service. Because `EmptyService` is defined in SAF.WindowsService's configuration file, `EmptyService` will be loaded into SAF.WindowsService automatically. All that `EmptyService` does is to write the current time to a file called `EmptyService.txt` under in the `C:\Temp` folder every few seconds. You can change its "RunAs" section in the configuration file and file access security in the physical `EmptyService.txt` file to test how the user account under which the service is running affects write access to the file. Each time you change the configuration setting, you must restart SAF.WindowsService for the configuration changes to take effect.

Summary

In this chapter we first learned at some basic threadings feature in .NET, such as creating a new thread, blocking a thread, and aborting a thread. We then talked about Windows service applications, their benefits, and how to create one in .NET. Later in the chapter, we learned about the SAF.WindowsService component, which allows developers to take advantage of Windows service applications without the overhead of creating and deploying a service application. SAF.WindowsService uses the .NET threading and platform invoke features to create a consolidated Windows service through which customized business components can be started and run along with SAF.WindowsService.

CHAPTER 9

Message Queue Services

THE MESSAGE QUEUE is a wonderful invention in the field of computer technology. If you haven't heard about message queues or worked with them in the past, this chapter is the chance for you to come up to speed on this topic.

Message queues offer many benefits to applications. When implemented correctly, they provide significant increased scalability and fault tolerance to your application. Having a message queue as part of your toolset is essential in planning and implementing high-volume and high-availability applications in various business scenarios. And the best part about message queues is that they are extremely easy to understand and implement. The idea behind the message queue is simple. A message queue is a pool into which data can be dropped and from which data can be removed. Figure 9-1 illustrates the concept of a message queue.

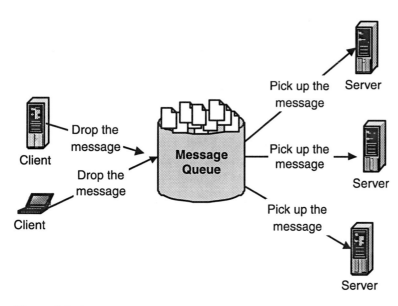

Figure 9-1. A message queue

A typical usage scenario of a message queue is that a client application drops a message into the pool and a server application picks up the message from the pool and processes it. Unlike traditional client/server programming, in which the client application sends data to the server application directly, an application that uses a message queue breaks the direct link between client and server. Decoupling, a schema that has appeared over and over again in this book, is indeed the essence of message queuing, and pooling. By decoupling the client and server, the possibilities are endless as to how a message can be processed. For example, you can achieve load balance by deploying multiple servers to process the message outside the queue, so that the load on each individual server is reduced. You can achieve fault tolerance by assigning more than one server to process messages in the queue. In case one server is down, any server can still keep pulling messages out of the queue and continuing with the service. A message queue can also help you make your application more scalable by controlling the demand on system resources. For instance, when the number of requests sent by clients increases dramatically, you can use a message queue as a buffer zone so that the high demand in client requests will not translate into high demand on the rest of the system, causing it to slow to a crawl.

Another major benefit of message queues is their ability to assist application integration on a single platform or different system platforms. Because message queue technology is well supported on a number of platforms, it is used as a common protocol for transmitting data between applications on different platforms. For example, Microsoft Windows clients can read and write messages from the IBM MQSeries on a mainframe or Unix system, thereby enabling applications on different platforms to send and retrieve data between them. Even on the same platform, a message queue's ability to decouple the data provider and data consumer eases the integration of applications that have very little knowledge of each other. In many ways, a message queue is able to achieve many integration goals that a Web service is created to provide.

In this chapter, we will be looking at the SAF.MessageQueue service, which allows developers to send and retrieve messages easily from different message queue implementations, such as MSMQ and MQSeries. The SAF.MessageQueue service also leaves room for extension through implementation of additional message queue technologies.

Motivation and Goals

Developers often need to deal with a number of message queue products when building applications that take advantage of a message queue. The two most common of these are Microsoft's MSMQ and IBM's MQSeries. In certain situations, you may also need to develop your own custom message queue. For example, you can create a database table that is used as a message pool so that client applications and server applications can communicate with each other by adding and reading records to and from the data table. Although these implementations are based on the principle of message queuing regardless of whether they are third-party or homemade products, the API, or application programming interface, of these message queue technologies are very different from each other. A developer who wishes to use these message queues in an application must be fluent in the APIs that come with each of these message queue technologies.

This often results in long learning curves for the additional APIs. Having different sets of message queue APIs also introduces a great deal of maintenance effort into the application when certain changes are required. For example, if you decided to move from the MQSeries to a custom database queue, you would have to change every line of code from the MQSeries API to accommodate your custom database queue API throughout the application. Wouldn't it be great if we had one common set of APIs that could handle the message queue regardless of the type of implementation we want to use? In fact, this is exactly what the SAF.Message-Queue service offers. With SAF.MessageQueue, your development team needs to learn only a single set of APIs for dealing with message queues regardless of the type of message queue technology that is being used. SAF.MessageQueue achieves this goal through the use of yet another GOF design pattern: the "bridge." You will learn more about the bridge design pattern and its implementation in the SAF.MessageQueue service later in the chapter. First we need to become familiar with the use of some common message queue technologies in .NET.

.NET Technology Overview

In the next few sections, we will look at how to send and receive messages using MSMQ and MQSeries. As we go over the various APIs, you will notice their differences. Later in the chapter, we will discuss how we can develop a common API for all the message queue technologies.

MSMQ

MSMQ is Microsoft's offering in message queuing technology. MSMQ is also part of the Windows operating system, so that you don't have to acquire additional software to send and retrieve queued messages on a Windows platform. Although MSMQ comes with Windows, it is not installed as part of the default Windows setup. Installation of MSMQ is done through the "Add or remove Windows component" wizard under the control panel. You can find out more details on the installation of MSMQ through Window's on-line help.

After the MSMQ has been successfully installed, you will find a new item labeled "Message Queuing" under the computer management control, as shown in Figure 9-2.

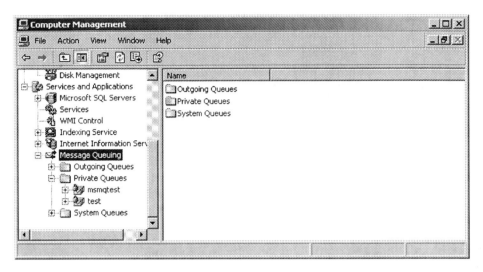

Figure 9-2. The MSMQ console

There are four kinds of queue in MSMQ, namely, outgoing queues, public queues, private queues, and system queues.

Outgoing queues are used to store messages temporarily before they are sent to their destinations. If the network is down, MSMQ will defer sending out messages in the outgoing queues until a later time, when the network is up again.

The public queues that are registered with the active directory and can be accessed without explicit knowledge of the physical location of the message queue. Client applications can query a public queue to retrieve information such as the physical location of the message queue at run time.

> **NOTE** *The computer must be part of the active directory in order to have a public queue. If the computer is installed as a standalone server, the public queue is not supported by MSMQ.*

A private queue can be accessed only if the application wishing to access it knows the queue's physical location, since it is not published in the active directory. To access a private queue on the system, you must know the name of the machine on which the message queue is located and the name of the message queue.

The system queues contain journal messages, dead-letter messages, and transactional dead-letter messages. Journal messages contain outgoing messages sent from the system. Journal messaging is disabled by default. To enable it, the application that sends out the messages has to enable it programmatically. Dead-letter messages store undeliverable and expired nontransactional messages. The transactional dead-letter queue stores undeliverable and expired transactional messages.

Message Sending

Sending a message to MSMQ is a very easy job using the System.Messaging name space in .NET. It involves four simple steps: Create the queue object; create the message object; send the message; and close the queue.

In order to use a message queue, a queue object must first be opened. Creating a queue object requires that one "FormatName" the queue. FormatName is a special MSMQ term to describe the location of the queue. The following are some examples of FormatName:

FormatName:
```
FormatName:Direct=TCP:127.0.0.1\MyPublicQueue
FormatName:Direct=TCP:127.0.0.1\private$\MyPrivateQueue
FormatName:Direct=OS:MyServer\private$\MyPrivateQueue
FormatName:Direct=OS:.\private$\MyPrivateQueue
```

Another way to locate the queue is through the queue's path. The queue's path is similar to FormatName, except that it is the logical name of the queue and requires the active directory on the network to obtain the physical location of the queue. You should try to avoid referencing the queue through "path" to reduce the dependency of the active directory and the network connectivity on the domain controller that hosts the active directory. I will use FormatName to reference the message queue throughout this chapter.

With a format name, you can open a queue with following code:

```
MessageQueue mq = new MessageQueue(@"FormatName:DIRECT=OS:.\private$\MSMQTest");
```

When a MessageQueue object is created, the next step is to create a message object that encapsulates the data you want to send to the queue:

```
Message message = new Message();
message.Label = "Test";
message.Body= "This is test!!!";
```

This code shows the simplest form of a message object. There are quite a few additional properties that you can set on the message object to take advantage of the many additional features of MSMQ. For instance, you can assign a correlation ID for a given message object so that you will have the option of retrieving a specific message from the queue later based on such ID. You can also send more complex data than a simple text message to the queue. In fact, you can send a custom business object as a message to the queue and retrieve it later as the same type of business object. For example, the following code will create message object that encapsulates a purchase order:

```
Message message = new Message();
message.Label = "Test";
message.Body= new PurchaseOrder();
```

With both queue and message ready, message sending is matter of one line of code, as in the following example:

```
mq.Send(message);
```

After the message has been sent, you should close the connection with the Close() method of the MessageQueue object. If we put everything together, we then have the following bare-bones code for sending a message to the MSMQ:

```
MessageQueue mq = null;
try
{
    mq = new MessageQueue(@"formatName:DIRECT=OS:.\private$\MSMQtest");
    Message message = new Message();
    message.Label = "Test";
    message.Body= "This is test!!!";
    mq.Send(message);
    // or mq.Send("Test","This is a test ");
}
finally
{
    mq.Close();
}
```

You should always use the finally block to ensure that the connection is closed down.

Message Retrieving

Retrieving a message from MSMQ is just as easy as sending one. It involves three steps: Create the queue object; retrieve the message; and close the queue. The following sample code shows how you can retrieve a single message from MSMQ:

```
MessageQueue mq = null;
try
{
    mq = new MessageQueue(@"formatName:DIRECT=OS:.\private$\MSMQtest");
    ((XmlMessageFormatter)mq.Formatter).TargetTypeNames = new String[1] {
                    typeof(string).ToString() };
    Message message = mq.Receive();
    Console.WriteLine(message.Label + " : " + message.Body);
}
finally
{
    mq.Close();
}
```

The Receive() method of the MessageQueue object will return a message object if there is any message in the queue. Otherwise, the Receive() method will block the running thread and will not continue until there is a message in the queue. You can also set a timeout value for how long the Receive() method should wait before throwing an exception by calling Receive(TimeSpan ts).

When a message is retrieved from the queue, the MessageQueue object will construct a Message object to contain the message from the queue. As part of the message construction, MessageQueue will set the Message.Body property with the original object sent to the queue. This requires that the receiver know the type information of the message. The MessageQueue.Formatter property provides a means for you to provide the type information needed by the MessageQueue object to construct the Message.Body. In our example, because the message we are sending to the queue is a text message, the TargetTypeName should contain the System.String type name in order for the message to be retrieved successfully. If we send a message that is other than a text message, we will need to add an additional type name to the TargetTypeNames property. The following code shows such a scenario:

```
((XmlMessageFormatter)mq.Formatter).TargetTypeNames = new
    String[2]{typeof(System.String).ToString(),typeof(PurchaseOrder).ToString()};
Message message = mq.Receive();
PurchaseOrder po = (PurchaseOrder)message.Body;
//access the member of po
```

As you can see, by adding more type names to the TargetTypeNames array, you provide MessageQueue type information this is used to construct the PurchaseOrder object in the sample code.

MQSeries

Unlike Microsoft's MSMQ, which is available only on the Windows platform, IBM's MQSeries is supported on many platforms, such as Mainframe, Unix, Linux, and Windows. Because of MQSeries's multiplatform support, it can be used to enable application integration in many heterogeneous environments. In the next section we will look at some how to send and receive messages to and from MQSeries in .NET.

We saw earlier that the System.Messaging name space provides all the classes we need to interact with MSMQ. The situation is bit different in the case of MQSeries. The .NET framework doesn't come with any .NET components that you can use with MQSeries. However, MQSeries's functionalities are available in a COM component, and you can use .NET's "interop" feature to access the functionalities in the COM component and hence access MQSeries from the .NET application. We will look at this in more detail later, but first, we need to install MQSeries.

In order to access MQSeries from a Windows platform, you need to install MQSeries on a Windows system. You can download a 90-day trial version from IBM's Web site. During the installation of MQSeries, the installation wizard will walk you through a number of steps for initial configuration. After you have successfully installed the software, you can start adding message queues by opening the WebSphere MQ explorer as shown in Figure 9-3.

In Figure 9-3, MQSeriesTest is a queue created under the MQ_Local queue manager. After you have installed MQSeries on the system, the next step is to create an interop assembly for MQSeries's COM component so that you can access MQSeries in .NET.

MQAX200.dll, a COM DLL installed as part of MQSeries, provides all the functionality we need to program against the MQSeries. MQAX200.dll is located in the Program Files\IBM\WebSphere MQ\bin folder (the default installation folder). You can create the Interop for MQAX200.dll either manually through the tlbimp utility or automatically through VS.NET.

Tlbimp.exe creates a .NET interop assembly (RCW, or runtime callable wrapper) that wraps around the COM DLL and makes it accessible to .NET applications. Figure 9-4 shows how you can create an RCW using tlbimp.exe.

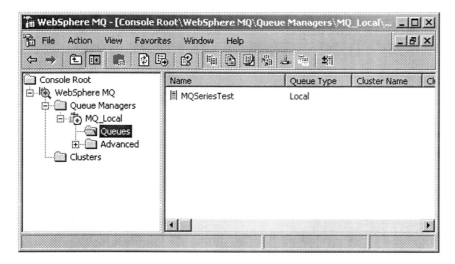

Figure 9-3. The WebSphere MQ explorer

```
C:\WINDOWS\System32\cmd.exe
C:\Program Files\IBM\WebSphere MQ\bin>tlbimp mqax200.dll /out: Interop.mqax200.dll
Microsoft (R) .NET Framework Type Library to Assembly Converter 1.0.3705.0
Copyright (C) Microsoft Corporation 1998-2001.  All rights reserved.

Type library imported to C:\Program Files\IBM\WebSphere MQ\bin\Interop.mqax200.dll

C:\Program Files\IBM\WebSphere MQ\bin>
```

Figure 9-4. Using tlbimp *to create a runtime callable wrapper for* mqax200.dll

After the new RCW is created, you can add the RCW (or interop.mqax200.dll in my case) to the project using the "Add Reference" feature in VS.NET.

Another option is simply to add mqax200.dll as a COM reference to the project. VS.NET automatically creates the RCW for you and adds it to the project reference.

With the MQSeries setup and the .NET RCW created, let's take a look at how to send and receive messages via MQSeries.

Message Sending

Sending a message to MQSeries also involves four major steps: Open the queue; create a message; send the message; and close the queue.

Before we can open a queue, we need to provide two pieces of information to locate a queue: the message queue manager and the queue name. The following code shows how you can open a queue using the MQSeries API:

```
Using MQAX200;
...
MQSession queueSession = new MQSessionClass();
MQQueueManager mqm = queueSession.AccessQueueManager("MQ_Local");
MQQueue queue =
        mqm.AccessQueue("MQSeriesTest",(int)MQ.MQOO_INPUT_AS_Q_DEF,"","","");
queue.Open();
```

After the queue has been opened, we need to create a message object that encapsulates the data we want to send to the queue. The following code shows how you can create a message and message option that carries additional information on how the message is sent:

```
MQMessage message = (MQMessage)queueSession.AccessMessage();
message.WriteString("This is test!!")
MQPutMessageOptions messageOption =
(MQPutMessageOptions)queueSession.AccessPutMessageOptions();
```

Sending the message involves one line of code:

```
queue.Put(message,messageOption);
```

After you are done with the queue, you should always close the open connection in the "finally" block as follows:

```
MQQueueManager mqm = null;
MQQueue queue =  null;
try
{
    mqm = ...;
    queue = ....;
    queue.Open();
    .....
}
finally
{
```

```
        if (queue != null)
        {
            queue.Close();
        }
        if (mqm != null)
        {
            mqm.Disconnect();
        }
}
```

Message Retrieval

Retrieving a message from MQSeries involves four steps: Open the queue; create an empty message; retrieve the message; and close the queue. The following code shows a simple message retrieval sample:

```
MQSession session = new MQSessionClass();
MQQueueManager mqm = null;
MQQueue queue = null;
try
{
    mqm = session.AccessQueueManager("MQ_Local");
    queue = mqm.AccessQueue("MQSeriesTest",(int)MQ.MQOO_OUTPUT,"","","");
    queue.Open();
    MQMessage message  = (MQMessage)queueSession.AccessMessage();
    MQGetMessageOptions messageOption =
        (MQGetMessageOptions)queueSession.AccessGetMessageOptions();
    queue.Get(message,messageOption,System.Reflection.Missing.Value);
    string content = message.ReadString(message.MessageLength);
    Console.WriteLine(content);
}
finally
{
    if (queue != null)
    {
        queue.Close();
    }
    if (mqm != null)
    {
        mqm.Disconnect();
    }
}
```

Unlike MSMQ, where the Receive() method will block the thread if there is no message in the queue to be retrieved, the Get() method in the MQSeries API doesn't block the thread even when the queue is empty. Instead, the Get() method will throw an exception to the caller to indicate that there is no message to retrieve. Because of the different behavior for retrieving the message, you should put in a catch block to handle message retrieval when the queue is empty. After you obtain the message from the queue, you can retrieve its data by calling its ReadString() method, which will return the data stored in the message.

By comparing the API of MSMQ and MQSeries through the past several sections, you can see the different sets of APIs used in each technology that developers have to learn in order to work with those message queues. In the next section, you will learn about SAF.MessageQueue and see how it is able to provide a common set of APIs to interact with message queues regardless of their implementation technologies.

Code Sample Walkthrough

How can we provide a common API that can work with different types of implementations of similar technology? Our goal is to create a set of APIs that developers can learn for all types of message queue implementations. We also want to make sure that as more message queue implementations are added, developers can easily adapt the new implementation without having to learn another set of APIs. GOF's bridge design pattern provides us an excellent architecture upon which the SAF.MessageQueue service is developed.

Bridge Design Pattern

To quote from GOF's book: The bridge pattern decouples an abstraction from its implementation so that the two can vary independently.

The bridge pattern is focused on the interface. It is actually very similar to the design we often use to separate the interface from its underlying implementation. Figure 9-5 shows the typical way an interface is used in most of our programs.

In Figure 9-5, the client wants to access the methods in an implementation class. However, the client doesn't directly bind itself to the implementation class. Doing so would make the client subject to frequent changes when the underlying implementation class varies. Instead, the client binds itself to the interface through which it accesses the underlying methods in the implementation classes. By adding an interface layer, the implementation classes can vary without affecting the client, because as far as the client is concerned, it works only with the interface layer.

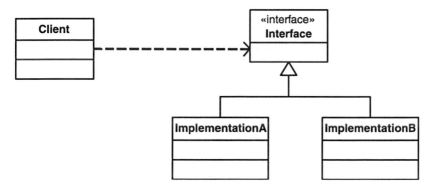

Figure 9-5. A common use of an interface

The design is simple and satisfies most of the architecture scenario we face in building an application. This type of design is based on the assumption that the interface will never change. However, if you step back and think about interfaces you have developed in the past, you will probably notice that many of those interfaces are method signatures of the underlying implementation. I wouldn't say that the interface is coupled to a particular implementation, but the interface is a very close representation of the underlying implementation. In some cases, binding to a representation of a detailed implementation is a point of inflexibility. This is a very abstract concept. Let's take a look at a real-life analogy that paraphrases the point I am making here.

When you begin a new development project, the first thing you need to do is gather the business requirements from the business users. During this phase, you will talk to the business users and figure out what exactly they want out of the project. At the end of this phase you will come up with a business requirement document that describes the high-level goals for the application, such as whether the user is able to send confirmation to the customer through a Web application and whether the user will be notified by e-mail when the ordering process fails. At this moment, you really don't know or care anything about any aspect of implementation, not even the high-level architecture of the final application. Only after the business user ratifies the business requirement document will you start thinking about the design aspect of the application. During this phase you will decide on the overall architecture of the application, the types of components, and their interfaces, and eventually create the application design document. Now, let's go back the diagram in Figure 9-5. Binding the client to the interface is like handing a design document to a business user and obtaining agreement on your design. Business users don't care or understand about the implementation. (The design document is a close representation of the actual implementation.) Business users do care about the results, not about a set of high-level instructions on how to achieve those results.

So if we add the "business requirement document" back into Figure 9-5, you in fact create a "bridge" that links the "client," who cares about the result, and the "interface," which cares about the high-level features of the underlying implementation. Figure 9-6 shows a new diagram with the "bridge" in it.

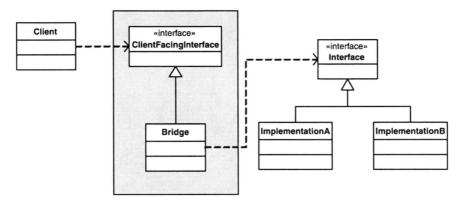

Figure 9-6. The bridge design pattern

ClientFacingInterface describes the high-level service that is available to the client. The bridge class holds the reference to the interface that describes the actual implementation. It also implements the ClientFacingInterface to provide the actual work to produce the result expected by the client. As you can see from the diagram, the bridge is the linkage between a "client-friendly" high-level interface and a low-level interface that describes the actual implementation. You can also think of the bridge design pattern as a way of providing an interface to an interface.

A low-level interface changes much less than its implementation, but it can still change due to new features and functionalities added to the underlying implementation. By placing the bridge class between the two interfaces, the low-level interface on the implementation side can vary without affecting the client application as long as the bridge can absorb the changes and shield them from the client application.

SAF.MessageQueue comes with two sample implementations of the IMessageQueue interface: one for MSMQ and the other for MQSeries. You can also create other implementations of queuing programs and plug them into the SAF.MessageQueue service. Figure 9-7 shows the SAF.MessageQueue service's class structure.

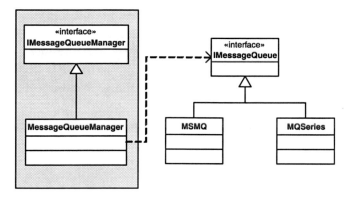

Figure 9-7. The SAF.MessageQueue *service's class structure*

IMessageQueueManager provides the interface of a simple message queue operation that the client application needs to interact with. It is defined as follows:

```
public interface IMessageQueueManager
{
    void SendMessage(Message message);
    Message RetrieveMessage();
    void RegisterMessageArrivalHanlder(MessageArrivalHandler mah);
    void OpenConnection();
    void CloseConnection();
}
```

SAF.MessageQueue also comes with IMessageQueue that describes the functionalities of implementation for various message queue technologies.

```
public interface IMessageQueue
{
    void Send(Message message);
    Message Retrieve();
    event MessageArrivalHandler MessageArrival;
    void Open();
    void Close();
}
```

IMessageQueueManager focuses on providing an easy interface to the client, and IMessagingQueue focuses on providing the signatures of the various implementations of the message queue. These two interfaces don't have to match.

Besides defining the methods for sending and retrieving messages, IMessageQueue also defines an event for which the client registers to receive messages as they arrive at the message queue instead of constantly checking the queue for new messages. We will see more about this event later in the chapter.

The following sample code demonstrates how we can use the SAF.MessageQueue service to send a message to MSMQ:

```
//bind the message queue implementation with MessageQueueManager
IMessageQueue queue = new MSMQ("QueueA");
IMessageQueueManager mqm = new MessageQueueManager(queue);
//create a new message
Message m = new Message();
m.Label = "test";
m.Content ="this is test";
try
{
    mqm.OpenConnection();
    mqm.SendMessage(m);
}
finally
{
    //close down the connection
    mqm.CloseConnection();
}
```

Because the client is using the IMessageQueueManager interface, a change from sending messages to MSMQ to sending them to MQSeries is a matter of one line of code. The following code shows the difference between sending a message to MSMQ and sending one to MQSeries:

```
MSMQ:
IMessageQueue queue = new MSMQ("QueueA");
IMessageQueueManager mqm = new MessageQueueManager(queue);
//… the rest of the code


MQSeries:
IMessageQueue queue = new MQSeries("QueueB");
IMessageQueueManager mqm = new MessageQueueManager(queue);
// … the rest of the code
```

QueueA and QueueB represent the logical names of the message queues you want to connect. The detailed connection information is stored in the configuration file as follows:

```
<Framework type="SAF.Configuration.ConfigurationManager,SAF.Configuration">
    <SAF.MessageQueue>
        <Queue name="QueueA" technology="MSMQ">
        <FormatName>FormatName:DIRECT=OS:.\private$\MSMQTest</FormatName>
            <SleepTime>1000</SleepTime>
        </Queue>
        <Queue name="QueueB" technology="MQSeries">
            <QueueManager>MQ_Local</QueueManager>
            <QueueName>MQSeriesTest</QueueName>
            <SleepTime>1000</SleepTime>
        </Queue>
    </SAF.MessageQueue>
</Framework>
```

With the SAF.MessageQueue service, developers can work with different types of message queuing technologies without knowing different sets of APIs accompanying such technologies. You can also develop additional IMessageQueue implementations and bind them to the ImessageQueueManager, with which developers are already familiar. By adding the bridge between the two interfaces, SAF.MessageQueue can also provide considerable flexibility in how message queues are used. For example, you can create additional constructors in SAF.MessageQueue.MessageQueueManager that take two parameters, one for the queue to which you send the message and another for the queue from which you retrieve the message, so that you can use receive messages from MSMQ and send messages through MQSeries with very little work on the developers' part. The following sample code shows this:

```
MSMQ incomingQueue = new MSMQ("QueueA");
MQSeries outgoingQueue = new MSMQ("QueueB");

IMessageQueueManager mqm = new MessageQueueManager(incomingQueue, outgoingQueue);
mqm.SendMessage(…);
Message m = mqm.RetrieveMessage();
```

In addition to the basic queue operations of sending and retrieving messages, the SAF.MessageQueue service also provides the ability for the client to register for the event of the arrival of new messages to the queue. The message-retrieval behavior in many queue technologies results in a block on the running thread when the message queue is empty. This behavior often leads client applications to "wait" on the method call that retrieves the message. SAF.MessageQueue solves this problem with the MessageArrival event, which notifies the client when a message arrives, thereby eliminating the need for the client to "wait" for the message.

The following sample shows how you can use the feature from the client application:

```
static void Main(string[] args)
{
    IMessageQueue msmq = new MSMQ("QueueA");
    IMessageQueueManager mqm = new MessageQueueManager(msmq);
    mqm.RegisterMessageArrivalHanlder (new MessageArrivalHandler(RecieveMessage));
}


public static void RecieveMessage(Message message, string queueName)
{
    Console.WriteLine(message.Content.ToString());
    Console.WriteLine(" from " + queueName);
}
```

RegisterMessageArrivalHandler is implemented in the MessageQueueManager as follows:

```
public MessageQueueManager : IMessageQueue
{
    private IMessageQueue mq;
    //... code omitted
    public void RegisterMessageArrivalHanlder(MessageArrivalHandler mah)
    {
        mq.MessageArrival += mah;
    }
}
```

When MessageQueueManager adds the handler to the underlying event defined in IMessageQueue, the message queue implementation will start to listen to the given message queue and fire the event when a new message arrives at the queue. A MessageArrival event is defined as follows in the SAF.MessageQueue.MSMQ class:

```
public class MSMQ
{
    //... some code omitted
    public event MessageArrivalHandler MessageArrival
    {
        //when new handler is registered for the event, start the listener
        //if it is not yet started
```

```
add
{
        handler += value;
        if (queueListenerStarted != true)
        {
                //create a new thread to listen on the queue
                ThreadStart ts = new ThreadStart(StartQueueListener);
                Thread t = new Thread(ts);
                t.Start();
        }
}
remove
{
        handler -= value;
        //stop the listener if no handler is listed
        if (handler == null || handler.GetInvocationList().Length <= 0)
        {
                StopQueueListener();
        }
}
    }
}
```

The advantage of using an event instead of a delegate is that you have the opportunity to perform some work when a delegate object is added to the delegate chain. When you define an event object in .NET, you can implement its "Add" and "Remove" actions. In our case, when a client registers for the event, the "Add" block is executed to start the queue listener. When the client unregisters for the event, the "Remove" block will remove the client delegate from the delegate chain and stop the queue listener if the delegate chain is empty at that time.

The StartListener() method creates a new connection to the queue and listens for the arrival of a new message with a while loop. When a message arrives, it will fire the MessageArrival event with the arrived message.

The concept behind SAF.MessageQueue service can also be applied in creating a data access component that allows developers to work with multiple database technologies, such as SQL server, Oracle, and Sybase, without having to learn different sets of data provider APIs. Similar to SAF.Messaging, the data access component will have a DatabaseManager class with which developers will interact and a set of database classes with which DatabaseManager interacts to provide specific behavior in accessing certain database servers.

Testing Project

The Test.SAF.MessageQueue project contains a console application that shows how to use the SAF.MessageQueue service to send messages to different queues in MSMQ and MQSeries. You don't have to install both MSMQ and MQSeries to run the demo, but you need to install one of them in order to run the part of the demo that uses the installed message queue technology. Please refer to early sections of this chapter for more detailed instruction on installation of MSMQ and MQSeries.

You also need to create the necessary queue described in the configuration file before you run the demo. The message queues must be created before any message can be sent to them.

After you have created the necessary message queues, you can run the demo by opening the solution under "Test.SAF.MessageQueue" and hitting F5.

Summary

In this chapter, you learned about message queues and their benefits in developing scalable applications and integrating applications in a heterogeneous environment. We looked briefly at how to send and retrieve messages via MSMQ and MQSeries in .NET. We also introduced the SAF.MessageQueue service, which provides a single API for interacting with different message queue technologies. You also learned about GOF's bridge design pattern, its advantage in decoupling the client interface and the interface of the implementation. At the end of the chapter, you learned how this pattern is implemented through the code walkthrough of the SAF.MessageQueue service.

CHAPTER 10

Authorization Service

THERE IS OFTEN some confusion about the difference between *authentication* and *authorization*. Authentication is a process that identifies who the caller/client is and verifies the client or caller's authenticity. This process normally involves some type of user ID and password checks. If the user ID and password match, authentication succeeds. The caller/client usually receives a security token from the authentication process so that its identity will not have to be validated again. Authorization is the process that checks the level of access to certain underlying resources for a given identity. In other words, it checks whether a particular caller or client that has already been authenticated successfully has permission (i.e., authorization) to access certain resources, such as reading a file, querying a database, or accessing a business component.

In this chapter, you will learn how to perform security authorization on .NET components. We frequently want to provide different levels of access to our business components. For example, we may have regular employees access generic information, while managers are able to access more sensitive information. In such a scenario, the level of access to the application depends on the group to which a particular user belongs.

Motivation and Goals

The .NET framework offer the attribute class System,Security.Permission.Security-Attribute, which allows you to mark the methods inside your class with an attribute tag to enforce role-level security authorization. When using SecurityAttribute, you must define which users or user roles are allowed to enter each method you want to protect. This approach works, but close coupling between the access permissions and actual implementation of the business component makes it difficult to change who can access particular components and their methods after the application has been deployed. If the capability of reassigning the component's access permission without modifying or recompiling the code is important to you, you need to develop a customized security attribute to handle the security permission check yourself. The SAF.Authorization service provides you just that, a customized security attribute that allows you to change the component's permissions with configuration changes instead of code compilation.

SAF.Authorization achieves the goal of separating the access permission declaration from the underlying business component with the .NET attribute and .NET declarative security permission model. It also allows you to plug in your own customized authentication logic to determine the access permission on underlying resources. Let's begin with a brief look at these two technologies.

.NET Technologies Overview

.NET Attributes

Let's first take a look at the .NET attribute. In .NET, an attribute can be applied to an assembly, class, method, property, field, etc. When you apply an attribute to such a class member, you basically provide a bit of metadata about such members. It is like sticking sticky notes on those members. You can later retrieve this attribute information for each member programmatically for decision-making purposes.

Marking some classes or methods with an attribute provides information only about those classes and methods. It is up to the consumer of the classes/methods to decide what to do with the additional information presented in the attribute. The .NET framework comes with a number of predefined attributes. The .NET language compiler and CLR commonly perform certain actions based on the information provided in these predefined attributes. The following are some examples:

```
[Serializable]
public class CustomerInfo{…}

[Transaction(TransactionOption.Supported)]
public class MyTransaction{…}

[PrincipalPermission(SecurityAction.Demand, Role=@"users")]
public void SecretMethod(){…}
```

SerializableAttribute informs the CLR that the class can be serialized into a stream. TransactionAttribute indicates the transaction property of certain classes when they are registered into COM+ service. PrincipalPermission tells the .NET compiler to inject certain security permission codes into the IL code for the underlying method during code compilation. The above are some examples of native attribute objects.

CLR and the .NET language compiler are hardwired to perform certain additional tasks based on certain attribute data. This is not the case when you want to create your own custom attributes. When you create a custom attribute from scratch, you normally have to write your own "consumer" to read and act on the information stored in the customized attribute.

An attribute is no different from a regular class. In fact, you must inherit from a System.Attribute class when you want to develop a custom attribute. Let's first see an example of a custom attribute class. Later, we will see how to retrieve the attribute information using reflection. The following is a customized attribute class:

```
[AttributeUsage(AttributeTargets.Class | AttributeTargets.Method)]
public class SampleAttribute : System.Attribute
{
    private string description;
    private string author;
    public string Description
    {
        get {return description;}
        set {description = value;}
    }
    public string Author
    {
        get {return author;}
        set {author = value;}
    }
    //constructor
    public SampleAttribute(string desc)
    {
        description = desc;
    }
}
```

To create a customized attribute, we first need to make the class extend the System.Attribute class and then mark the class with the AttributeUsage attribute as shown in the example. AttributeUsage specifies the types of members to which the customized attribute can apply. For instance, the compiler will throw an exception if you attempt to add the SampleAttribute to property as follows:

```
[Sample("this is test property", Author = "Xin")]
public string SomeProperty
{
    get {return "ok";}
    set {;}
}
```

Because SampleAttribute is allowed only in class and method definition, you will get an error saying, "'SampleAttribute' is not valid on this declaration type. It is valid on 'class, method' declarations only."

After you have created the Attribute class, you can apply it to whatever member is specified by AttributeUsage, as in the following example:

```
[Sample("this is Test method", Author = "Xin")]
public void Test()
{
}
```

[Sample(…)] is shorthand and is equivalent to [SampleAttribute(…)]. The previous code instructs the compiler to create an attribute object by calling its constructor and passing in the string value and then setting its property "Author" to "Xin." You can set additional property values by adding more key-value pairs in the form "PropertyName = PropertyValue," separating each key-value pair with a comma. After all these are done, the compiler associates the attribute object with the underlying method and stores them together in the assembly's metadata.

We can later retrieve the attribute information that binds to the test method through reflection. As you may recall from the discussion on .NET reflection in Chapter 4, some of the methods of the Type class help us to inspect the information stored inside a class, such as method information, property information, and attribute information. The following example shows how you can use reflection to retrieve the attribute information stored within a class:

```
static void Main(string[] args)
{
    Type type = typeof(TestApp);
    MethodInfo[] methods = type.GetMethods();
    foreach (MethodInfo method in methods)
    {
      object[] attributes = method.GetCustomAttributes(false);
      foreach (object o in attributes)
      {
        if(o.GetType() == typeof(SampleAttribute))
        {
          SampleAttribute sa = (SampleAttribute)o;
          Console.WriteLine(method.Name + " method has following attribute data");
          Console.WriteLine("Description: " + sa.Description);
          Console.WriteLine("Author:" + sa.Author);
        }
      }
    }
}
```

Using .NET reflection, we can retrieve the MethodInfo[] object, which contains all the methods defined in the class. We can then use the MethodInfo.GetCustom-Attribute() method to retrieve an object array containing the attribute's classes associated with the underlying method. If the attribute class is of SampleAttribute type, we can cast the object into the SampleAttribute class and access its properties. In the previous example, it will print out the following lines:

```
Test method has following attribute info
Description: this is test method
Author: Xin
```

This example shows how to set and retrieve the attribute data. I have to say that it is not a particularly interesting way to use attributes. Although the usage of this example is not as interesting as that of many predefined attributes, it follows the same principle as those of the predefined attribute classes that come with the .NET framework.

This chapter is about security authorization, so we want to focus on things that are security related. The .NET framework comes with an attribute class that can help us set the access permission for our class and the methods used in our application. The following section will give you an overview of this attribute class, and later, we will look at how to create a customized permission attribute through the code sample of the SAF.Authorization component.

PrincipalPermissionAttribute

System.Security.Permission.PrincipalPermissionAttribute is one of those attributes for which the .NET framework has been wired up internally to perform some interesting work for us. To better understand what PrincipalPermissionAttribute can do for us, let's look at the following example:

```
static void Main(string[] args)
{
    try
    {
        SecureMethod();
    }
    catch(System.Security.SecurityException ex)
    {
        Console.Write(ex.Message);
    }
}
```

```
[PrincipalPermission(SecurityAction.Demand,Role = @"BUILTIN\Administrators")]
public static void SecureMethod()
{
    Console.WriteLine("Access the method successfully");
}
```

If you run the Main() method, you get a security exception that says, "Request for principal permission failed." This is because SecureMethod() has been marked with the PrincipalPermission attribute, which demands that the caller be a member of a group called BUILTIN\Administrators to access SecureMethod. CLR checks the caller's membership by getting the principal information of the caller's thread and checking whether it is a member of the "BUILTIN\Administrators" group. The following code is similar to the code that CLR calls at runtime to determine whether the caller is permitted to access the method:

```
IPrincipal p = Thread.CurrentPrincipal;
if (! p.IsInRole(@"BUILTIN\Administrators"))
{
    throw new System.Security.SecurityException("Request for principal permission
                                                failed");
}
```

Because the role information defined in the attribute is stored as part of the metadata for SecureMethod(),CLR will be able to retrieve the role information at runtime and validate the caller's principal information against the role information.

Let us now return to the earlier sample code and see how we can make it work. When we start an application in .NET, the CLR creates a new thread to execute our application. This new thread doesn't have any .NET security information attached to it by default even through its underlying Win32 thread contains the identity information about the caller. However, we can assign a WindowsPrincipal object to the thread that reflects the actual caller that starts the application. The following code shows how to attach a Windows principal to a thread:

```
WindowsPrincipal wp = new WindowsPrincipal(WindowsIdentity.GetCurrent());
Thread.CurrentPrincipal = wp;
```

WindowsIdentity.GetCurrent() is a static method that returns the IIdentity object representing the Windows account of the user who is starting this application. We have seen this method in Chapter 8, where we had to create a new WindowsIdentity object from scratch with a given Windows user name and password. After we obtain the WindowsIdentity object for the current user, we can create a WindowsPrincipal object from it. This WindowsPrincipal object contains the current user's membership information. We can then bind the current thread with a new principal object by setting the CurrentPrincipal property.

Now let's add the two lines of code that we just saw to the original Main() method. You should log onto the system with a local administrator account and run it again. This time, SecureMethod() is successfully called, and this time the console will print out "Access the method successfully." The following is the new Main() method:

```
static void Main(string[] args)
{
    try
    {
        WindowsPrincipal wp = new
        WindowsPrincipal(WindowsIdentity.GetCurrent());
            Thread.CurrentPrincipal = wp;
        SecureMethod();

    }
    catch(System.Security.SecurityException ex)
    {
        Console.Write(ex.Message);
    }
}
```

Although we used WindowsPrincipal in this example, the PrincipalPermission attribute doesn't limit its check to WindowsPrincipal. Instead, this attribute can check the permission on every object that implements the System.Security.Principal.IPrincipal interface. This includes WindowsPrincipal, GenericPrincipal, and custom principal objects that you create. In fact, if you replace the first two lines of code in the Main() method with the following code, you will still be able to access the method successfully even though the principal of the current thread is not a Windows principal at all. This is because the PrincipalPermission attribute and the CLR check the membership of the caller at the interface level (IPrincipal) at runtime:

```
GenericIdentity gi = new GenericIdentity("FakeUser");
GenericPrincipal gp =
                new GenericPrincipal(gi,new String[1]{@"BUILTIN\Administrators"});
Thread.CurrentPrincipal = gp;
```

> **NOTE** *Be careful when using the* `PrincipalPermission` *attribute to protect your method or class from being accessed by unauthorized users. Because the* `Principal-Permission` *attribute works with all* `IPrincipal` *objects, users can pretend that they belong to certain groups by creating a generic principal with the matching Windows group name, thereby bypassing the Windows authentication process. We will look at how SAF.Authorization can prevent this type of problem later in the chapter.*

The `PrincipalPermission` attribute offers the good basic functionality of authorizing callers as they access a method and class, but it would be ideal if we could define a customized permissions logic for deciding whether to accept or reject certain calls and making CLR run our customized logic at runtime. For example, you could store the user identity and membership information inside a database server and use the information inside the database to determine the permissions on certain methods or classes.

The .NET framework comes with an abstract class and an interface that allows us to develop our own authorization logic and, most importantly, to wire it up with CLR so that our authorization logic will be executed automatically at runtime.

CodeAccessSecurityAttribute and IPermission

The .NET framework has hardwired some predefined attribute classes so that they can perform special services on members that are labeled with such attributes. `CodeAccessSecurityAttribute` is one of these predefined and prewired attribute classes. It notifies the .NET language compiler to add code that can perform a permission check on the callers. This sounds very much like `PrincipalPermission-Attribute`. In fact, CodeAccessSecurityAttribute is the parent of `PrincipalPermission-Attribute`. The following is the class definition of `PrincipalPermissionAttribute`:

```
public sealed class PrincipalPermissionAttribute : CodeAccessSecurityAttribute
```

By marking a member with `PrincipalPermissionAttribute` or an attribute class that derives from `CodeAccessSecurityAttribute`, you effectively tell the .NET language compiler that you need to perform a permission check on the marked member. However, there still needs to be some entity that is actually responsible for performing such a check.

You can specify how you want to handle the permission check by implementing the `CreatePermission()` method. Here is its definition:

```
public abstract IPermission CreatePermission();
```

CreatePermission() follows the "factory method" design pattern in GOF's book. Its sole purpose is to produce a Permission object, which is how the attribute class binds to a specific permission class. For a class to qualify as a permission class, the class must implement the System.Security.Permission.IPermission interface. The most interesting method in this interface is the Demand method. The IPermission.Demand() method is the one that decides whether a particular caller can access the resources that are marked with the permission attribute. Permission to the underlying resource is granted if the Demand() method returns without an exception. If the demand method raises an exception, then permission is denied and a SecurityException is sent to the caller. This is the method in which you want to start your permission logic and decide whether to throw a Security exception based on the caller's credentials.

Now let's look at a concrete example of the relationship between the attribute class and the permission class. Recall the earlier example of PrincipalPermission-Attribute:

```
[PrincipalPermission(SecurityAction.Demand,Role = @"BUILTIN\Administrators")]
public static void SecureMethod()
{
    Console.WriteLine("Access the method successfully");
}
```

The permission class that pairs with the PrincipalPermissionAttribute class is called System.Security.Permissions.PrincipalPermission. It is the one that actually performs the permission check with the information provided by the attribute tag. The definition for the PrincipalPermission class is as follows:

```
public sealed class PrinciplePermission : CodeAccessPermission,
IUnrestrictedPermission
```

Although the PrincipalPermission class doesn't implement the IPermission interface directly, its parent class CodeAccessPermission does. Now that we know about the attribute class and its counterpart permission class, let's take a close look at how these two classes interface with .NET at both design time and runtime. Figure 10-1 shows what is happening behind the scenes when you compile an application that contains the PrincipalPermission attribute.

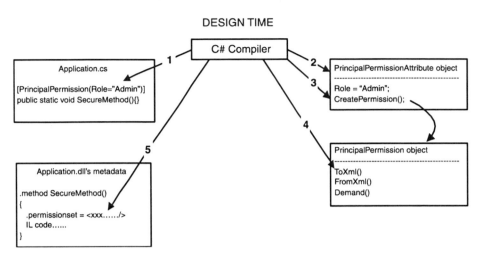

Figure 10-1. Security permission during design time

Figure 10-1 shows what happens when you compile an application that contains the PrincipalPermission attribute. There are five major steps during code compilation. First, the .NET language compiler looks through the source code of your application and locates the attributes that are of CodeAccessSecurityAttribute type. Second, the compiler creates the attribute object and assign the values of the specified properties on the attribute tag in the source code. Third, the compiler calls the CreatePermission() method on the attribute object. The CreatePermission() method creates a new concrete permission object, passes the attribute information into the permission object via its public fields or properties, and then returns it to the compiler. Fourth, the compiler calls the ToXml() method on the newly created permission object. The ToXml method returns a SecurityElement object, a special XML object that contains all the information CLR needs to determine the caller's permission status to access a particular class or method. Some of this information is the type information on the permission class that handles certain permission attributes and the attribute property data defined on the attribute tags, such as role name in the case of PrincipalPermissionAttribute. In the last step, the compiler streams the object returned from the ToXml() method into XML data and stores these data as part of the application's metadata. The XML data that are stored in the metadata are always associated with the members that are tagged with the corresponding attribute. For example, the XML data are stored as part of the metadata for the method SecureMethod() in Figure 10-1 because the SecureMethod() method has been tagged with the SecurityPermissionAttriubte in the source code of the application. The end result of compilation shown in Figure 10-1 is that the compiler injects the application's metadata with an "instruction" regarding which permission class will be responsible for the permission check on the underlying members as well as certain parameters needed by the permission class to do its job. Figure 10-2 shows the actual permission-related metadata stored with SecureMethod using `ildasm.exe`.

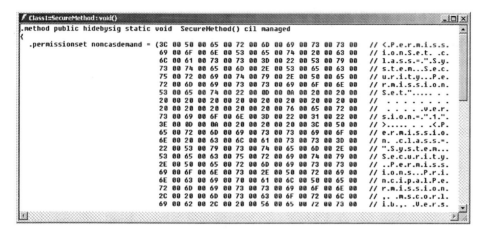

Figure 10-2. Metadata for the method marked with the permission attribute

We learned that the Demand() method is the method that determines whether a caller has permission to access a certain resource. So how does a call initialized by the caller end up calling the Demand() method? Figure 10-3 illustrates what happens when a caller calls the method that is tagged with CodeAccessPermissionAttribute.

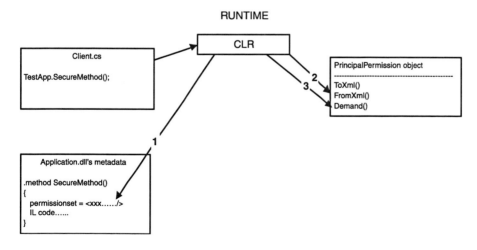

Figure 10-3. Security permission at runtime

The process shown in Figure 10-3 begins when a caller makes a call to SecureMethod(). CLR will first load the assembly that contains the method if it is not already loaded. Then CLR will locate the metadata for SecureMethod() in the assembly. If SecureMethod() were not tagged with CodeAccessSecurityAttribute, CLR would have to go right to the IL code to execute the method. However, SecureMethod() is tagged with CodeAccessSecurityAttribute, so there are quite a few things that need to happen before the IL code can be executed. In our case, SecureMethod() contains permission-set information (XML data returned by the IPermission.ToXml() method) that is generated by the compiler, as we saw earlier. When CLR sees the permission-set information, it will first create a permission object based on the type information stored in the XML data. Next, CLR will call the FromXml method on the permission object and pass in the XML data stored in the metadata for SecureMethod(). This method effectively sets the public fields and properties of the permission object with the attribute's property value, such as Role. (Recall the process on how the metadata is generated in the first place.) After all the properties of the permission object are set, the CLR will call its Demand() method. If the Demand() method returns without an exception, CLR will continue on to execute the IL code for the method. Otherwise, SecurityException is returned to the caller.

Now that you have learned quite a bit of theory about how attribute classes and permission classes can work together to carry out some very interesting declarative role-based security in .NET, it is time to see how to implement a customized attribute and permission class from scratch. For the rest of chapter, we will look at the implementation of the SAF.Authorization component, which contains a customized attribute class and permission class.

SAF Code Sample Walkthrough

One of the goals of SAF.Authorization is the separation of the permission settings from the application code, so that we can change the permission information on the methods or classes without application code changes and recompilation of the code. Instead of storing the authorization information inside the application code, the authorization component moves such information to the configuration file, where it can be modified to reflect the latest access permissions on the resource throughout the application.

The difference between SAF.Authorization and PrincipalPermission is illustrated in the following comparison:

```
[PrincipalPermission(SecurityAction.Demand,Role = @"BUILTIN\Administrators")]
public static void SecureMethod(){...}
```

```
[SAFSecurity(SecurityAction.Demand, Name="MyAssembly.MyType.MyMethod1")]
public static void SecureMethod(){...}
```

As you can see, the second attribute, SAFSecurity, contains no user role information, but rather a logical name that represents the underlying method. The Name
property doesn't have to follow any particular format. However, it is easier to identify names uniquely by combining the assembly name, class name, and method
name.

Accompanying SAFSecurityAttribute are the configuration data that perform
the authorization information necessary for the permission object to perform its
permission check on the underlying resource. The following code shows the section for the SAF.Authorization component in the configuration file:

```
<configuration>
  <configSections>
    <section name="Framework" type="..." />
  </configSections>

  <Framework type="SAF.Configuration.ConfigurationManager,SAF.Configuration">
    <SAF.Authorization>
        <Providers>
            <Provider name="Generic"
type="SAF.Authorization.GenericAuthorizationProvider,SAF.Authorization" />
            <Provider name="Windows"
type="SAF.Authorization.WindowsAuthorizationProvider,SAF.Authorization" />
        </Providers>
        <Permissions>
            <Allows>
                <Allow name="MyAssembly.MyType.MyMethod1" roles =
                  "BUILTIN\Administrators, MyDomain\Managers" provider="Windows" />
            </Allows>
            <Denies>
                <Deny name="MyAssembly.MyType.MyMethod2" roles="Anonymous"
                            provider="Generic" />
            </Denies>
        </Permissions>
    </SAF.Authorization>
  </Framework>
</configuration>
```

The Permissions element under `<SAF.Authorization>` contains two sections: Allows and Denies. The Allows section defines who can access which resources. The Denies section defines who is forbidden to access which resources. Each entry in the Allows and Denies sections also contains the provider information. The Provider represents the authorization provider that is responsible for determining whether a particular caller has permission to access the resource. By providing support for multiple authorization provider classes, you are free to use additional types of authorization mechanisms beyond just checking the generic principal and Windows principal. For instance, you may store the user's membership and privilege information in a database, in which case, you can create your own authorization provider to check the database for a given user to determine whether to grant permission.

You have just seen how the SAFSecurityAttribute is used and permission information stored in the configuration file. It is time to tackle the most important classes: SAFSecurityAttribute and SAFSecurityPermission. The following is a portion of the code for the SAFSecurityAttribute class:

```
[AttributeUsageAttribute(AttributeTargets.All, AllowMultiple = true)]
public class SAFSecurityAttribute : CodeAccessSecurityAttribute
{
    private string name;
    public SAFSecurityAttribute( SecurityAction action ) :
                                 base( SecurityAction.Demand )
    {
        // Provide unrestricted access to the resource protected by the permission
        this.Unrestricted = true;
    }
    public override IPermission CreatePermission()
    {
        //create the new permission object
        SAFSecurityPermission permission = new SAFSecurityPermission();
        //set the property of the permission object
        permission.Name = this.Name;
        permission.Unrestricted = this.Unrestricted;
        return permission;

    }
    public string Name
    {
        get{return name;}
        set{name = value;}
    }
}
```

SAFSecurityAttribute extends CodeAccessSecurityAttribute and overrides the CreatePermission() method to create a new instance of its counterpart permission object SAFSecurityPermission. The CreatePermission() method also transfers the attribute property values to the newly created permission object so that the property information will be streamed into the metadata later, during compilation.

SAFSecurityPermission has a few more methods, three of which are of particular interest: ToXml(), FromXml(), and Demand(). Here are their implementation:

```
public SecurityElement ToXml()
{
    // SecurityElement is a speical XML object containing
    // encoded security attribute values.
    SecurityElement securityElement = new SecurityElement("Permission");
    Type type = this.GetType();
    //add important permission info to Xml
    securityElement.AddAttribute("class", type.AssemblyQualifiedName);
    //the attribute name that has been added must match
    //the actual property names.
    securityElement.AddAttribute("Unrestricted", Unrestricted.ToString());
    securityElement.AddAttribute("Name",Name);
    return securityElement;
}


public void FromXml(SecurityElement securityElement)
{
    //retrieve the info from the metadata
    string flag = securityElement.Attribute("Unrestricted");
    Name = securityElement.Attribute("Name");
    if(flag != null)
    {
        this.Unrestricted = Convert.ToBoolean(flag);
    }
}


public void Demand()
{
    //get the configuration object for permission
    ConfigurationManager cm =
            (ConfigurationManager)ConfigurationSettings.GetConfig("Framework");
    AuthorizationConfiguration ac = cm.AuthorizationConfig;
    //get the allowed and denied roles arrays
    string[] allowedRoles = ac.AllowedRoles(Name);
```

```
    string[] deniedRoles = ac.DeniedRoles(Name);
    //get an authorization provider to perform the permission check
    IAuthorizationProvider ap = (IAuthorizationProvider)
                            ac.GetAuthorizationProvider(Name);

    ap.Authorize(allowedRoles, deniedRoles);
}
```

ToXml() and FromXml() are called at design time and runtime by the .NET framework to serialize and deserialize the security attribute information as described
in Figures 10-1 and 10-3, which we saw earlier in the chapter. Inside the ToXml()
method, we want to store the security attribute information in the SecurityElement
object. In the FromXml() method, we want to do the opposite, that is, to retrieve the
attribute information from the SecurityElement and place it in the class fields. The
Demand() method deserves some explanation. It first retrieves the authorization
configuration object, which contains methods that return string arrays of both the
allowed and denied roles for a given name defined on the attribute property. This
name doesn't have to match the actual method name. It is merely a logical name
used to identify a protected method in the class. Using the earlier sample, the
name would be MyAssembly.MyType.MyMethod1. The Demand method then calls another
method on the authorization configuration object to obtain a reference to the
authorization provider object that handles the particular resource. In our example,
the provider for MyAssembly.MyType.MyMethod1 is "Windows," which is referred to as
the SAF.Authorization.WindowsAuthorizationProvider class in the <Providers> section
in the configuration file.

All authorization providers implement the IAuthorizationProvider interface,
which contains a method defined as follows:

```
namespace SAF.Security.Library
{
    public interface IAuthorizationProvider
    {
        void Authorize(string[] allowedRoles, string[] deniedRoles);
    }
}
```

If the authorization provider decides that the current caller has permission
to access the underlying resource, the Authorize method will return without an
exception. Otherwise, it should throw a SecurityException to indicate that authorization has failed. Because the Authorize() method is called inside the Demand()
method, any exception in the Authorize method will bubble up to the Demand
method, which will cause access to the underlying resource to fail. The following
code shows an example of what you can do within an authorization provider:

```csharp
public class WindowsAuthorizationProvider : IAuthorizationProvider
{
    public void Authorize(string[] allowedRoles, string[] deniedRoles)
    {
        bool allowed = false;
        WindowsPrincipal wp = null;
        //make sure we are dealing with the Windows principal only
        if(Thread.CurrentPrincipal.GetType() != typeof(WindowsPrincipal))
        {
            wp = new WindowsPrincipal(WindowsIdentity.GetCurrent());
        }
        else
        {
            wp = (WindowsPrincipal)Thread.CurrentPrincipal;
        }
        //check the deniedRole first.
        if (deniedRoles != null)
        {
            foreach (string role in deniedRoles)
            {
                if (wp.IsInRole(role))
                {
                    throw new System.Security.SecurityException("Access
                            denied to account " + WindowsIdentity.GetCurrent().Name;
                }
            }
        }

        if (allowedRoles != null)
        {
            foreach (string role in allowedRoles)
            {
                if (wp.IsInRole(role))
                {
                    allowed = true;
                    break;
                }
            }
        }
        //if current call doesn't belong to allowed role either, reject the call.
        if (allowed ==false)
        {
            throw new System.Security.SecurityException("Access
                    denied to account " + Thread.CurrentPrincipal.Identity.Name);
        }
    }
}
```

During the discussion on SecurityPermissionAttribute earlier in the chapter, we saw that SecurityPermission doesn't distinguish between GenericPrincipal and WindowsPrincipal. This leads to a security problem in which a caller's generic principal may gain access to a resource restricted to Windows users. We can solve this problem by specifying WindowsAuthorizationProvider as the authorization provider for a given "Name" in the configuration. WindowsAuthorizationProvider ensures that only the Windows principal is used during the permission check, thereby removing the security risk in the PrincipalPermission class. As you can see, the SAF.Authorization service allows you to customize the access control of resources based on the user's membership information stored in various sources, such as Windows Active Directory, databases, etc.

The Testing Project

The Test.SAF.Authorization project contains a demo application that shows how you can use SAFSecurityAttribute in your application code. There is no additional setup needed to run the demo. You need, however, to make sure that the information in the configuration file is appropriate for your local computer, such as role information for the user account.

> **NOTE** *Because the .NET language compiler needs to load* SAF.Authorization.dll *in order to generate the security metadata, you should avoid adding the* SAF.Authorization *project as part of the* Test.SAF.Authorization *solution. Otherwise, you will receive a compiler error, since the compiler tries to compile* SAF.Authorization.dll *and load it at the same time. A workaround to this problem is to add a reference to the file* SAF.Authorization.dll *in the* TestConsole *project inside the solution so that* SAF.Authorization *is not compiled again when you run the demo application. This is also how the* Test.SAF.Authorization *is set up. You should still be able to step into* SAF.Authorization's *code during debugging.*

To run the demo, open the solution under Test.SAF.Authorization and hit F5 to run it.

Summary

In this chapter, you first learned about the .NET attribute and some of its applications in security authorization, such as `PrincipalPermissionAttribute`. We then looked more closely at security permissions in .NET through examples of the `CodeAccessSecurityAttribute` class and `IPermission` interface. You learned how .NET achieves the application's security permission check using the attribute-permission class pair and how the .NET language compiler and CLR interact with the attribute-permission class pair to perform the permission check. In the second part of the chapter we talked abut the `SAF.Authorization` framework component, which provides a customized security attribute class and permission class that developers can use to perform customized permission-checking logic in the application, allowing them to extract the user's role information from the application code so that security permissions can be changed on the underlying resource without changes in application code or code recompilation.

CHAPTER 11

Authentication Service

AN AUTHENTICATION SERVICE is the foundation of every security system. In order to protect a resource against unauthorized users, we must first identify each user and verify that he or she is indeed who they say they are. This process of identifying a given user is called authentication. There are many forms of authentication that we encounter in everyday life. We are authenticated through a user ID and password when we log onto a computer. We are authenticated through our driving license when we are asked to show identification at an airport. We are authenticated through our voice when we speak over the phone with our friends. Just as there are many ways to identify who you are in "real life," there are many ways to identify a particular user in the digital world. Different applications use different mechanisms to identify a particular user. Some depend on the Windows Active Directory, while others depend on some type of custom code, such as code that compares the user ID and password presented with those stored in a database, or code that inspects a user's digital signature.

In this chapter, we will focus on how authentication works and how we can customize the authentication process to make it easy to work with among multiple applications.

Motivation and Goals

When every component inside an application uses the same mechanism to identify the user, authentication is not something developers need to think about. For example, if you are developing an application that runs in a Windows domain environment, all the components in your application will use the Windows Active Directory to authenticate users. However, applications often consist of many subsystems, each of which has its own way of identifying users. To make all the subsystems work together, we need first to make sure that each subsystem will be able to authenticate users as requests flow back and forth among the subsystems. This commonly involves writing a lot of code to present the user's security credentials to each of the subsystems of the application that employs an authentication mechanism. For example, one part of the application might use Windows authentication, and while another part of the application uses an SQL server database to store the application's users that are not Windows, and yet another part of the application depends on yet a third set of user accounts. You can imagine the amount of code you have to write to map the security credentials among different part of the application.

A more personal analogy is the trouble people go through to keep track of all their user names and passwords to access various Web sites on the Internet. You have to identify yourself to different Web sites using different credentials. Wouldn't it be better if we could use one set of credentials to identify ourselves once and log onto all the Web sites without presenting different credentials over and over again?

In fact, there are already technologies that allow us to do just that. Microsoft Passport does this, it by providing a passport with which the user signs onto the computer just once and then can access all Web sites that support Passport technology without the need to use different sets of credentials. In other words, it achieves the effect of single sign-on.

This concept of single sign-on is very useful not only to users who want to avoid the hassle of remembering different sets of user names and passwords, but also for developers who are tired of writing the tedious and repetitive authentication code to allow authentication requests to flow freely among the different parts of an application, each of which understands only a specific set of user accounts.

The SAF.Authentication service sets out to provide this single sign-on service for applications. SAF.Authentication will perform coordination among different parts of the application to make sure that once a user is authenticated, it is "trusted" by the other parts of the application despite the differences in the way they identify a users. Figure 11-1 illustrates what SAF.Authentication sets out to do.

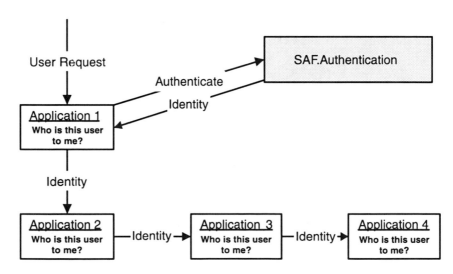

Figure 11-1. SAF.Authentication

Using Figure 11-1 as an example, a user request must pass through four applications to complete the call. Each application uses a different user authentication service to identify the user. Normally, the user must carry four types of credentials, one for each application it accesses. Each application must also present the credentials to the next application in line so that the call can be successfully passed down. However, with a centralized authentication service, we can simplify application development by removing the need for multiple authentications in different applications. In essence, each application will honor the single credential presented by the centralized authentication service as the request passes through it. We see later in this chapter how to implement this centralized authentication service using .NET.

.NET Technology Overview

The SAF.Authentication service relies on the System.Security.Principal name space for its features. It is built on the concept of the Principal object in the .NET Framework. Before we look at the implementation of this service, we need to understand the .NET principal.

.NET Principal

In discussing authentication, we need first to understand two concepts: identity and principal. A user's identity simply answers the question, "Who is the user?" The principal is a combination of user identity information and a number of roles associated with the user. Because the role information is commonly associated with some special privilege to do something (for example, the Administrator role has the ability to delete other users), we can also regard the principal as something that answers the question, "What can the user do?"

Identity always comes before the principal: Without user identity information, the user principal doesn't make any sense. There are four types of identity objects in the .NET Framework: FormIdentity, GenericIdentity, PassportIdentity, and WindowsIdentity. All of them implement the System.Security.Principal.IIdentity interface. One of the properties of this interface is Name, which represents the user name. It is important to recognize that there is no password information in the identity. Password information is commonly used in the process of obtaining an identity, and plays no role in the resulting identity object.

The .NET framework also has two types of principal: GenericPrincipal and WindowsPrincipal. They both implement the System.Security.Principal.IPrincipal interface. This interface has two members: the Identity property and the IsInRole() method. The Identity property represents the underlying user, and the IsInRole() method provides a way to verify whether the user is part of a given user role.

GenericPrincipal allows us to bind an identity object, regardless of the authentication mechanism used, to a list of user roles that a particular identity belongs to. In other words, you can create a generic principal on any of the four types of Identity objects in the .NET framework or any custom Identity object. WindowsPrincipal is a somewhat special case of GenericPrincipal, since it works only with WindowsIdentity. The benefit of using WindowsPrincipal is that you can leverage your existing Windows security infrastructure, such as Active Directory, to obtain the role information associated with a given user. When you create a WindowsPrincipal, you need to provide only the WindowsIdentity object, and WindowsPrincipal will automatically pull the user membership information from the user account repository (e.g., Active Directory), whereas in the GenericPrincipal scenario, you must provide a list of user roles information yourself. The following sample illustrates these differences:

```
GenericIdentity gID = new GenericIdentity("Mike");
string[] roles = new String[3]{"Users","Managers","Administrators"};
GenericPrincipal gPrincipal = new GenericPrincipal(gID,roles);
if(gPrincipal.IsInRole("Administrator")){Console.WriteLine("super user!");}

WindowsIdentity wID = WindowsIdentity.GetCurrent();
WindowsPrincipal wPrincipal = new WindowsPrincipal(wID);
if(wPrincipal.IsInRole(@"MyDomain\Administrator"))
                          {Console.WriteLine("super user!");}
```

The WindowsIdentity.GetCurrent() method returns the WindowsIdentity object of the current user who is executing the code. You can also get the WindowsIdentity object for a user other than the current user by using P/Invoke on the LogonUser() method in advapi.dll. If you recall the SAF.WindowService from Chapter 8, it uses the LogonUser() method to instantiate different services using different user accounts.

We frequently cannot rely on the Windows Active Directory for authentication service and role membership management. For example, we sometimes need to use a database server to validate users. We want to store role membership information in a database which can be accessed at run time to check whether a user is associated with a certain role. To achieve this goal, we need to create the custom Identity and Principal objects that access the user information stored in the external database. I will show you some code for these custom classes. But first, let's see how we can make our custom Identity object talk to an external database:

```
public class SQLIdentity : IIdentity
{
    private string name;
    public SQLIdentity(string userName, string password)
    {
        string sql = "select user from UserInfo where userid ='" + userName +
                "' and password ='" + password + "'";
        //ADO.NET code to execute the query and check whether any row is returned
        if (dtUser.Rows.Count == 0)
        {
            throw new Exception("Invalid user name or password");
        }
        name = userName;
    }

    public string AuthenticationType
    {
        get{return "Basic authentication";}
    }
    public bool IsAuthenticated
    {
        get{return true;}
    }
    public string Name
    {
        get{return name;}
    }

}
}
```

In the above example, the user's credentials are validated before an Identity object is created. Within the constructor, we can perform some ADO.NET code that verifies whether the user name and password are a valid combination in the user table. After we obtain an Identity object, we can derive its Principal object, which binds a user to a list of user roles stored in the database. The following example shows how we can create a custom principal class that collects the role membership information from an external database:

```
public class SQLPrincipal : IPrincipal
{
    private IIdentity identity;
    private string[] roles;
```

```csharp
public SQLPrincipal(IIdentity id)
{
    identity = id;
    //get the role information
    string sql = "select role from Membership where userid ='" + identity + "'";
    roles = ...//some ADO.NET code to retrieve the roles
}
public IIdentity Identity
{
    get{return identity;}
}
public bool IsInRole(string role)
{
    bool isInRole = false;
    //check if the user is member of a given role
    foreach (string r in roles)
    {
        if (r == role)
        {
            isInRole =true;
            break;
        }
    }
    return isInRole;
}

}
```

The SQLPrincipal performs its work in two steps. First, we create an SQLPrincipal object by calling its constructor and passing it the IIdentity object; the constructor will make database calls to retrieve a list of roles of which the given identity is a member, and store the list to a string array to be used later. Second, we need to implement the IsInRole() method in the SQLPrincipal. After we have a string array that contains all the role information for a given user, IsInRole() would simply loop through the roles array and check for a match. If a match is found, IsInRole() returns true; otherwise, it will return false. You can also potentially use some data-caching techniques to reduce the number of data queries for certain commonly used user accounts.

The example above shows how we can create custom identities and custom principals that rely on the database for user authentication and user membership information.

SAF Code Sample Walkthrough

In order to create a single sign-on process among different applications, we need first to ensure that all the applications that participate in the single sign-on trust a "common" identity, which I call the SAF identity. The following code illustrates how this works:

```
<Identities>
   <Identity name="SAF-Administrator">
      <Application name="ADApp" id="NY\HR-admin" />
      <Application name="SQLApp" id="dbuser" />
   </Identity>
</Identities>
```

The above configuration contains the user information mapping between the common identity or SAF identity and the user identity at each application level. In other words, if the application detects that the request is made by SAF-Administrator, the application can find out who this user actually is in relation to it by looking up the mapping. For example, when a user who carries the SAF-Administrator identity makes a request to the SQLApp application, SQLApp will treat the request as if it were made by dbuser, a database user account. Similarly, when the request arrives at ADApp, the application will treat the request as if it were made by "NY\HR-admin." One key concept is that each application that participates in the single sign-on process will honor the SAF identity. The request carries the SAF identity as it passes through different applications, which will be able to determine what this SAF identity means to them.

The idea of single sign-on is based on the concept of one commonly agreed-upon identity. SAF.Authentication comes with an IIdentity class called SAFIdentity, a class that provides the foundation of the authentication service. SAFIdentity provides a feature for authenticating a user with given credentials and allowing the application to query on what application-level user account it maps to SAFIdentity is shown in the following code:

```
public class SAFIdentity : IIdentity
{
   protected string applicationName;
   private string name;
   protected string ApplicationName
   {
      get {return applicationName;}
   }
```

```
public string Name
{
   get {return name;}
}

//...more code omitted...
}
```

The `Name` property represents an application-specific identity name. The `ApplicationName` property represents the name of the application with which the identity is associated. `SAFIdentity` acts as a base class. Its child classes may contain the authenticating code to validate whether the user name and its credentials match. The following is the sample code for `ADIdentity`, an identity class that is used to represent a Windows user account. You don't have to put authentication code inside the constructor, but so doing ensures that the users are who they say they are:

```
public class ADIdentity : SAF.Authentication.SAFIdentity
{
        public ADIdentity(string userid, string password, string domain, string
                          applicationName)
        {
           //check if the userid and password are valid.
           SecurityUtility su = new SecurityUtility();
           su.ValidateUser(userid,password,domain);
           //set the application name and userid of the identity object
           this.applicationName = applicationName;
           this.name = userid;
        }
}
```

`ADIdentity`'s constructor does two things. First, it calls the `ValidateUser()` method in the `SecurityUtility` class to perform the "LogonUser" action to ensure that the name and password are a valid match. Second, it will set the value of two properties: `Name` and `ApplicationName`. With `Name` and `ApplicationName` we should have enough information to locate its SAF identity in the configuration file shown earlier. From a client perspective, creating an `SAFIdentity` involves one line of code, as shown here:

```
SAFIdentity SAFID = new ADIdentity("xin","password","MyHome","ADApp");
string AppUser = SAFID. Name;
string AppName = SAFID.ApplicationName;
```

SAFIdentity provides us a "universal" identity across multiple applications. Providing an application-specific identity alone only solves part of the problem. Many applications depend for their business logic and access on a combination of user identity and membership information. We need to have a principal class that provides the membership information that is specific to a given application so that each application can query on what roles a specific user belongs to at run time. SAFPrincipal provides us the ability to bind the application-specific user roles to a given SAFIdentity:

```csharp
public class SAFPrincipal : IPrincipal
{
   private IIdentity identity;
   //internal application-specific principal object
   private IPrincipal currentApplicationPrincipal;
   private string safUser;

   public SAFPrincipal(SAFIdentity sid)
   {
      //retrieve the authentication configuration from the configuration file
      ConfigurationManager cm =
               (ConfigurationManager)ConfigurationSettings.GetConfig("Framework");
      AuthenticationConfiguration ac = cm.AuthenticationConfig;

      identity = sid;
      safUser = ac.GetSAFUserName(sid.Name,sid.ApplicationName);
      //set the application information of the SAFPrincipal
      SetApplication(sid.ApplicationName);

   }

   public bool IsInRole(string role)
   {
      return currentApplicationPrincipal.IsInRole(role);
   }
   public IIdentity Identity
   {
      get {return identity;}
   }
   public string SAFUser
   {
      get {return safUser;}
   }
```

```
        public void SetApplication(string application)
        {
           ConfigurationManager cm =
        (ConfigurationManager)ConfigurationSettings.GetConfig("Framework");
           AuthenticationConfiguration ac = cm.AuthenticationConfig;
           //retrieve the type information for the principal object of a given
        application
           string typeName = ac.GetPrincipalTypeForApplication(application);
           string appUserName =
        cm.AuthenticationConfig.GetIdentityForApplicaiton(safUser,application);
           SAFIdentity safIdentity = new SAFIdentity(appUserName,application);
           Type type = Type.GetType(typeName);
           object[] parameters = new object[1]{safIdentity};
           //set the new object to the internal principal object
           currentApplicationPrincipal =
        (IPrincipal)Activator.CreateInstance(type,parameters);
           identity = (IIdentity)safIdentity;
        }
}
```

SAFPrincipal has a constructor that takes SAFIdentity as its parameter. SAF-Principal then extracts the application name information from SAFIdentity and uses such information to obtain an IPrincipal object that knows how to retrieve the membership information for that application. In other words, SAFPrincipal doesn't provide any role membership check for a given application. Instead, it will delegate it to a specific principal class that knows how to perform the actual check. For example, in order for the application to determine what roles an ADIdentity belongs to, we need to develop an ADPrincipal class to check the roles using Windows security. The following code shows how this is done:

```
public class ADPrincipal : IPrincipal
{
   private IIdentity identity;
   private string searchQuery;
   public IIdentity Identity
   {
      get {return identity;}
   }

   public ADPrincipal(string userid, string applicationName)
   {
      identity = new ADIdentity(userid,applicationName);
```

```
    ConfigurationManager cm =
            (ConfigurationManager)ConfigurationSettings.GetConfig("Framework");
    XmlNode providerData
        =cm.AuthenticationConfig.GetProviderConfigurationData(applicationName);
    searchQuery = providerData.SelectSingleNode("ADDirectoryEntry").InnerText;
}


    public bool IsInRole(string role)
    {
        StringCollection groupCollection = new StringCollection();
        DirectoryEntry obEntry = new DirectoryEntry(searchQuery);
        //search on the user name. if user doesn't exist,
        //an exception will be thrown
        DirectoryEntry obUser = obEntry.Children.Find(identity.Name,"user");

        //retrieve the group information for the given user
        object groups = obUser.Invoke("Groups");
        //loop through each group object to retrieve the group name
        foreach (object o in (IEnumerable)groups)
        {
            DirectoryEntry group= new DirectoryEntry(o);
            groupCollection.Add(group.Name);
        }

        //check whether the role is part of the groups to which the user belongs
        return groupCollection.Contains(role);
    }
}
```

ADPrincipal implements the IPrincipal interface and contains special logic to check the membership information. ADPrincipal uses System.DirectoryServices to retrieve the membership information for a specific user. Another option for retrieving membership information is through WindowsPrincipal. However, creating WindowsPrincipal requires you first to create WindowsIdentity, which in turn requires you to know the password of the user in order to create a WindowsIdentity object via LogonUser, as we saw in an earlier chapter. We want to avoid such dependency on user credentials information when creating a principal object, since the principal itself shouldn't carry the responsibility of user authentication.

We can redraw the diagram shown in Figure 11-1 to obtain a better picture of how SAF.Authentication fits among applications, as shown in Figure 11-2.

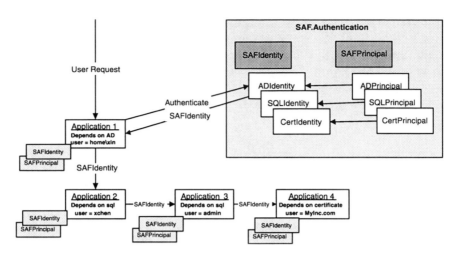

Figure 11-2. SAF.Authentication

The SAF.Authentication service works as follows: A user sends a request or invokes a method on Application 1. Because Application 1 is the first application that accepts the user request, it may ask to authenticate the user against the authentication service it may use. In Figure 11-2, Application 1 uses the Active Directory to authenticate the user. Therefore, an SAFIdentity (ADIdentity type) is created for the current user if its user ID and password match. Application 1 can then create the corresponding SAFPrincipal (ADPrincipal type) object for the SAFIdentity, and then check on the role membership of the user to determine the appropriate action to perform. To complete the user's request, Application 1 must also call Application 2 for its service. Because all the applications that participate in the single sign-on must honor the SAFIdentity, Application 2 will not authenticate the user again. Instead, it will query the configuration settings to obtain an application-specific identity that is mapped to the given SAFIdentity. It will then get a SAFPrincipal (SQLPrincipal type) object that knows how to query the database for the user's membership information. If Application 2 needs to call Application 3, the process will continue in a similar fashion. To summarize, as requests enter an application, the application will retrieve the SAFPrincipal from the thread, set its application context, and query the membership information that is specific to a given user in a given application.

The following example shows how developers can use the SAF.Authentication service in the code to achieve the single sign-on effect across multiple applications:

```
//First Application, Authenticate
SAFIdentity safID = new ADIdentity("xin","password","NYDomain","Application1");
SAFPrincipal  sp = new ADPrincipal(safID);
Console.WriteLine("SAF Identity name is " + sp.SAFUser);
Console.WriteLine(sp.Identity.Name + " is accessing Application 1");
Console.WriteLine("Is " + sp.Identity.Name + @" member of NYDomain\AdminGroup? "
                + sp.IsInRole(@"MyHome\AdminGroup"));
Thread.CurrentPrincipal = sp;


//Second Application, Get application-specific user name and principal object
AuthenticationManager am = new AuthenticationManager();
SAFPrincipal sp = Thread.CurrentPrincipal;
Sp.SetApplication("Applicaiton2");
Console.WriteLine("SAF Identity name is " + sp.SAFUser);
Console.WriteLine(sp.Identity.Name + " is accessing Application 2");
Console.WriteLine("Is " + sp.Identity.Name + " member of HR-Group? +
                sp.IsInRole("HR-Group"));


//Third Application, Get application-specific user name and principal object
AuthenticationManager am = new AuthenticationManager();
SAFPrincipal sp = Thread.CurrentPrincipal;
Sp.SetApplication("Applicaiton3");
Console.WriteLine("SAF Identity name is " + sp.SAFUser);
Console.WriteLine(sp.Identity.Name + " is accessing Application 3");
Console.WriteLine("Is " + sp.Identity.Name + " member of HR-Group?
                + sp.IsInRole("Sale-Group"));
```

The sample contains three code blocks; each simulates an application. In the first code block, an SAFPrincipal is created from the ADIdentity object. The SAF-Principal is then attached to the thread. In the second code block, SAFPrincipal is extracted from the thread object and is switched to a different application context using the SetApplication() method. After SetApplication() is called with a different application name, sp.Identity and sp.IsInRole() will retrieve the user and membership information specific to the new application. In the third code block, the steps in the second code block are repeated with yet another application name; the user and membership information in the third code block will again be specific to the new application name. The example presented will need to depend on some configuration settings, shown in the following code, that indicate the relationship between an SAF identity and the application-specific identities, as well as the Identity class and Principal class used by each application:

```
<SAF.Authentication>
   <Applications>
      <Application name="Application1" identity_type="...ADIdentity,..."
                      principal_type="...ADPrincipal,..." />
      <Application name="Application2" identity_type="...SQLIdentity,..."
                      principal_type="...SQLPrincipal,..." />
      <Application name="Application3" identity_type="...SQLIdentity,..."
                      principal_type="...SQLPrincipal,..." />
   </Applications>
   <Identities>
      <Identity name="SAF-Administrator">
         <Application name="Application1" id="NYDomain\xchen" />
         <Application name="Application2" id="HR-chen" />
         <Application name="Application3" id="Sale-chen" />
      </Identity>
   </Identities>
</SAF.Authentication>
```

As you can see, three application-specific users are mapped to a single SAF identity: SAF-Administrator. If you use this client sample code, the console will produce the following output, which further shows how SAF.Authentication works:

```
SAF Identity name is SAF-Administrator
xchen is accessing application 1
Is xchen member of NYDomain\AdminGroup? true

SAF Identity name is SAF-Administrator
HR-chen is accessing application 2
Is HR-chen member of HR-Group? true

SAF Identity name is SAF-Administrator
Sale-chen is accessing application 3
Is Sale-chen member of Sale-Group? True
```

Testing Project

The Test.SAF.Authentication project contains a console application that demonstrates how to use SAF.Authentication in the application code. There is no additional setup for the project, except that some references need to be added to the user account in the configuration file and the console application needs to be modified to fit your computer environment.

To run the demo, open the solution in the Test.SAF.Authentication folder and hit F5 to run.

Summary

In this chapter, you learned about .NET Framework's IIdentity and IPrincipal interfaces. We looked at how some Identity and Principal classes in .NET Framework work, such as GenericIdentity and GenericPrincipal. We also looked at how to create a custom identity class and principal class to authenticate users and verify user membership information. In the second half of the chapter, we introduced the single sign-on concept and showed how to create a single sign-on service through the SAF.Authentication service, allowing multiple applications to use their own mechanisms to store and retrieve user and role information and to communicate with one another without having to authenticate user requests multiple times.

CHAPTER 12

Cryptography Service

WHEN PEOPLE TALK about application security, they are usually referring to authentication of users and the types of information that should be provided to a particular authenticated user. There is, however, another aspect of security that increasingly demands our attention during the course of application development: cryptography, or the use of codes to convert data so that only a specific recipient will be able to read it.

Cryptography has been used to secure information for thousands of years, long before the development of computers. The methods used by the ancients to encode their information so that an enemy would be unable to understand it were primitive by today's standards. A simple rearrangement of words and letters was good enough to ensure the secrecy of a message against an unsophisticated populace. Of course, to decode such a message, you would first have to capture the encoded message, which was a nontrivial task when communication was via a human messenger. In the early twentieth century, messages began being sent over the airwaves, which allowed communication from opposite corners of the earth. However, that gave easy access to anyone with a radio receiver, including one's wartime enemies. The failure to secure information could determine the outcome of a war. With the arrival of the information age and the Internet, where messages are exchanged across a vast global network, it has become easier than ever for someone to capture the information you send. There are even those calling themselves hackers who consider it their duty to intercept our messages, read them, and do their best to cause trouble at our expense. As developers, it is our duty to use available tools to protect our data and make hacking a frustrating hobby. In this chapter, we will learn about how we can keep our data secret.

Motivation and Goals

Keeping data secret is easier said than done. To encrypt a piece of data, developers need to understand the principle of some basic modern cryptographic mechanisms, namely, secret key, symmetric cryptography, asymmetric cryptography, digital signature, certificate, and certificate authority. `SAF.Cryptography` offers a shortcut to protecting data. It offers a set of classes that simplify encrypting and decrypting data, so that developers can keep sensitive information secret without having to learn about data cryptography on their own and to write tedious code to carry out such encryption and decryption. Besides offering some handy helper classes to en/decrypt data easily, SAF.Cryptography also provides a feature that allows you to abstract the cryptographic code out of your application code. Because the goal of cryptography is simply to keep data secret and has nothing to do with the specific business logic of the underlying data, I consider cryptography an infrastructure-level service, something that shouldn't be blended with the application code that performs the business logic. The SAF.Cryptography component includes a pair of customized .NET remoting channel sinks that allow you to encrypt and decrypt data transmitted between client and server via .NET remoting. This pair of remoting channel sinks provides cryptography service as an infrastructure-level service, meaning that you don't have to modify your application code to use the additional cryptography services provided in this framework component.

.NET Technology Overview

There are quite a few technologies that SAF.Cryptography references. In the next several pages, I will prepare you with some of its key concepts and .NET technologies you need to know to implement cryptography in your application and help you understand how the SAF.Cryptography component is built. The following is a list of the points that we will discuss next:

- Cryptography fundamentals

- .NET Cryptography support

- WSE Cryptography support

- Customized .NET remoting sinks

Cryptography Fundamentals

Cryptography is the process of encoding a message in such a way that only the intended recipient can read it. It is about engaging in a secure communication in which only you and your intended recipient understand the message. To achieve this goal, there are some fundamental premises that have to be met. As technical as computer cryptography may sound, it is rooted in human experience as to how to keep a message secret between its sender and recipient. We communicate with others in our daily lives using different variations of cryptography more often than we think. We can certainly draw a number of parallels between computer cryptography and human cryptography if we look more closely. The following example is one of my favorite analogies to illustrate this parallelism.

I met a Chinese woman named Sherry on campus while I was in school, and planned to call her to invite her for a chat. I knew that she had a couple of roommates, and I wanted to keep our conversation private. Normally, if I had something to hide, I could call her up with a quick "hello," hoping that the person on the other end of the line would say something like, "Who is this?" I could then identify whether the voice was Sherry's before saying anything really embarrassing. If the voice was not hers, I could hang up the phone and try later, or ask to talk to Sherry.

After confirming that the person I was talking with was Sherry, I could start a private conversation with her. But what if her roommates decided to spy on us by picking up another phone on the same line to listen to our conversation? I certainly had no wish to make my tender romantic side the butt of jokes on campus. A good way to defend against such intrusion into privacy would be to talk with Sherry in some sort of encrypted language. Chinese is just about the most encrypted language you can get for Americans, since few Americans study it, and English and Chinese belong to completely different language families. So I could start speaking Chinese with her. Of course, if her roommates were also Chinese, then there would be really nothing I could do about the situation, and some degrading joke against me would be bound to happen sooner or later, as indeed it did.

The moral of this story is that there are two important principles you want to enshrine to ensure secure communication. First, you want to identify the person you are communicating with. Second, you want to make sure that your communication cannot be understood by third parties who may be eavesdropping on you.

You will find that these two principles also apply to secure communication in the digital world. For example, when you are making purchase on the Amazon.com, you want to make sure that the site you are visiting is indeed the real Amazon.com rather than some hacker's phony site that tricks your Web browser into believing that it is the Amazon site. You also want to make sure that the credit card and order information you send to Amazon.com will not be understood by some hacker who is network sniffing, that is, capturing network data packages as they travel to their destination. As you can see, only when both of these principles are satisfied can you ensure secure communication.

But enough of theory! Let's look at how we can achieve secure communication from a technical perspective. Implementations of cryptography revolve around three important concepts: symmetric cryptography, asymmetric cryptography, and digital signatures.

Symmetric Cryptography

To keep third parties from interpreting our messages, we need to encrypt them, which normally involves an algorithm and a secret key. The algorithm describes how to encrypt or decrypt a message with a given key. Because such algorithms are predefined and commonly known, it is the key that must be kept secret in order to prevent third parties from decrypting and reading the message.

The question, however, is how to get the key to the intended recipient so that he or she can use this key for decryption. You must somehow communicate this key securely before you can communicate the message securely. So what do you send first? As you can imagine, it is a Catch-22. The assumption for this type of secure communication is that you have somehow securely given the intended recipient the secret key so that he or she can read your messages. This is called secret key cryptography or symmetric cryptography. Figure 12-1 shows how symmetric cryptography works.

Figure 12-1. Symmetric cryptography

Asymmetric Cryptography

The issue of how to send a secret key securely is called the key distribution problem. This problem was solved by two professors at Stanford University in 1976 when they introduced public key cryptography, or asymmetric cryptography. The idea is that in order for two parties to engage in a secure communication, each of them must have two keys: one public and one private. A message encrypted by a private key can be decrypted only by a public key, and a message encrypted by a public key can be decrypted only by a private key. The private key is always kept secret by the owner. The public key is made accessible to the public.

Figure 12-2 illustrates one use of asymmetric cryptography, which guarantees that only the intended recipient will be able to decrypt a message. If I decided to send a message to my friend Sherry, inviting her to dinner, I would use Sherry's public key to encrypt the message before I send it. After Sherry received the message, she would have to decrypt it using her private key before she could understand what I was saying. In this scenario, because I encrypted the message with

Sherry's public key, only Sherry's private key would be able to decrypt the message. Since only Sherry has her private key, we can be just about absolutely sure that only Sherry herself can read the encrypted message. Had someone gained access to the message I sent to Sherry, the message would be completely useless, since the interceptor wouldn't know the key to decrypt it.

Figure 12-2. Asymmetric cryptography

The same principle is used when Sherry decides to send a message exclusively to me. In that case, she would first use my public key to encrypt her message and send it to me. When I receive the message, I will use my private key, which is only known to me, to decrypt the message. Figure 12-3 shows the message that is sent back to me.

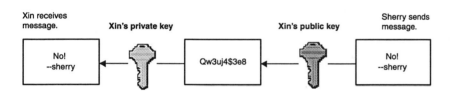

Figure 12-3. Asymmetric cryptography

Although the above communication through asymmetric cryptography guarantees that no one other than the intended recipient can understand the encrypted message, there is no way for the recipient to know who sent the message. Because the recipient's public key is accessible to the public, anyone can use the recipient's public key to encrypt a message and send it. In our example, there could be twenty people who use Sherry's public key to encrypt messages and send them to her. Any one of them could sign a letter with my name, and Sherry would have no way of knowing whether such a message was really from me or from an imposter.

To satisfy one of the two principles of secure communication, we must find a way to identity the owner of the message. Digital signatures do exactly that.

Digital Signatures

A digital signature is analogous to a human signature. When you sign your name on a piece of paper, you associate yourself with the paper. When you "sign" a piece of data through a digital signature, you associate your identity with the data. Digital signatures are also based on asymmetric cryptography. Compared with the data encryption example using asymmetric cryptography we just saw above, digital signatures use the public/private key pair a bit differently. Figure 12-4 shows how to use these keys to verify the origin of the message.

Figure 12-4. Another use of the public/private key pair

At first glance, Figure 12-4 may look like Figure 12-2. But in fact, the key usage is different in the two figures. In Figure 12-2, I encrypt the message with Sherry's public key. However, in Figure 12-4 I encrypt the message with my private key. This is an important distinction. Because the message is encrypted using my private key, as shown in Figure 12-4, Sherry can use my public key to decrypt the message. The fact that Sherry can decrypt the message using my public key tells Sherry that the message must have originated with me, because only my public key can decrypt a message encrypted by my private key. Of course, this benefit comes at a price. The price is that my message is no longer secret, since anyone with my public key can decrypt the message I sent to Sherry. In other words, the key usage shown in Figure 12-4 doesn't keep the communication private from third parties, but it does allow the recipient of the message to be sure of the identity of the sender.

Digital signatures use the same principle shown in Figure 12-4 with a minor twist, whereby the digital signature allows the sender of the message to be identified without encrypting the message.

Since using a private key to encrypt a message doesn't keep the message secret from third parties, there is no reason to encrypt the whole message. Encryption and decryption using a public/private key pair is a very time-consuming process, and we want to find a way to minimize this process as much as possible. Digital signatures provide a solution for minimizing this process with the help of a hashing technology.

To hash something is to produce a very small digest, usually about 128 or 160 bits long, from a large chunk of data. A very small change in the source data will generate a massive change during the hashing of the data, so by comparing the digest of the message before and after transmission, you can ensure that the message data wasn't tampered with during transmission. In other words, the digest will ensure the integrity of the data.

Figure 12-5 shows how a digital signature is generated.

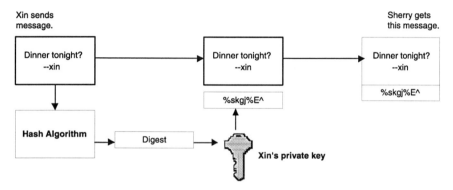

Figure 12-5. Creation of a digital signature

There are three major steps involved in signing a message. First, the sender creates a digest by hashing the original message. Second, the sender uses its private key to encrypt the digest. Because the digest is very small, encrypting it has very little overhead on our resources. The last step is to combine the original message with the encrypted digest and send it to the recipient. As you can see in the Figure 12-5, signing the message doesn't prevent anyone from seeing what is in the message. This is the intended result, since digital signatures are not designed to keep a message secret, but to ensure the integrity of the message and identify the sender to the recipient. Let's see how these two goals are achieved through Figure 12-6.

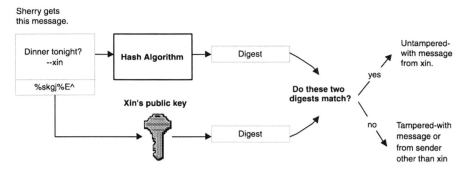

Figure 12-6. Verifying a digital signature

When Sherry receives the message, she will first use the same hash algorithm to create a digest of the message part of the data. She will also need to use my public key to decrypt the encrypted digest located at the end of my message. If the digest she generates on her end is same as the one I sent in my message, she can be sure of two things: First, the message came from me, because she used my public key to decrypt the encrypted digest; and second, the message, "Dinner tonight?" has not been tampered with. If the message had been tampered with, the two digests would not match.

To summarize: If you have your private key, you can send authenticated messages that others can be sure come from you. If you have someone else's public key, you can send an encrypted message only that "someone else" can read. To do both these things and achieve truly secure communications, you need to combine the different applications of these two keys and hash technology. For example, you can encrypt the message using the recipient's public key and then attach the sender's digital signature to the encrypted message. This way, you not only make the message readable only to the intended recipient, but you also allow the recipient to verify the identity of the sender, thereby satisfying the two requirements for secure communication.

In reality, however, the public/private key pair is not used to encrypt/decrypt the actual messages that travel back and forth between sender and recipient due to the fact that the algorithm involved in asymmetric cryptography is extremely complex and requires significant resources to compute. For this reason, asymmetric cryptography is commonly used to solve only the "key distribution" part of the problem during a secure communication. The sender usually starts the communication by generating a secret key and passing this secret key to the recipient, who will use this secret key for further communication. In order to deliver the secret key securely, the sender will use the approach of asymmetric cryptography through the use of a public/private key pair. In other words, the sender and recipient will use the asymmetric cryptographic approach at the beginning of the communication, and then use the symmetric cryptographic approach for the rest of the communication. Because the vast majority of encryption and decryption occurs in the symmetric pattern through a secret key, this process requires far fewer resources than if the whole communication had undergone public/private key encryption/decryption.

You should also note that my earlier arguments have been based on an important assumption: that Sherry's public key, which I used to encrypt the message, does indeed come from Sherry. However, unless she physically handed her public key to me, that assumption isn't safe. In today's e-commerce applications, public keys are transmitted over the Internet and are as subject to tampering as the messages they are designed to protect. This brings us the topic of certificates and certificate authorities, or CAs.

Certificate and Certificate Authority

A certificate is a piece of data that is used to identify a person or an entity. It can contain the public key, the private key, and other information that is used to prove its owner's identity. A certificate also identifies its certificate authority (CA), which is the organization that issues this certificate. The relationship between the CA and the certificates is like that between a department of motor vehicles (DMV) and a driver's license. Before a CA issues a certificate to someone, it makes some background checks to make sure that the identity information in the certificate is correct. Some well-known CAs, such as VeriSign and Thawte, charge money for performing the background check and issuing the certificate. In order for Sherry to get a certificate from a CA, she would probably need to use her driver's license or birth certificate to prove that she is indeed Sherry. After the background check, her name and other identity information would be added to the certificate. In order for me to obtain her public key, I would request her certificate, which contains her public key. If the name in the certificate is correct, I could then trust that this certificate is indeed from Sherry and that the public key in the certificate also comes from Sherry. The important step here is to verify the information inside the certificate before extracting the public key for use. However, I still have to make one assumption that will never go away: I have to assume that the CA does do background checks rather than blindly issuing certificates to whoever pays. In the case of well-known CAs, this is a valid assumption.

.NET Cryptography Support

The .NET framework comes with a comprehensive toolkit for cryptographic programming through the System.Security.Cryptography name space. System.Security.Cryptography consists of implementations for four different symmetric cryptography algorithms and two asymmetric cryptography algorithms. We will need to use these concrete cryptography algorithms within our application to encrypt and decrypt messages. Figure 12-7 shows these implementations and their parent abstract classes.

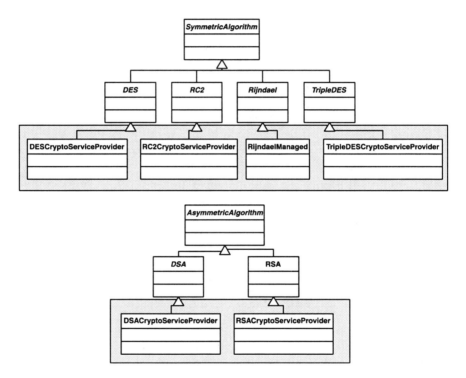

Figure 12-7. .NET cryptography classes

The cryptography classes are categorized into three groups. The roots are AsymmetricAlgorithm and SymmetricAlgorithm. They are both abstract classes. The group beneath them is a series of algorithm-specific abstract classes, such as DES and DSA. The third group consists of the implementation classes. These are the classes you can use to instantiate and encrypt and decrypt messages. Many of the cryptography classes belong to the .NET wrapper of the CryptoAPI, a set of Win32 APIs that allows developers to add cryptographic functionality to an application. These wrapper classes are indicated with the "CryptoServiceProvider" suffix on the class name, such as DESCryptoServiceProvider, DESCryptoServiceProvider. There are classes that are completely written in .NET. For such cryptography classes, the "Managed" suffix is added, such as in the RijndaelManaged class.

Now let's see how these cryptography classes work in action. .NET cryptography has taken a stream-based approach to encrypting and decrypting data through the use of the System.Security.Cryptography.CryptoStream class. As data passes through the CryptoStream class, it will be encrypted or decrypted. The constructor for CryptoStream is as follows:

```
public CryptoStream(
    Stream stream,
    ICryptoTransform transform,
    CryptoStreamMode mode
);
```

The first parameter is the stream object, representing the output stream in an encryption scenario and input stream in a decryption scenario. The second parameter represents the algorithm service provider, and the last parameter represents whether the action performed on the stream object is read or write.

Figure 12-8 illustrates the use of the CryptoStream class.

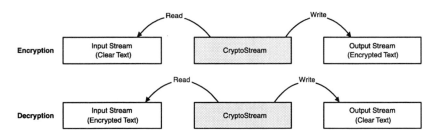

Figure 12-8. The CryptoStream *class*

Let's take a look at how to use CryptoStream combined with the cryptography Algorithm class to encrypt and decrypt data in .NET.

Symmetric Example (Encryption)

The following is an example using symmetric cryptography:

```
//create a TripleDES provider
SymmetricAlgorithm provider = SymmetricAlgorithm.Create("TripleDES");
```

```
//specify the key and iv values; otherwise, a random key and iv are
//generated and used by the provider.
provider.Key = Encoding.Default.GetBytes("6HD+Ngi8JoGmDOg=");
provider.IV = Encoding.Default.GetBytes("gi8JoGmD");

ICryptoTransform encryptor = provider.CreateEncryptor();
string clearData = "This is test";
Console.WriteLine("Clear Data: " + clearData);
Stream clearData = new MemoryStream(Encoding.Default.GetBytes(clearData));
Stream encryptedData = new MemoryStream();

//create CryptoStream object to encrypt the data
CryptoStream cryptoStream = new
                    CryptoStream(encryptedData,encryptor,CryptoStreamMode.Write);
byte[] buffer = new byte[1024];
int count = 0 ;
//write the encrypted data to the outputStream through CryptoStream
while ((count = clearData.Read(buffer,0,1024)) > 0)
{
    cryptoStream.Write(buffer,0,count);
}
cryptoStream.FlushFinalBlock();
encryptedData.Position = 0;
byte[] encryptedDataArray = new Byte[encryptedData.Length];
//convert stream to byte array
encryptedData.Read(encryptedDataArray,0,encryptedDataArray.Length);
Console.WriteLine("Encrypted data: " +
                    Encoding.Default.GetString(encryptedDataArray));
```

The program starts by creating a service provider for TripleDES (symmetric).
It then set the two parameters of the provider: Key and IV. The key is the secret key
that you will use to encrypt the data. The IV (initialization vector, 64-bit data) is
used to conceal any repetitive patterns in the encrypted data. For example, if certain large blocks of the original data are identical, certain blocks of the encrypted
data would also look identical. This can potentially reveal a lot of information
about the data and increase the chance of someone not in possession of the secret
key being able to decrypt the data. As each block of data is encrypted, the IV value
is calculated based on the encrypted value of the previous block of data and used
to rearrange the data inside the current block so that even two identical data
blocks will appear completely different after encryption. Because the IV value is
based on the previous data block, you need only a secret key and very first IV value
to figure out the IV used on each block within the data. In other words, the sender
and recipient must both know the secret key and IV value in order to encrypt and

decrypt the data. The other name of IV is "salt," which can be found in much of the literature referring to the same concept.

Although the value of the key can vary, its size must be one of the supported key sizes for a given algorithm. In my example, I use a 128-bit key. You can increase it to 192 to increase security.

Because cryptography in .NET takes a stream-orientated approach, we need to use a while loop to read the data from and write it to the stream object used by the CryptoStream object. If you execute the program just presented, the console will display the encrypted string of the original data as shown in Figure 12-9.

Figure 12-9. CryptoDemo.exe

Symmetric Example (Decryption)

The decryption process looks very similar to that of encryption. Some differences are highlighted in the following sample code:

```
SymmetricAlgorithm provider = SymmetricAlgorithm.Create("TripleDES")
provider.Key = Encoding.Default.GetBytes("6HD+Ngi8JoGmDOg=");
provider.IV = Encoding.Default.GetBytes("gi8JoGmD");
ICryptoTransform decryptor = provider.CreateDecryptor();
//due to technical difficulty, the actual encrypted text can't
//be displayed properly here during the book editing process,
//hence the "?" is used to represent the encrypted text.
data = "?????????????";
Stream encryptedData = new MemoryStream(Encoding.Default.GetBytes(data));
Stream clearData = new MemoryStream();
//create CryptoStream object to decrypt the data
CryptoStream cryptoStream = new
CryptoStream(encryptedData,decryptor,CryptoStreamMode.Read);
byte[] buffer = new byte[1024];
int count = 0 ;
//Write the decrypted data to the stream through CryptoStream
while ((count = cryptoStream.Read(buffer,0,1024)) > 0)
{
```

```
        clearData.Write(buffer,0,count);
}
clearData.Position = 0;
byte[] clearDataArray = new Byte[clearData.Length];
clearData.Read(clearDataArray,0,clearDataArray.Length);
Console.WriteLine("original data: " + Encoding.Default.GetString(clearDataArray));
```

We have just seen how to encrypt and decrypt a piece of data using symmetric cryptography. Next, we will look at how to encrypt and decrypt a key using asymmetric cryptography.

Asymmetric Example (Encryption)

Because asymmetric cryptography relies on a public/private key pair to do its job, we need first to familiarize ourselves with the task of retrieving the key information from a certificate. The Certificate console, a snap-in for MMC, allows you to administer the certificates that are installed on your computer. Figure 12-10 is a screenshot of the Certificate console.

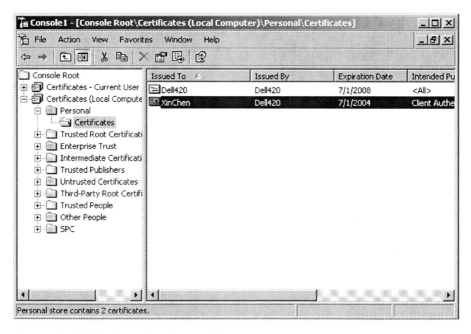

Figure 12-10. The Certificate *console*

System.Security.Cryptography has a certificate feature that allows you to retrieve information stored in a certificate. The following is an example of retrieving information from a certificate file:

```
X509Certificate cert = X509Certificate.CreateFromCertFile(@"c:\Temp\XinChen.cer");
Console.WriteLine("Issuer Name: " + cert.GetIssuerName());
Console.WriteLine("Subject Name: " + cert.GetName());
Console.WriteLine("Public Key: " + cert.GetPublicKeyString());
```

Although you can use System.Security.Cryptography to access the certificate information, it has limited features with respect to certificates. For example, there is no good way to retrieve the information in certificates if it is stored inside the certificate store as opposed in to a file, such as local store or current user store.

There are several ways to access the certificates in the certificate store. You can use P/Invoke with the CryptoAPI or CAPICOM, which provides many features inside the CryptoAPI through a COM interface, or WSE (Web Service Enhancements). We will review WSE and its security features in this chapter.

WSE is a set of classes that developers can use to enable many services such as security and routing on top of XML Web service calls. We will look at WSE in depth later in this chapter. For now, let's look at how we can leverage many certificate-related features in WSE to help us develop an asymmetric cryptographic application.

The following example shows how you can perform secret key exchange using asymmetric cryptography. There are four major steps to encrypting a message using asymmetric cryptography:

1. Retrieve the sender's private key and recipient's public key.

2. Encrypt the message using symmetric cryptography with a random key and IV.

3. Encrypt the key and IV using the recipient's public key.

4. Digitally sign the message using the sender's private key.

Step 1: Retrieve the Keys

The Microsoft.Web.Security.X509 name space allows the developer to query and retrieve information on certificates stored in various locations on the system. The X509CertificateStore class consists of a number of static methods that return the number of certificates stored on the system. With a given certificate store, you can search for a specific certificate using one of the "Find" methods. The following is sample code for achieving the first steps:

```
//get a reference to a specific certificate store
X509CertificateStore x509Store =
            X509CertificateStore.CurrentUserStore(X509CertificateStore.MyStore);
```

```
bool open = x509Store.OpenRead();
X509Certificate sender_cert = null;
X509Certificate receiver_cert = null;
if (open != true)
{
    throw new Exception("unable to open the certificate store");
}

    //Use the Find method to search for a specific certificate
    sender_cert = x509Store.FindCertificateBySubjectName("CN=XinChen,
                        E=none@none.com")[0];
    receiver_cert = x509Store.FindCertificateBySubjectName("CN=Sherry,
                        E=none@none.com")[0];


//obtain the private key and public key from the certificate object
RSAParameters sender_privateKey = sender_cert.Key.ExportParameters(true);
RSAParameters receiver_publicKey = receiver_cert.PublicKey.ExportParameters(false);
```

After you obtain the certificate objects for both sender and recipient, you need to retrieve the sender's private key and the receiver's public key. The sender's private key will be used to sign the message, and the receiver's public key will be used to encrypt the secret key, as you will see later in this section. The ExportParameters() method takes a Boolean parameter and returns an RSAParameters object. The RSAParameters object, like that of Key and IV in a symmetric cryptography scenario, is used by the algorithm service provider to encrypt and digitally sign the message. ExportParameters(true) means that the returned RSAParameters object contains the private key, hence can be used for digital signatures. ExportParameters(false) means that the returned RSAParameters object contains only the public key, and hence can be used for data encryption.

Step 2: Encrypt the Data Using Symmetric Cryptography

As we learned earlier, asymmetric cryptography is used to exchange the secret key between the sender and receiver in a secure manner. The underlying message itself is actually encrypted and decrypted using the secret key on both ends after the initial key exchange. In this step, we will generate a secret key and encrypt the underlying message with this secret key. The encryption that occurs in this step is symmetric:

```
//get a symmetric service provider to encrypt the message
SymmetricAlgorithm symmetricProvider = SymmetricAlgorithm.Create("TripleDES");
ICryptoTransform encryptor = symmetricProvider.CreateEncryptor();
Stream data = new MemoryStream(Encoding.Default.GetBytes("This is test"));
//create a CryptoStream to encrypt the message
CryptoStream encStream = new CryptoStream(data, encryptor, CryptoStreamMode.Read);
MemoryStream encrypted  = new MemoryStream();
byte[] buffer = new byte[1024];
int count = 0;
//Read the encrypted data into the new stream
while ((count = encStream.Read(buffer,0,1024)) > 0)
{
    encrypted.Write(buffer,0,count);
}
```

As you can see, this step is very similar to the symmetric encryption example shown earlier. The only difference is that we are creating an encryptor without specifying a secret key and IV value. In this case, a random key and IV value are generated and used to encrypt the underlying message. Of course, in order for anyone to decrypt the message, they must obtain this generated secret key along with the IV value. We are now talking about the key exchange. The next step shows how to use asymmetric cryptography to achieve this key exchange.

Step 3: Encrypt the Generated Key and IV

Recall Figure 12-2. We need to use the recipient's public key to encrypt the message to ensure that only the intended recipients can decrypt the message. In this case, we can encrypt the secret key and IV that are generated in step two. We will later need to ship out the encrypted key and IV so that recipients can decrypt them and use them to decrypt the actual message. The following code sample shows the asymmetric encryption process:

```
byte[] key;
byte[] iv;
RSACryptoServiceProvider asymmetricProvider = new RSACryptoServiceProvider();
asymmetricProvider.ImportParameters(receiver_publicKey);
key =  asymmetricProvider.Encrypt(symmetricProvider.Key,false);
iv = asymmetricProvider.Encrypt(symmetricProvider.IV,false);
```

Notice that after the code is executed, key[ ] and iv[ ] now hold the encrypted key and IV used to encrypt the underlying message using the recipient's public key. The last step is to create a digital signature for the encrypted message so that the recipient can identify the sender and determine whether the message has been tampered with.

Step 4: Create a Digital Signature

Creating a digital signature requires the sender to use its private key to encrypt the hash of the encrypted message. We need to pass into the ImportParameters() method an RSAParameters object that contains the private key. The following code shows how you can create a digital signature:

```
byte[] signature;
asymmetricProvider.ImportParameters(sender_privateKey);
signature = asymmetricProvider.SignData(encrypted.ToArray(),new
                                  SHA1CryptoServiceProvider());
```

After the four steps that we have just seen, there are four values that the sender needs to pass to the recipient in order for the recipient to decrypt the message. They are the encrypted message, the encrypted key, the encrypted IV, and the digital signature. In my example, they are the variables encrypted, key, iv, and signature, respectively.

Asymmetric Example (Decryption)

There are also four steps involved in decrypting a message using asymmetric cryptography:

1. Retrieve the sender's public key and the recipient's private key.

2. Verify the digital signature.

3. Decrypt the secret key and IV.

4. Use the decrypted key and IV to decrypt the message.

Retrieve the Keys

Decryption occurs on the recipient side, relatively speaking. The type of keys the recipient needs to retrieve are different from those needed by the sender during encryption. Instead of the sender's private key and the recipient's public key, we need to retrieve the sender's public key and the recipient's private key during the decryption process. The following code shows the type of key needed for decryption. Note that some of the code is omitted to avoid repetition:

```
byte[] key =… //get from the sender
byte[] iv =…//get from the sender
btye[] signature = …//get from the sender
Stream encryptedData = …//get from the sender

RSAParameters sender_publicKey =
                   senderCertificate.PublicKey.ExportParameters(false);
RSAParameters receiver_privateKey =
                   receiverCertificate.Key.ExportParameters(true);
```

Verify the Digital Signature

The next step is to determine whether the data has been tampered with during transmission. During the verification of the signature, we can also implicitly verify the identity of the sender by using the sender's public key to decrypt the encrypted hash value, as follows:

```
provider.ImportParameters(sender_publicKey);
bool verify = provider.VerifyData(encryptedData,new
                   SHA1CryptoServiceProvider(),signature);
if (verify == false)
{
    throw new CryptographicException("failed to verify the signature");
}
```

The VerifyData() method returns a Boolean value to indicate whether the signature verification was successful. If false is returned, we need to abort the operation and throw an exception, since there is no sense in continuing with decryption. If true is returned, it means that the data indeed comes from the sender and no tampering has occurred during transmission, and we can proceed to the next step.

Decrypt Secret Key and IV

The recipient's next step is to use its private key to decrypt the secret key and IV, since they were encrypted using the recipient's public key on the sender side:

```
provider.ImportParameters(receiver_privateKey);
byte[] decryptedkey =  provider.Decrypt(key,false);
byte[] decryptediv = provider.Decrypt(iv,false);
```

Now we have the original secret key and IV used to encrypt messages, we have all the information we need to decrypt the message

Decrypt the Message with Decrypted Key and IV

After we obtain the decrypted key and IV, the decryption process is no different from the ordinary symmetric decryption process we saw earlier in the chapter.

```
SymmetricAlgorithm symmProvider = SymmetricAlgorithm.Create("TripleDES");
ICryptoTransform  decryptor =
                        symmProvider.CreateDecryptor(decryptedkey,decryptediv);
CryptoStream decStream = new CryptoStream(encryptedData, decryptor,
                                        CryptoStreamMode.Read);
//... code omitted
```

Web Service Enhancements

We have just seen that WSE offers us an extended feature to access and search certificates in various certificate stores. However, what WSE offers goes beyond what we have seen so far. WSE 1.0 includes the implementation of four WS-I specifications: WS-Security, WS-Routing, WS-Referral, and WS-Attachment.

WS-Security was created to overcome the lack of security features provided by Web services. It provides Web services with three major benefits: credential exchange, or the ability to identify the participant of the Web service call; message integrity, or the ability to verify whether a Web service call has been tampered with during transmission; and message confidentiality, or the ability to encrypt the Web service call.

WS-Routing was created to provide Web services with the ability to route calls through different points within a system before reaching their final destination.

WS-Referral was created to work in conjunction with WS-Routing. It provides the logical message path of a Web service call, whereas WS-Routing specifies how the Web service calls are routed.

WS-Attachments was created to provide Web services with the ability to carry one or more file attachments without serializing the attachments into XML.

I will spend the rest of the section talking about the architecture of WSE and then focus on WS-Security and how we can use WSE to secure Web service calls.

Installation

WSE is not a part of the .NET Framework, as of .NET Framework 1.1, so we need to download the WSE from the Microsoft site and install it on the system before we can take advantage of its features. After installation, you will find that the "Microsoft.Web.Services" assembly appears in the "Add Reference" window in Visual Studio .NET.

Like other .NET services in the framework, WSE relies heavily on the information stored in the configuration file to do its work. Microsoft also ships a VS.NET add-in tool called "WSE Settings Tool for Visual Studio .NET," which makes it easier for you to configure the settings that are related to WSE. This tool is a separate download from WSE itself, and can be found on Microsoft's WSE Web site.

After you install the WSE settings tool, you will see an additional option in the Properties window (right-click on the project in Solution Explorer) for each project within a solution, called "WSE Settings...." Clicking on it will prompt you with the window shown in Figure 12-11.

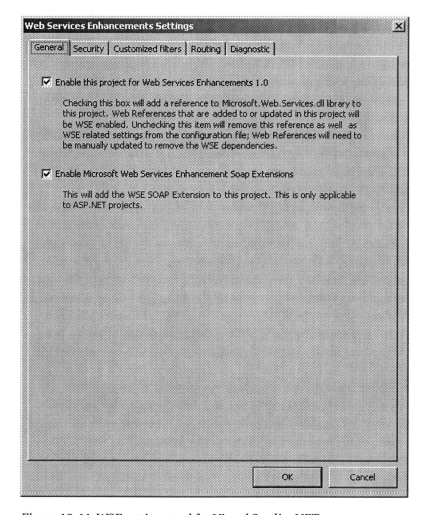

Figure 12-11. WSE settings tool for Visual Studio .NET

Each tab contains a number of WSE-specific configuration settings, such as which certificate store the service will use. All the changes you make through the WSE settings tool will be reflected in the application's configuration file. All the WSE-specific configuration settings will reside in the `<microsoft.web.services />` section.

WSE Architecture

We know that WSE makes it possible to add several services on top of Web services. How does WSE do it? It turns out that WSE has a very simple approach. It relies on two things to perform its work: SOAP headers and filters.

SOAP headers represent the information stored in the `<Soap:Header>` element in the SOAP message. WSE uses it to carry configuration information on how certain services should be carried out. For example, if I want to indicate that a certain portion of the SOAP message has been encrypted using symmetric cryptography, I need to say that somewhere in the SOAP header, so that the recipient of the SOAP message can react to the message accordingly. Figure 12-12 shows a Web service call using WSE caught on the wire; notice the different SOAP header information in the SOAP message.

To understand how these SOAP headers are added and how the services those headers are associated with are carried out on both ends of a Web service, we need to look at the WSE filter pipeline. Figure 12-13 shows the filter that participates in providing the additional service on top of the Web service.

Filters are grouped into output filters and input filters. Output filters will write the additional SOAP headers and modify sections of the body when the SOAP message goes out. Input filters, on the other hand, will read the SOAP message, seek out the special header information, and take appropriate actions toward it.

Reading and writing the SOAP message at the byte level is not very developer-friendly. In order to alleviate the development effort of implementing advanced Web services, WSE relies on the `SoapContext` object and `Filter` objects to shield developers from directly accessing the SOAP message, hence removing the need for developers to perform the tedious and repetitive reading and writing of SOAP messages.

To access the `SoapContext` from the user code, you must make sure that the Web service proxy is extended from `System.Web.Service.WebServicesClient-Protocol`. `WebServicesClientProtocol` has two properties: `RequestSoapContext` and `ResponseSoapContext`; both are of the `SoapContext` type. By extending your Web service proxy class from `WebServicesClientProtocol`, you can have access to the `SoapContext` object, which is important in determining what each filter will do as SOAP messages pass through them.

Figure 12-12. A SOAP message using WSE

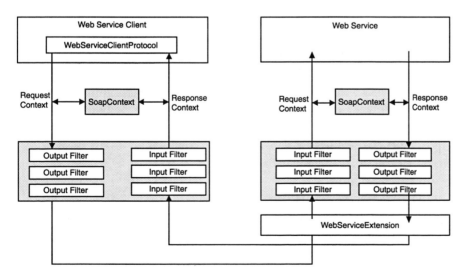

Figure 12-13. WSE filters

> **NOTE** *VS.NET will automatically generate a Web service proxy that extends* SoapHttpClientProtocol *if* Microsoft.Web.Service *isn't initially referenced in the current project. To change that, you need first to add Microsoft.Web.Service to the project reference and then manually change the Web service proxy's inherited class from* SoapHttpClientProtocol *to* WebServicesClientProtocol.

WSE Output Filters

WSE output filters, whose job is to generate a WS-* compliant soap message, rely on SoapContext to do their work. It works like this: When developers are making the SOAP call through the Web service proxy, they will specify what additional WS-* service they want to apply to the call by setting the properties of SoapContext. As the clients are making Web service calls at run time, each of the WSE's output filters will examine the SoapContext object and perform the low-level SOAP message manipulation to change its headers and body so that it is compliant with the WS-* specification. For example, the following code will result in the additional security SOAP header and replacement of a section of SOAP body with the encrypted data as shown in Figure 12-12:

```
//...some code omitted, serviceProxy is the proxy object
// for the external Web service.
SoapContext requestContext = serviceProxy.RequestSoapContext;
SymmetricEncryptionKey key=
                new SymmetricEncryptionKey(TripleDES.Create(), keyBytes);
EncryptedData ed = new EncryptedData(key);
requestContext.Security.Elements.Add(ed);
```

From the developer's perspective, the above code is about all they need to do to encrypt the soap body with the secret key. Of course, one of the filter objects (Microsoft.Web.Services.Security.SecurityOutputFilter) has to do the dirty work of adding the security-related SOAP head and encrypt the SOAP body. Table 12-1 shows the output filters that come with WSE 1.0.

Table 12-1. Output Filters Provided with WSE 1.0

Filter	Description
ReferralOutputFilter	Adds referral headers and data to outgoing messages if there are Referral objects in the Referrals collection of the SoapContext.

(continued)

Table 12-1. Output Filters Provided with WSE 1.0 (continued)

Filter	Description
RoutingOutputFilter	Adds routing information to the WS-Routing header of the outgoing message from the Path of the SoapContext.
SecurityOutputFilter	Adds the security headers to the outgoing messages, based on the contents of the SoapContext.Security and SoapContext.ExtendedSecurity properties.
TimestampOutputFilter	Adds time-related information to the WS-Timestamp header of the outgoing messages from the Timestamp in the SoapContext.
TraceOutputFilter	Saves the outgoing message to the diagnostic input file specified in the configuration file. (The default input file name is OutputTrace.Webinfo in the application directory.) It is turned off by default.

WSE Input Filter

WSE input filters process the incoming SOAP message by examining the SOAP headers and performing the appropriate actions accordingly. For example, if the SOAP headers indicate that the message has been signed and encrypted, an input filter (Microsoft.Web.Services.Security.SecurityInputFilter) will use the sender's public key to determine whether the message has been tampered with and use the recipient's private key to decrypt the message as the soap message flows through it. Input filters are also responsible for setting the SoapContext properties so that the recipient of the SOAP message is able to extract the information stored inside the SoapContext and perform some business logic accordingly. For example, the following Web method will extract the attachment data in the SOAP message via SoapContext and store it somewhere:

```
[WebMethod]
public void StoreFile()
{
    String content= null;
    SoapContext requestContext = HttpSoapContext.RequestContext;
    Stream incomingFileStream = requestContext .Attachments[0].Stream;
    StreamReader stream = new StreamReader(incomingFileStream );
    content = stream.ReadToEnd();
    //code to store the file to some location...
}
```

Table 12-2 shows the input filters that come with WSE 1.0.

Table 12-2. Input Filters Provided by WSE 1.0

Filter	Description
ReferralInputFilter	Inspects incoming messages for referrals and processes them, adding Referral objects to the Referrals collection of the SoapContext.
RoutingInputFilter	Inspects incoming messages and processes the WS-Routing header, removing it from the SOAP header and adding a Path to the SoapContext.
SecurityInputFilter	Inspects incoming messages and processes the security header for the node. This includes verifying signatures and decrypting data.
TimestampInputFilter	Inspects incoming messages and processes the WS-Time stamp header, adding time-related information to the Time stamp of the SoapContext.
TraceInputFilter	Saves the incoming message to the diagnostic input file specified in the configuration file. (The default input file name is InputTrace.Webinfo in the application directory.)

In essence, SoapContext provides a communication bridge between the user code (on either end of the Web service) and filter objects that performs the actual work of providing the additional service on Web service calls. Input filters read the information stored in the SoapContext and write out the corresponding SOAP headers to the outgoing SOAP messages. Output filters read the information stored in the incoming SOAP messages, perform some tasks accordingly, and then make them available to the recipient through the SoapContext object.

Extensibility of WSE Filters

WSE uses the filter approach to greatly increase the extensibility of WSE. As a developer you can create your own customized input filter and output filter and plug them into the filter pipeline on either side of the Web service call. As a SOAP message passes through the filters, the customized filter object will be executed in the same manner as those of the native filters as part of WSE. As more WS-* specifications are implemented in WSE in the future, more filters will be added to WSE to provide those additional services. Figure 12-14 shows how a customized filter and a WSE native filter can work together to process the SOAP messages.

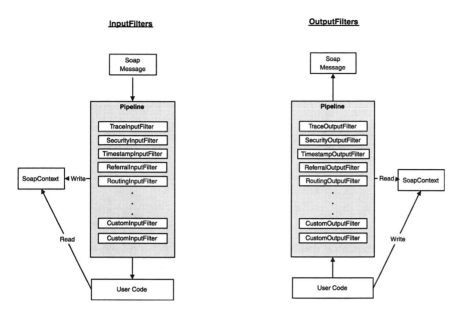

Figure 12-14. Custom filters in the pipeline

To create a custom filter, you must create a class that extends from SoapOutput-Filter or SoapInputFilter, depending on the purpose of the filter. Each filter performs its work by overriding the ProcessMessage() abstract method on the SoapInput(Output)Filter class. The following is the method signature of the ProcessMessage():

```
public abstract void ProcessMessage(SoapEnvelope envelope);
```

The SoapEnvelope object is passed into the method as the parameter. The SoapEnvelope object has three properties you can access to determine what you want to do as the SOAP message goes out of and comes into the pipeline. SoapEnvelope.Context returns the SoapContext object. SoapEnvelope.Body returns an XmlElement object that represents the SOAP body. SoapEnvelope.Header returns another XmlElement object that represents the SOAP header.

Installing the custom filter to the pipeline is done through the application's configuration file. For example, the following configuration indicates that you want to make the outgoing SOAP request pass through the MyCustomOutputFilter object between being processed by the WSE native output filters:

```
<configuration>
    <configSections>
        <section name="microsoft.web.services"
```

```
                type="Microsoft.Web.Services.Configuration.WebServicesConfiguration,
                    Microsoft.Web.Services, Version=1.0.0.0, .. PublicKeyToken=…" />
    </configSections>
    <microsoft.web.services>
     <filters>
         <output>
             <add type="MyCustomFilterLibrary.MyCustomOutputFilter,
                 MyCustomFilterLibrary"/>
         </output>
     </filters>
     </microsoft.web.services>
</configuration>
```

You can also achieve the same result using the WSE setting tool, which provides a nicer GUI interface for adding filters to the configuration file.

.NET Remoting Channel Sink

With the arrival of WSE, developers can now easily add many additional services to Web services with little or no code change by "plugging and playing" the input and output filters to the pipeline. In the area of Web service security, this has significantly reduced the amount of effort required by developers to ensure the secure communication of SOAP messages between client and server. Developers need do very little besides making sure that WSE's security input and output filters are enabled to process the SOAP message. Unlike Web services, there isn't a convenient way to enable secure communication in a .NET remoting situation. This would have added considerable development burden to developers if they had to secure the .NET remoting calls between different systems. Although .NET remoting doesn't come with security support natively, we can definitely extend the existing .NET remoting framework to support various security features. SAF.Cryptography contains a couple of classes that are built on top of .NET remoting's extensibility, allowing developers to enable the security of .NET remoting calls with simple configuration settings.

Before we can extend the .NET remoting system, we need first to learn about the existing components involved in making the remoting call possible. The following is a very simple remoting configuration that specifies that the client will use the http protocol for the remoting call and that the data sent across the wire will be in binary format:

```
<configuration>
    <system.runtime.remoting>
      <application>
```

```
  <client>
    <wellknown url="http://localhost:8989/BusinessObjectA.rem" type="..." />
      </client>

  <channels>
      <channel ref="http" port="4000">
          <clientProviders>
              <formatter ref="binary"/>
          </clientProviders>
      <channels>
    </application>
  </system.runtime.remoting>
</configuration>
```

In Chapter 4, we talked about how the remote invocation will pass through a transparent proxy, a real proxy, and a series of message sinks before it hits the other end of the remoting call, as shown Figure 4-4. In this section, we will talk about what happens when a real proxy passes the IMessage object to a chain of message sinks and how we can extend .NET remoting with customized message sinks.

Figure 12-15 shows how the message sinks convert an IMessage object to the data stream that is sent out using various network protocols.

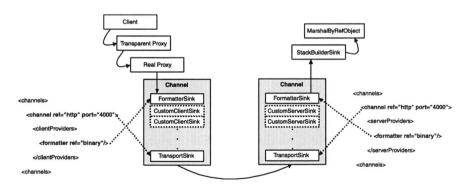

Figure 12-15. Different message sinks involved during a remote invocation

Now let's see how each sink in the channel contributes to the invocation calls. When a client make a remoting call, the transparent object will generate an IMessage object for the remoting call and pass it to the real proxy. The real proxy then will look into the remoting configuration settings associated with a particular remote object to determine what message sinks it needs to load in order to serve the remoting call.

There are at least two message sinks that the real proxy needs to load. One sink is the formatter sink, which is responsible for serializing the IMessage object to a data stream. This data stream will eventually be transmitted over the wire. The .NET framework comes with two formatter sinks: SoapFormatter and Binary-Formatter. The other sink is the transport sink, which is responsible for transporting the data stream to the destination, or the remoting server. The .NET framework also comes with two transport sinks: TcpChannel and HttpChannel. For example, using Figure 12-15, the real proxy would load the BinaryFormatter sink and the HttpChannel sink because of <formatter ref = 'binary' /> and <channel ref = 'http' port = '4000'> in the configuration.

Of course, you can have many message sinks between the formatter sink and the transport sink. Adding customized message sinks between these two sinks is how we extend .NET remoting to perform an array of customized actions.

After we have created the customized message sink, we must chain it to the existing message sinks. How does .NET remoting chain various message sinks so that each message sink in the chain has an opportunity to process the message in the correct order? The .NET framework achieves this through the IClient(Server)ChannelSink interface. Every message sink that comes with .NET Framework and your custom sink must at least implement this interface. This interface contains a number of members, but one is of particular interest:

```
void ProcessMessage(
    IMessage msg,
    ITransportHeaders requestHeaders,
    Stream requestStream,
    out ITransportHeaders responseHeaders,
    out Stream responseStream
);
```

One of the input parameters of ProcessMessage() is the Stream type. It represents the data stream of the serialized IMessage object by the formatter sink. The ProcessMessage() method also has an output Stream type parameter. It represents the response IMessage object from the remoting server.

In order to form a message sink chain, each message sink is responsible for figuring out the identity of the next message sink and passing the data to the ProcessMessage() method of the next message sink. Figure 12-16 can help in visualizing this effect.

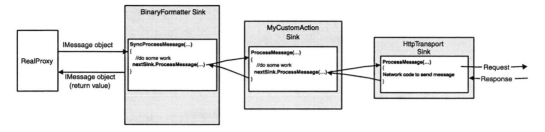

Figure 12-16. A message sink chain

The very first message sink in the channel is the formatter sink, which is a bit special in comparison to the other sinks in the channel. Its job is to serialize the IMessage object into the data stream and pass it down to the next sink in the chain. When the return value is returned, the first message sink will deserialize the return value from data stream to an IMessage object before returning it to the real proxy. The method on the binary formatter to perform this task is IMessageSink.SyncProcessMessage(). This is its signature:

```
public IMessage SyncProcessMessage(IMessage msg);
```

Notice that the formatter's SyncProcessMessage() method triggers the next sink by calling nextSink.ProcessMessage(…), which itself is responsible for triggering its next sink by calling nextSink.ProcessMessage(), as shown in Figure 12-16. This type of chainlike approach to processing a piece of data with a series of components is known as the "decorative design" pattern. We will learn more about this pattern in Chapter 14.

Obviously, keeping track of where nextSink points is critical. To cut a long story short, the CLR determines which sink comes after the formatter sink by looking at the .NET remoting configuration section. For the following sample settings, the CLR will put the TcpChannel sink right after the formatter sink, since there is no custom sink specified in between:

```
<channels>
    <channel ref="http" port="4000">
        <clientProviders>
            <formatter ref="binary"/>
        </clientProviders>
    <channels>
```

However, you can install additional sinks to the chain with the following changes:

```
<channels>
    <channel ref="http" port="4000">
        <clientProviders>
        <provider type="xx.MyCustsomClientSinkProvider, xx">
            <formatter ref="binary"/>
        </clientProviders>
    <channels>
```

The .NET Framework requires you to specify your custom sink's provider instead of the custom sink itself when adding it to the chain. The provider is nothing more than an abstract factory. By using the abstract factory pattern, the CLR avoids binding to a specific class type. The sink's provider class has two simple members:

```
IClientChannelSinkProvider Next {get; set;}
IClientChannelSink CreateSink(
    IChannelSender channel,
    string url,
    object remoteChannelData
);
```

The CLR will call the Next property of the provider object at run time to set the next sink in the chain. The CLR will always set it to the last sink, a transport sink. CreateSink() is also called by the CLR at run time. This method, a factory method, returns a new instance of the custom sink to the CLR. The CLR will then put it right behind the formatter sink in the chain. The CreateSink() method is also responsible for passing the value of the Next property to the custom sink object so that the custom sink can use it in its ProcessMessage() method to trigger the next sink.

> **NOTE** *It is bit hard to grasp how the "NextSink" is communicated throughout the chain. It is not something I can most easily explain in words. If you have a hard time understanding how* NextSink *is determined at each step of the process, you can run the remoting sample for this chapter and debug through the various sinks in the sample to see how the value of* NextSink *is set at each step.*

SAF Code Sample Walkthrough

It has been a long time coming to reach this section. You have learned quite a bit in terms of how cryptography works, how we can leverage WSE for its security features, and how we can extend .NET remoting to provide additional services, such as cryptographic services on top of the default message sink chain. In this section, we will see how all this theory plays out in the field. We will look at how SAF.Cryptography is implemented using the concepts and .NET technologies learned in the previous pages.

The following list quickly recaps what SAF.Cryptography offers:

- A helper class to ease the effort of performing data encryption and decryption.

- A pair of remoting sinks that provide the infrastructure-level cryptography service to protect data transmitted using .NET remoting without the need of a change remoting client and remoting server.

Cryptography Helper Class

SAF.Cryptography comes with an Encryption class and a Decryption class. The Encryption class provides the methods to perform symmetric and asymmetric encryption. The Decryption class provides the methods to perform symmetric and asymmetric decryption. The method signatures for Encryption are as follows:

```
//For symmetric encryption:
public static string Encrypt(string data, string profile)
public static Stream Encrypt(Stream data, string profile)

//For asymmetric encryption:
public static string Encrypt(string data, string profile,
                        out byte[] key, out byte[] iv, out byte[] signature)
public static Stream Encrypt(Stream data, string profile,
                        out byte[] key, out byte[] iv, out byte[] signature)
```

Depending on whether the source data is of string type or stream type, the developer can choose the appropriate method overload. Each method takes a security profile name as its parameter. The security profile represents the security configuration necessary for the Encryption class to do its work. Here is what this configuration looks like:

```
<SAF.Cryptography>
  <Profiles>
    <Profile name ="Profile1" symmetric="true" algorithm="TripleDES">
     <SecretKey>6HD+Ngi8JoGmDOg=</SecretKey>
     <IV>gi8JoGmD</IV>
     </Profile>
    <Profile name ="Profile2" symmetric="false" algorithm="RSA">
    <SenderCertificate store="CurrentUser">CN=CompanyA,...</SenderCertificate>
    <ReceiverCertificate store="LocalMachine">CN = CompanyB,
                                      ...</ReceiverCertificate>
    <SymmatricAlgorithm>TripleDES</SymmatricAlgorithm>
    </Profile>
    </Profiles>
</SAF.Cryptography>
```

Accompanying the System.Cryptography name space is the SAF.Configuration.CryptographyConfiguration class, which provides easy access to the cryptography-related information stored in the configuration file.

The decryption class takes a similar approach to that taken by the class responsible for the security profile information in collecting security information so that it can decrypt the data. The following are the signatures for the decryption methods:

```
// For symmetric decryption:
public static string Decrypt(string data, string profile)
public static Stream Decrypt(Stream data, string profile)


// For asymmetric decryption:
public static string Decrypt(string data, string profile,
                         byte[] key,  byte[] iv,  byte[] signature)
public static Stream Decrypt(Stream data, string profile,
                         byte[] key,  byte[] iv,  byte[] signature)
```

The implementation of the Decryption and Encryption methods is very similar to the encryption/decryption sample code shown earlier in the chapter, except that the security-related information is stored externally instead of hard-coded in the sample.

Using SAF.Cryptography, developers can significantly reduce the amount of code they need to perform encryption and decryption. The following sample code shows the amount of code needed to perform asymmetric cryptography:

```
byte[] key;
byte[] iv;
byte[] signature;
string sample = "this is test";
string encryptedData = Encryption.Encrypt(sample,"Profile-1",
                                    out key, out iv, out signature);
string originalData =
              Decryption.Decrypt(encryptedData,"Profile-2", key, iv, signature);
Console.WriteLine(orginalData + " is encrypted to " + encryptedData);
```

With the Encryption and Decryption helper classes in SAF.Cryptograpahy, we can now start building some cryptographic solutions to leverage what is offered in these helper classes. One goal I want to achieve in SAF.Cryptograpahy is to turn the responsibility of securing the data transmission to an infrastructure-level service. When developers write .NET remoting applications, they don't have to worry about how the invocation call is delivered to its destination, since the .NET remoting service has already taken care of all the low-level plumbing through the proxies and message sinks. This has helped keep the development simple for .NET remoting applications. The developer now can set up remoting through the configuration file. We can apply the same approach to make securing .NET remoting communication an infrastructural-level service that developers don't have to worry about. We will look at how we can achieve this using custom .NET remoting sinks.

Cryptography Remoting Sinks

SAF.Cryptography contains a pair of channel sinks: CryptoRemotingClientSink and CryptoRemotingServerSink. This pair of sinks will be installed as part of the remoting sink chain. They perform data encryption and decryption for remoting calls so that the message that the remoting client sends out and the message with which the remoting server replies are encrypted at all times. Figure 12-17 shows how the CryptoRemotingXxxSinks appear in the remoting sink chain.

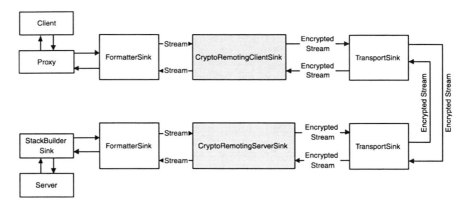

Figure 12-17. CryptoRemoting *sink pair*

As you can see from the figure, by plugging a sink between the formatter sink and transport sink, we now have an opportunity to perform a particular cryptography service on the data stream passing between the client and server. The CryptoRemotingClientSink on the client side is responsible for encrypting the request and decrypting the response from the remoting object. The CryptoRemoting-ServerSink on the server side is responsible for decrypting the client's request and encrypting the response before sending it back to the client. The result is that the data stream on the right side of both CryptoRemotingXxxSinks has become encrypted. Let's first look at how the work is done in the client-side sink.

CryptoRemotingClientSink

The following is the method inside our custom sink that performs encryption and decryption on the data stream:

```
private  static ConfigurationManager cm =
            (ConfigurationManager)ConfigurationSettings.GetConfig("Framework");
private  static CryptographyConfiguration cc = cm.CryptographyConfig;

public void ProcessMessage(
    IMessage msg, ITransportHeaders requestHeaders, Stream requestStream,
    out ITransportHeaders responseHeaders, out Stream responseStream)
{
    string identity =cc.GetIdentity();
    //add the identity information to the request header so that the other side
    // knows whose security profile will be used to decrypt the data
    requestHeaders["Identity"] = identity;
```

```
//encrypt the data stream based on the identity's
//security profile
Stream encryptedStream =
        helper.EncryptStream(identity,sinkType,requestHeaders,requestStream);

//call the next sink when the request data has been encrypted
next.ProcessMessage(
     msg, requestHeaders, encryptedStream,
     out responseHeaders, out responseStream);

//retrieve the identity information of the remote server
identity = responseHeaders["Identity"].ToString();
//decrypt the response data based on the security profile
//associated with the remote server
Stream decryptedStream =
        helper.DecryptStream(identity,sinkType,responseHeaders,responseStream);
responseStream = decryptedStream;
}
```

The code may look intimidating, but it is in fact very simple. It involves the following four steps:

- Identify the security profile to be used to encrypt the data.

- Encrypt the request stream.

- Identify the security profile to be used to decrypt the data.

- Decrypt the response stream.

Identify the Security Profile for Encryption

Because this custom sink will used to talk with multiple remote objects that may require different cryptographic algorithms, we must provide a way for our custom sink to switch among different algorithms and security profiles when dealing with communication with different servers. One way to achieve this goal is to carry the identity information of the client or server on every request and response so that the custom sink can determine at run time how to encrypt and decrypt the message. We also need to set up the configuration file to allow the sink to determine dynamically the identity that the message should carry with a mapping between the logical identity name and the identity of the current thread. The following is an example of the configuration settings:

```
<CryptoRemotingClientSink>
    <Identity name = "ClientA"  uri="http://localhost:4000/Class1.rem" >
        <EncryptProfile name ="Profile1" />
        <DecryptProfile name ="Profile2" />
    </Identity>
     <Identity name = "ServerA" >
        <EncryptProfile name ="Profile3" />
        <DecryptProfile name ="Profile4" />
    </Identity>
</CryptoRemotingClientSink>
```

In this example, when the remoting call is made to `http://localhost:4000/`
`Class1.rem`, the custom sink will add "ClientA" as the identity field on the request
header. The custom sink will also query as to which security profile to use during
encryption and decryption. In my example, we will use "Profile1" to encrypt the
message and "Profile2" to decrypt the message.

When the message is passed to the remote server side, the server-side sink
will determine that the message is coming from "ClientA" by checking the request
header. Of course, the server-side sink will have to load the security profile based
on this identity name and use it to verify whether the remoting message is indeed
coming from "ClientA." We will see how this is done later.

Encrypt the Request Stream

After the custom sink has figured out what security profile to use, it can start
encrypting the request stream by calling the cryptography helper class that
we have seen earlier. After the encryption is performed, a new data stream is
generated that contains the encrypted request stream. The sink then calls the
`ProcessMessage()` method of the next sink and passes in the decrypted request
stream.

Identify the Security Profile for Decryption

After `next.ProcessMessage(…)` is returned, we will then have an output parameter
`responseStream` that contains the response data from the remoting server. In order
to ensure that the response data from the remote server is secure and protected,
the remoting server should also encrypt the response data. In that case, `response-`
`Stream` will contain the encrypted stream. We must first decrypt it using the appropriate security profile. The server-side sink is responsible for adding the identity
information to the response header so that the client can determine what security
profile to use by looking up the configuration file. Using the sample configuration
above, for example, if the `Identity` field in the response header is "ServerA," the
client-side sink will use "Profile4" to decrypt the response stream.

Decrypt the Response Stream

With the knowledge of the security profile to be used to decrypt the response, the sink will call the helper class again and generate a decrypted response stream. The custom sink then sets responseStream equal to the newly generated decrypted response stream. At this moment, the work for our custom sink is done. The responseStream will eventually be serialized by the formatter sinks into an IMessage object and returned to the proxy.

Now let's look at what we need to do inside the server-side sink, which is responsible for decrypting the remoting message from the client and encrypting the response message.

CryptoRemotingServerSink

The concept and implementation of CryptoRemotingServerSink is almost the same as that of CryptoRemotingClientSink, since both are about encrypting and decrypting data streams. The most significant difference is he order of encryption and decryption applied inside the ProcessMessage() method. The following is the implementation of that method in the server-side sink:

```
public ServerProcessing ProcessMessage(
                    IServerChannelSinkStack sinkStack,
                    IMessage requestMsg, ITransportHeaders
                    transportHeaders, Stream targetStream,
                    out IMessage responseMsg,
                    out ITransportHeaders responseHeaders,
                    out Stream responseStream)
{
    //retrieve the client identity, which is used to find the security profile
    //extract the identity information from the header
    string identity = transportHeaders["Identity"].ToString();
    LocalDataStoreSlot dataSlot = null;
    //create a thread data slot
    dataSlot = Thread.GetNamedDataSlot("Identity");
    //put the identity information to the data slot so that server program can
    //determine who made the request
    Thread.SetData(dataSlot,identity);
    // Push this onto the sink stack, required for the server sink
    sinkStack.Push(this, null);

    Stream decryptedStream =
            helper.DecryptStream(identity,sinkType,transportHeaders,targetStream);
```

```
//indicate the status of the processing
ServerProcessing processingResult;

//trigger the next sink on the chain
processingResult = next.ProcessMessage(
                sinkStack, requestMsg, transportHeaders, decryptedStream,
                out responseMsg, out responseHeaders, out responseStream);
Stream encryptedStream =
        helper.EncryptStream(identity,sinkType,responseHeaders,responseStream);
//get the identify information for the server
string serverIdentity = cc.GetServerSinkIndentity();
responseHeaders["Identity"] = serverIdentity;
responseStream  = encryptedStream;
return processingResult;
}
```

The server object can retrieve the identity of the caller by retrieving the information stored in the thread's data slot during the remoting. For example, the following code shows how we can determine the identity of the caller in the remoting server object:

```
public class SampleBusiness : MarshalByRefObject
{
    public string SayHelloWorld()
    {
        //retrieve the data slot that contains the sender's identity information
        LocalDataStoreSlot dataSlot = Thread.GetNamedDataSlot("Identity");
        string sender = (string)Thread.GetData(dataSlot);
        //... more code....
    }
}
```

Installing the Sinks

After we create our custom sinks class and its associated provider class, we must install it to the chain. This task is achieved through the configuration file settings. The following code contains all the remoting settings you need in order to include our CryptoRemotingClientSink and CryptoRemotingServerSink in the remoting chain.

Here is the configuration on the remoting client side:

```
In the Remoting Client's configuration file:
<system.runtime.remoting>
<application>
  <client>
    <wellknown
      Type="Test.BusinessLibrary.SampleBusiness, Test.BusinessLibrary"
                url="http://localhost:4000/SampleBusiness.rem" />
  </client>
  <channels>
    <channel ref="http">
    <clientProviders>
      <formatter ref="binary" />
      <provider type=
          "SAF.Cryptography.CryptoRemotingClientSinkProvider, SAF.Cryptography" />
    </clientProviders>
    </channel>
  </channels>
</application>
<system.runtime.remoting>
```

Here is the configuration on the remoting server side:

```
In the Remoting Server's configuration file:
<application>
  <service>
    <wellknown
    type="BusinessLibrary.SampleBusiness, Test.BusinessLibrary"
    objectUri="SampleBusiness.rem"
    mode="Singleton" />
  </service>
  <channels>
    <channel ref="http" port="4000">
        <serverProviders>
         <provider type=
          "SAF.Cryptography.CryptoRemotingServerSinkProvider,SAF.Cryptography" />
          <formatter ref="binary" />
        </serverProviders>
    </channel>
  </channels>
</application>
```

The Testing Project

The demo for SAF.Cryptography requires you to run the client project (Test.Client.SAF.Cryptography) and the server project (Test.Server.SAF. Cryptography) at the same time in order to demonstrate how CryptoRemoting sinks work during .NET remoting calls.

Before you can run the demo, you must first install the certificates into the certificate store. Open an instance of MMC by entering mmc at the command prompt. After the management console is opened, add a "Certificates" snap-in for both the computer account and the current user account. Figure 12-18 shows what the console looks like after the two certificate console snap-ins have been added.

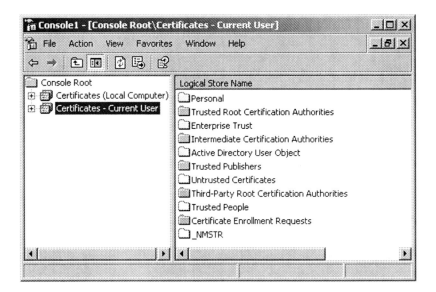

Figure 12-18. MMC with certificate console snap-in

Open the "Personal" folder under Certificate (Local Computer). Right click on the folder and then select All Tasks -> Import. A certificate import wizard will appear. You need to import two certificate files (CompanyA.pfx and CompanyB.pfx) from the Setup\Certificate folder in the source code folder. These two certificates contain the public key as well as the private key of the certificate. During the importation, you will see a screen as shown in Figure 12-19 that asks for the password. Type in "password" and then check the checkbox next to "Mark this key as exportable…," and then click Next until the wizard finishes its work.

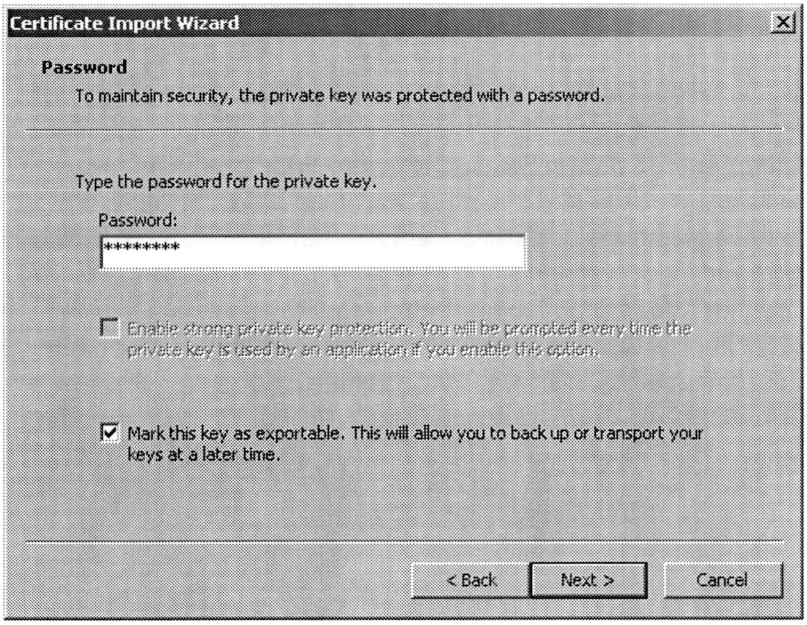

Figure 12-19. Certificate import wizard

After you have imported the certificate into the personal folder under Certificates (Local Computer), you need to import the CompanyA_PublicKey.cer and CompanyB_PublicKey.cer files to the personal folder under Certificate (Current User). These two certificates contain only the public key and don't require a password during the importation procedure. After the certificates have been installed into the certificate store, you are ready to run the demo.

First, open the solution in the Test.Server.SAF.Cryptography folder and hit F5 to start it and wait until the server console application is blocked at Console.ReadLine().

Second, open the solution in the Test.Client.SAF.Cryptography folder and hit F5 to run the client console application.

After these steps have been completed, you should have two instances of VS.NET running side by side. The first test of the client console application encrypts and decrypts some data through both symmetric and asymmetric cryptography. Its second test is to make a call to a remoting object via the remoting sinks that perform the data encryption/decryption on the remoting call. You can test out both symmetric and asymmetric scenarios over the remoting call by swapping certain sections of the configuration file. Please refer to the instruction in the app.config files for more detail.

Summary

In this chapter, we have focused on cryptography in .NET. You have learned about many cryptographic concepts, such as symmetric and asymmetric cryptography and digital signatures. We looked at how secure communication can be ensured using these concepts. We also spent a large portion of the chapter going over some of the .NET technologies related to the cryptography: how to implement encryption, decryption, and digital signatures using the `System.Security.Cryptography` name space. We then looked at Web service enhancements and their ability to ensure the security of Web services. At end of the chapter we looked at an implementation of the components inside `SAF.Cryptography`: a cryptography helper class and a pair of remoting sinks to ensure secure communication for .NET remoting.

CHAPTER 13

Transaction Service

IT IS ALMOST CERTAIN that there is some type of transactional processing involved in every enterprise application. Although there are several interpretations of what a transaction is, they are all variants of one sort or another of the original definition: the act of transferring money and goods between a seller and a buyer. A transaction involves two units of work: the transfer of money from the buyer to the seller and the transfer of goods from the seller to the buyer. The transaction is canceled if either part is not carried out. The concept of all operations being performed as a unit or not at all is widely used in application development to ensure that certain tasks are considered complete only when all the necessary steps within the task have been completed. In the case of failure of a single step, the whole series of steps that have been completed are to be rolled back. Treating a series of processes as a single unit achieves data consistency throughout an application.

One of the most common examples of transactions in an application is that of carrying out modifications to data across multiple tables and databases. Although the concept of transactions is easy to grasp, implementing them requires significant effort from developers to ensure that every operation within a transactional unit is rolled back in case of failure. Because transactions are widely used in enterprise applications, many software vendors have baked the transactional feature into their product so that developers don't have to worry about how to commit or roll back their transactions. For example, all major database applications allows developers to achieve transactions with a modest amount of code. Other software vendors enable developers to extend the boundary of a transaction across multiple databases and other transactional resources by adding an extra layer between the application code and the target data source. Microsoft COM+ is one such example. In this chapter, we will look at how transactions are achieved in .NET and how we can develop a transaction service (SAF.Transaction) that further eases application development involving transactions.

Motivation and Goals

The .NET framework provides its transaction service through the System.Enterprise-Services.ServicedComponent class. It is fairly easy to develop business components that support transactions in .NET; however, there are several limitations in developing transactional components using ServicedComponent. First, a class must inherit from the ServicedComponent class to participate in a transaction. This makes it impossible to extend a class from other classes, since .NET languages support only single class inheritance. Second, one frequently requires the flexibility to combine multiple methods into a single transaction during development. The .NET framework does not have an out-of-the-box approach to grouping several methods into a transaction in a flexible manner; it often requires developers to create additional methods inside the ServicedComponent to produce such a result. This usually will change the normal process flow of your application and require additional coding to regroup the methods. You will find out more about this limitation later in the chapter. Third, transactional attribute information is directly bound to the ServicedComponent object and can't be changed at runtime, which means that if we want a component to present a different transactional behavior in the application, we would have to create duplicated components differing only in the transactional attributes. As you can imagine, this limitation can potentially cause an explosion in the number of transactional components that have to be created and maintained.

The SAF.Transaction service has been created to resolve these limitations. SAF.Transaction is built on top of ServicedComponent and the distributed transactional concept. It allows developers to combine multiple methods into transactions. Using SAF.Transaction service, developers are no longer required to create ServicedComponents to achieve the transaction. You can also specify different transactional attributes without creating duplicated transactional components through the SAF.Transaction service.

.NET Technologies Overview

SAF.Transaction relies on several concepts and .NET technologies. The following are the ones we will look at in this section:

- Transactions and the distributed transaction coordinator (DTC)

- ServicedComponent

- Registration of a ServicedComponent

COM+ Transactions

ACID, an acronym for *atomic, consistent, isolated, and durable*, represents the four requirements that every transaction must satisfy.

The *atomic* requirement requires that all updates either complete or roll back. It is equivalent to the concept of "all or none."

The *consistent* requirement mandates that a transaction leave a system in a consistent state. What constitutes the consistency of the system is very broad. For example, if a database transaction is committed, but it fails to maintain the referential integrity of the updated data, then the transaction doesn't meet the requirement for consistency.

The *isolation* requirement says that while a transaction is being executed, the changes that it makes to the system should be isolated or hidden from the rest of the system until the transaction has been either committed or rolled back. If another part of the system were able to see the changes before the transaction was completed, it may make decisions based on the data that may or may not be rolled back. In other words, a failure to isolate a transaction can introduce the possibility that the rest of the system may act on invalid information.

The *durable* requirement says that all changes made by a transaction should be written to a durable storage medium that can survive a failure, such as a network or system failure. If a transaction writes its changes only to system memory and not to some durable storage medium, an unexpected system crash could erase all the committed changes and leave the system in an inconsistent state.

MTS, or Microsoft Transaction Server, was the first attempt to provide developers an easy approach to using transactions within applications on the Microsoft platform. It was also the predecessor of COM+, which also provides a transaction service, an object management service, and many other services for the .NET framework. In order to use transaction services more effectively in a .NET application, we first have to understand the transaction service model provided in COM+, whose transactions consist of four important concepts: a resource manager, happy/done/doom bits, the DTC (distributed transaction coordinator) /two-phase commit protocol, and transaction attributes.

Resource Manager

A resource manager is a piece of software that knows how to commit and roll back updates that occur on the underlying data store, make the change persistent, and lock the data so that other transactions are unable to see it until the transaction is complete. In essence, the resource manager fulfills the list of transaction requirements we saw earlier on its underlying data source. A resource manager also knows how to join itself to a COM+ transaction; in other words, it knows how to follow the commands of a COM+ transaction as to whether a transaction should be committed or rolled back. Every transactional data resource that is able to participate in a COM+ transaction needs a resource manager. For example, an MS-SQL server has its resource manager; an Oracle database and IBM's DB2 have their own resource managers. Resource managers are not limited to database systems. MSMQ and IBM's MQSeries also have their own resource managers and can participate, like an MS-SQL server, in COM+ transactions.

Figure 13-1 illustrates the resource manager's relation to a COM+ transaction.

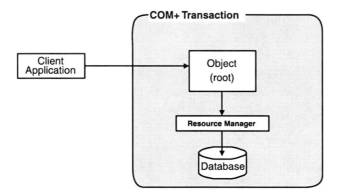

Figure 13-1. Resource manager

It is important to note that developers don't interact directly with the resource manager; instead, they interact with the COM+ transaction by asking the transaction to commit or abort. It is the responsibility of COM+ to command the resource manager to either commit the changes it has made to the underlying data source or to roll back the changes in their entirety. So what happens when developers ask COM+ to commit or abort? This leads us to our next topic: happy/done bits.

Happy/Done/Doom Bits

A COM+ transaction's fate is determined by the values of three bits. The developer controls the fate of a transaction by controlling the *happy*, *done*, and *doom* bits. In a nutshell, these bits have the following meanings:

- Happy bit: The object that participates in the transaction has no objection (and so is happy) to committing the transaction if the happy bit is set to true.

- Done bit: The object is done and ready to be deactivated if the done bit is true.

- Doom bit: The transaction is to be committed if the doom bit is false.

To be precise, a transaction's fate is determined by the doom bit alone, but the doom bit's value is determined by the happy/done bits of participating objects. Figure 13-2 illustrates how these bits can determine the fate a transaction.

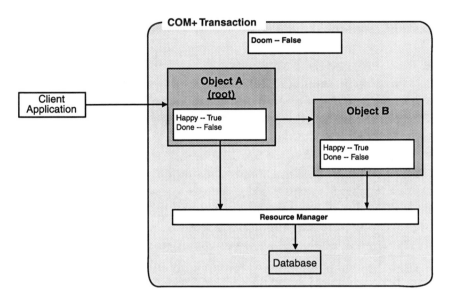

Figure 13-2. Happy/done/doom bits

Figure 13-2 shows a typical transaction scenario in which a client application calls Object A, which creates a new transaction. Object A performs a database update and then calls another object (Object B), which will perform an additional update under the same transaction.

Each object that participates in the transaction is associated with a happy bit and a done bit. The happy bit indicates whether the object has an objection to committing the transaction in which it is involved. The done bit indicates whether the object is ready to be deactivated. A transaction often involves multiple objects, each of which performs a particular data update. COM+ determines the state of the transaction by examining the happy bit of each participating object. For example, if Object B throws an exception during its database update, we want to make sure that the data update made by Object A is rolled back. To do that, we need to set Object B's happy bit to false, indicating that it is not happy about the current transaction. COM+ will record the happy bit of Object B when Object B's done bit is set to true. The done bit is set to true when the object deactivates. However, COM+ will not do anything special other than recording the happy bits of the objects in the transaction. This situation changes when the root object (Object A in my case) deactivates. The root object is the object that starts the transaction, and it thus plays a special role in a COM+ transaction. When the root object's done bit is set to true, it triggers a series of actions. First, COM+ is notified that all objects within a given transaction have deactivated, and so it is time to check the recorded happy bits and make a decision on the fate of the transaction. If all the happy bits have been set to true, COM+ will set the doom bit of the transaction to false. A false doom bit causes the COM+ to commit the transaction (which, in turn, will cause the resource manager to commit the transaction) and then release the transaction. However, if one of the happy bits is false, the transaction's doom bit is set to true. A true doom bit causes COM+ to abort the transaction (which in turn will cause the resource manager to abort the transaction) and then release the transaction. As you can see, whether a transaction is committed or aborted is triggered when the root object deactivates.

As a developer, you can control the fate of a transaction by controlling these bits. The ObjectContext is accessible to the participating objects within a transaction. It contains a number of methods and properties that we can use to determine the status of the current transaction as well as to set those important bits. We will see how to access ObjectContext from .NET applications later in this chapter. Here is a brief description of the methods we can use to set those bits:

- DisableCommit(): Calling this method will set the object's happy bit to false.

- EnableCommit(): Calling this method will set the object's happy bit to true.

- SetComplete(): Calling this method will set the happy bit and done bit to true, thereby committing and releasing the transaction immediately.

- SetAbort(): Calling this method will set the happy bit to false and done bit to true, thereby aborting and releasing the transaction immediately.

SetComplete() and SetAbort() will force the transaction to complete and hence free up the resource held by the transaction quickly. DisableCommit() and Enable-Commit() do not force the transaction to complete. Instead, they simply cast their vote on the fate of the transaction. In other words, calling DisableCommit() and EnableCommit() seal the fate of the transaction, but the transaction can still live and hold the resource for some time before the transaction is released.

> **NOTE** *You should always call* SetComplete() *or* SetAbort() *on the root object instead of a secondary object in a transaction. Calling the* SetComplete() *or* SetAbort() *on a secondary object causes the transaction to release the root object and leave it in an unstable state, where it will try to commit or abort a transaction that has been committed or aborted by another object.*

Two-Phase Commit Protocol and the Distributed Transaction Coordinator

The scenario in Figure 13-2 is fairly simple, involving only one resource manager that handles all the data updates. In practice, however, applications often span transactions across different data sources, possibly on multiple servers. With multiple resource managers at different locations involved in a single transaction, COM+ transactions can no longer simply ask one resource manager to commit or abort, since the work performed by other resource managers in the transaction also determines the final outcome of the transaction. To make all the resource managers work together with the COM+ transaction when it comes to committing or rolling back all the updates, we need a coordinator that is capable of controlling multiple resource managers. This is where the distributed transaction coordinator (DTC) comes in. Figure 13-3 shows the role the DTC plays in a COM+ transaction.

Figure 13-3 shows a typical scenario of a transaction that involves multiple resource managers on multiple machines. The client calls Object A, which in turn calls Object B on Machine B and Object C on Machine C. Because the transaction spans multiple machines, each machine will start a DTC service to communicate with other DTC services in the transaction.

To complete the transaction, COM+ initiates a two-phase commit process, which works as follows: when the transaction is done, the root DTC, which is located on the machine where the root object is located, starts collecting the transaction votes from the other DTCs within the transaction to determine whether to commit or roll back. The DTC on each machine is responsible for determining its vote by examining the happy bits of the participating objects on that machine. After the root DTC has retrieved all the votes from the other DTCs in the transaction, it can then determine the fate of the transaction. If one of the votes from the DTCs indicates that the transaction should be aborted, the root DTC will ask all the DTCs to roll back the change. If all the votes indicate commit, it is time for the first phase of the two-phase commit protocol. In this phase, the root DTC will ask each participating DTC whether it will have any problem committing the updates that it controls. The root DTC will then receive the votes from all the participating DTCs, and then the second phase starts. In the second phase, the root DTC will ask participating DTCs to commit the changes if none of the DTCs has indicated any problem in committing the changes. Otherwise, the root DTC will ask the participating DTCs to roll back the changes.

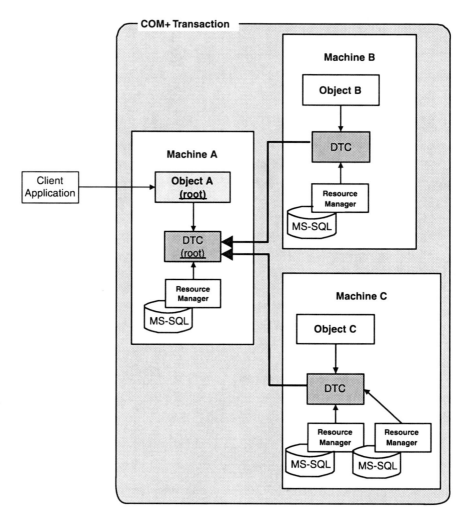

Figure 13-3. Distributed transaction coordinator

NOTE *It is important to note that when the DTC says that it does not have a problem committing the change during the first phase, it is assumed that the DTC will indeed not have any problems committing the change. The two-phase commit process is based on this assumption. It is up to the software vendor to implement the resource manager in such a way that satisfies this assumption.*

Transaction Attributes

When we create an object, we can specify how the object is to participate in trans-actions by providing one of five transaction attributes. These attributes determine whether the object creates a new transaction, participates in an existing transaction, or participates in no transactions. The following are the five attributes and their descriptions:

- Disabled: The object doesn't participate in any transaction.

- Not Supported: The object is created in context, but has no access to any transaction.

- Supported: Shares a transaction, if one exists.

- Required: Shares a transaction, if one exists, and creates a new transaction if necessary.

- Required New: Creates the component with a new transaction, regardless of the state of the current context.

Figure 13-4 illustrates the differences among these transaction attributes.

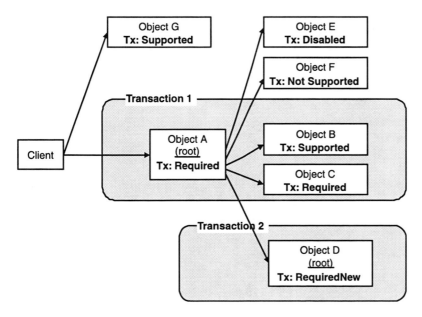

Figure 13-4. Five transaction attributes

Figure 13-4 shows how objects participate in a transaction according to their transactional attribute. If a client that doesn't belong to any transaction calls an object that is marked with the "Required" attribute, a new transaction is created to host the root object, such as Object A in Figure 13-4. The root object may instantiate multiple objects. Based on their attributes, such objects may participate in the same transaction as the root object (such as Objects B and C), or participate in a brand new transaction (such as Object D), or not participate in any transaction at all (such as Objects E and F). If the client creates an object that is marked as "Supported," then no transaction is created (such as with Object G), since the client doesn't reside within the transaction.

You have just learned about some important concepts of the transaction service in COM+; we will now take a look at how to leverage the transaction service provided in COM+ in .NET applications.

.NET Serviced Component

COM+ provides many services to applications, including object management, security, and transactions. In this section, we will be focusing on COM+'s transaction service in .NET.

The .NET framework provides us with many COM+ services through the System.EnterpriseServices name space. Among all the classes under this name space, two are the most commonly used, namely, ServicedComponent and ContextUtil.

When you develop a .NET class, you can enable the transaction support of the class by adding a Transaction attribute to the class definition. The following code shows an example of a transactional component:

```
using System;
using System.EnterpriseServices;
using System.Runtime.InteropServices;

namespace TxDemo
{
    [Transaction(TransactionOption.RequiresNew)]
    public class MyTransaction : ServicedComponent
    {
        public void TransferMoney(int amount)
        {
            //code to move money from checking
            //code to add money to savings
        }
    }
}
```

Creating a transactional component involves two simple steps. The first is extending the class from the System.EnterpriseServices.ServicedComponent class, and the second is marking the Transaction attribute on the class. The Transaction attribute marked on the MyTransaction class indicates that whenever an instance of MyTransaction is created, it will be created inside a brand new transaction. There are a total of five possible values for TransactionOption enumerations, matching exactly the five transaction attributes we talked about in the last section.

With that one and a half lines of code, we are halfway through writing a fully functional transactional component. The other half is to deal with how we control the commit and rollback of the transaction.

There are two ways to control the transaction. One is automated, and the other is manual, although it involves very little additional code. Let us continue using the sample code as the example for our demonstration.

The TransferMoney() method will call two additional methods: One moves money out of the checking account, and the other moves money into the saving account:

```
public void TransferMoney(int amount)
{
    TakeFromChecking(amount);
    AddToSaving(amount);
}
private void TakeFromChecking(int amount)
{
    //code to move money out from checking DB
}
private void AddToSaving(int amount)
{
    //code to add money to the savings DB
}
```

Clearly, in order for the TransferMoney() method to work properly, TakeFrom-Checking() and AddToSaving() must complete successfully, or else changes made by these methods must be rolled back completely.

One way to ensure that both methods work as a single unit is by adding the [AutoComplete()] attribute on the TransferMoney() method. For example:

```
[AutoComplete()]
public void TransferMoney(int amount)
{
    TakeFromChecking(amount);
    AddToSaving(amount);
}
```

By marking the TransferMoney() method with the AutoComplete attribute, COM+ determines the fate of the transaction by examining whether any unhandled exceptions have been thrown inside the method. Using TransferMoney() as an example, the current transaction will automatically be committed when Transfer-Money() completes without any unhandled exceptions being thrown inside the method. However, if an unhandled exception is thrown in the TransferMoney() method, the transaction will automatically abort, and the work performed so far will be rolled back. This is by far the most convenient way to control committing and aborting of transactions. For example, assume that the TakeFromChecking() method completes successfully but an exception is thrown inside the AddToSaving() method. The exception will then bubble back to TransferMoney() and cause it to throw an exception. Because we have labeled the TransferMoney() method with AutoComplete, COM+ will automatically roll back all the changes made so far by TakeFromChecking() and AddToSaving(), which is exactly the result we want. After the transaction has been completed, either through commit or abort, COM+ also deactivates the MyTransaction object.

> **NOTE** *You can still have exception handling code inside* AddToSaving()*, for example, to write an exception to a log. However, you must make sure that you throw the exception again in the* catch *block so that it can bubble up to the* Transfer-Money() *method, which will cause the transaction to roll back.*

The other way to control the transaction requires more programming, using ContextUtil, which provides every object that runs in a transaction the ability to explicitly commit or abort the transaction. Using the same TransferMoney() example, the following shows how ContextUtil is used to control the transaction:

```
public void TransferMoney(int amount)
{
    try
    {
        TakeFromChecking(amount);
        AddToSaving(amount);
        ContextUtil.SetComplete();
    }
    catch (Exception ex)
    {
        ContextUtil.SetAbort();
```

```
        //possible exception; rethrow to notify
        //the client about the error
    }
    }
    finally
    {
        this.Dispose();
    }
}
```

In this example, no `AutoComplete` attribute is used. Instead, the developer has full control over the fate of the transaction through the `SetComplete()` and `SetAbort()` methods. The key is to use the "try-catch" block to determine which method to call. When both the `TakeFromChecking()` and `AddToSaving()` methods have been processed successfully, the `ContextUtil.SetComplete()` is called, which will commit the transaction. However, if either method causes an exception, `ContextUtil.SetComplete()` will never be reached; instead, the `ContextUtil.SetAbort()` in the `catch` block will be called, which will roll back the transaction. Both the `SetComplete()` and `SetAbort()` methods also trigger the deactivation of the object that participates in the transaction (the `MyTransaction` object in our example).

We have just created a `ServicedComponent` class with COM+ transactions enabled. Unlike other .NET components, which we can use right away, `ServicedComponent` has its own special installation procedure that we have to follow in order to prepare the component for consumption, which we will look at next.

Registering a ServicedComponent

Every `ServicedComponent` needs a strong name. The .NET framework comes with a console program called `sn.exe`, which allows you to generate a key pair that can be used to provide a strong name for a given assembly. The following example shows how to generate a key pair with `sn.exe`:

```
c:\>sn -k mykey.snk
```

After you generate a key, you can bind it to the assembly that contains the `ServicedComponent` class by adding `[assembly: AssemblyKeyFile(@"c:\mykey.snk")]` to the `AssemblyInfo.cs` file and recompiling your class.

With the assembly strongly named, you can either register the component manually or register it through self registration.

Self registration does what the name implies. When the `ServicedComponent` object is created for the first time, COM+ will check whether the component is already registered, and if not, it will try to register the component to COM+. There

are a number of attributes that you can apply to the component to provide the
COM+ run time with the registration-related information, such as the application
name, the GUID for the class, and the ProgID inside the assembly. The following is
an example of the use of attributes to provide the COM+ registration information:

```
// In the class file
[assembly: ApplicationActivation(ActivationOption.Library)]
[assembly: ApplicationID("11169CB1-A111-11D0-111D-11C04FD111E1")]
[assembly: ApplicationName("Transaction.Demo")]
namespace
{
    [ProgId("MyTransaction")]
    [Guid("F55F5FFF-444B-4F20-AE66-B12A3C075555")]
    [Transaction(TransactionOption.RequiresNew)]
    public class MyTransaction : ServicedComponent
    {
        public void TransferMoney(int amount)
        {...}
    }
}
```

```
Inside the AssemblyInfo.cs file, add
[assembly: ApplicationName("MyTransactionDemo")]
```

> **NOTE** *you need to make sure that you provide a GUID and ApplicationID in the
> class file. Otherwise, COM+ will generate these unique IDs randomly every time
> the object is created and you will end up registering the same component multiple times.*

The second way to achieve the same result is through registering it using the
regsvcs.exe tool. For example, to install a serviced component TxDemo.dll into
COM+, use the following command at the prompt:

```
Regsvcs.exe TxDemo.dll
```

One thing you need to keep in mind regarding the registration of the Serviced-
Component is that you need administrator privileges to do so, either through automatic registration or menu registration using Regsvcs.exe. This security requirement
makes automatic registration impossible in most cases, since the user who runs the

application for the first time may not have security privileges to register the component. Therefore, it is recommended that you register the ServicedComponent via Regsvcs.exe as part of the application deployment effort.

You have just learned about the concept of transactions, COM+ transactions, and ServicedComponent. For the rest of the chapter, we will look at the SAF.Transaction service, which includes a number of ServicedComponent classes that provide features that allow us to use transactions more effectively in our .NET applications.

SAF Code Sample Walkthrough

With all our talk about transactions, we now have a fairly good grasp on the subject, and so it is a good time to revisit the problems that SAF.Transaction tries to solve in .NET applications.

Still using TransferMoney() as an example, in order to make the transaction work, you must put the TakeFromChecking() and AddToSaving() methods into the TransferMoney() method and mark the TransferMoney() method AutoComplete or use "try-catch" blocks combined with ContextUtil.SetComplete() or SetAbort() to control the transaction. In essence, we need to create a method that provides transaction-controlling code in a transaction-enabled serviced component that wraps around multiple methods that want to participate in the transaction. Creating this wrapping method in a serviced component doesn't seem to require a great deal of effort when you have only couple of methods to work with, but imagine that you have fifty methods throughout your application, and each performs a particular update to a particular data source. Some transactions require only a couple of methods that work as a unit, while others require five or ten such methods. Sometimes, you need to create wrapping methods for the wrapping methods to ensure the unity of the task. Depending on the business rules of the transaction involved in your application, you may end up with an overwhelming number of wrapping methods that you would have to create, each for a particular combination of the methods that needs to work as a single unit. Another shortcoming of the wrapping method is that it is not very flexible to changes to business requirements. For example, if you had a new transaction that requires a new combination of existing methods, you would have to modify your serviced components that host the wrapping method. This means that you would have to redeploy the changed serviced components, which would mean a step backward into the development, testing, and deployment phase.

In addition to the problems caused by the wrapping method, you may face an explosion in the number of serviced components you would have to create in a particular business case. If you recall how to define the transaction attributefor the serviced component, you may notice that the transaction attribute is hard-coded in the source code. This means that you would have to create two serviced components with identical content except for the different transaction attribute if you want the same methods to behave differently under different business scenarios. For example, say you have created two methods to allow users to buy stocks and options: BuyStock() and BuyOption(). If investors want to buy some stocks and some options at market prices, you would like to treat each stock and option purchase as a separate transaction. To achieve that, you would mark the serviced component that hosts these methods "RequireNew." But what if investors buy options to protect their purchase of some risky stock? In other words, an investor may wish to buy stocks and options together as a single trade. They want an all-or-none style trade. In that case, we can't use the BuyStock() and BuyOption() methods in the component that is marked "RequireNew." Instead, we need the identical methods in a component that is marked "Required" so that all the trades within the order to buy will be treated as a single transaction. One failed purchase will cause the entire order to be rolled back. This type of scenario is not often seen, but when you happen to run into it, you would end up writing and maintaining a lot of duplicated code.

Another issue about using transactions in .NET applications is that you have to extend your class from ServicedComponent. Due to the single-inheritance nature of .NET, we have to choose between extending from a class to inherit its functionality and extending from ServicedComponent so that we can enable the class for transactions. In other words, if you want the transaction, you will have to write a lot of code you otherwise wouldn't have to write by inheriting it from another class.

The following list summarizes these issues and problems in using Serviced-Component in .NET applications for transactional support:

- Overwhelming and inflexible wrapping methods

- Duplicate components to support multiple transactional behaviors

- Inability to extend from another class if it has already extended from ServicedComponent

With these issues in mind, let's look at how the SAF.Transaction service works to solve them. Figure 13-5 illustrates the SAF.Transaction's approach to solving these problems.

The SAF.Transaction service consists of four serviced components: *Support Transaction*, *Require New Transaction*, *Require Transaction*, and *No Transaction*. In contrast to the serviced components we normally create, such as the "MyTransaction" example shown earlier, which usually contain many business methods that will participate in the transaction, these four service components don't contain any business methods at all. Instead, they are equipped with functionality that enables them to execute external methods as part of the transaction that each of these components represents. This approach provides the foundation of the SAF.Transaction service and a resolution of the existing issues associated with the serviced components that we discussed earlier.

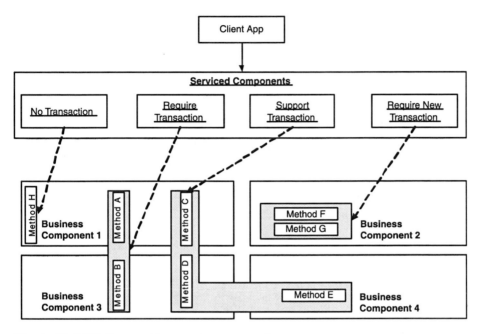

Figure 13-5. SAF.Transaction *service approach*

Figure 13-5 also shows how client applications can use the SAF.Transaction service. The business components at the bottom of the figure contain the business methods. These business components are not serviced components; in other words, they don't extend from the ServicedComponent class. Therefore, each business component has the freedom to extend from another class. In contrast to the traditional way business components are called, the client doesn't interact with the business component directly when using SAF.Transaction services. The client application will instruct the four serviced components located between the client and the business components on how the business method should participate in transactions. With SAF.Transaction, business methods from one or more business components can participate in a single transaction, thereby removing the need to create wrapper methods. Without wrapper methods, client applications can organize the scope of a transaction and its participating business methods in a much more flexible and comprehensive way. As new business components and methods are added, there are no new serviced components and methods to create; instead, client applications can immediately use the new business component, and it can participate in transactions. This again significantly reduces the amount of code that the developer has to write and maintain in order to react to the changes. Figure 13-6 shows the class hierarchy of the SAF.Transaction service.

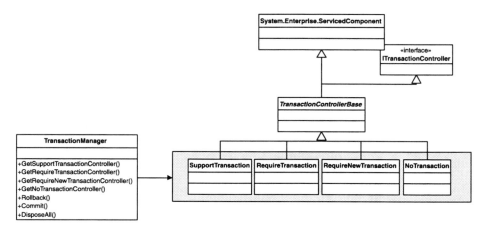

Figure 13-6. SAF.Transaction *service's class hierarchy*

The SAF.Transaction service consists of the following major pieces: Transaction-Manager on the left side of the figure consists of a number of factory methods that return the corresponding transaction controller objects to the clients. There are a total of four concrete transaction controller objects, namely, the SupportTransaction, RequireTransaction, RequireNewTransaction, and NoTransaction classes. Each concrete transaction controller is responsible for committing or rolling back its own transactions. You will see more about each of these classes later. Each of these concrete controller classes inherits from the TransactionControllerBase class, an abstract class that is responsible for executing the business method in a specific transaction context and managing the outstanding transactions. ITransaction-Controller is the interface that is implemented by TransactionControllerBase.

Now let's look at these classes one at time. We will use an example of a client application to see how to use the SAF.Transaction service. First, the Transaction-Manager class provides the client with the ability to obtain a transaction controller object with a specific transaction attribute:

```
public class TransactionManager
{
    public static ITransactionController GetSupportTransactionController()
    {
```

```
      return new SupportTransaction();
   }

   public static ITransactionController GetRequireTransactionController()
   {
      return new RequireTransaction();
   }

   public static ITransactionController GetRequireNewTransactionController()
   {
      return new RequireNewTransaction();
   }

   public static ITransactionController GetNoTransactionController()
   {
      return new NoTransaction();
   }

public static void Rollback(params ITransactionController[] txControllers)
{
   foreach (ITransactionController txController in txControllers)
   {
      if (txController != null)
      {
         txController.Rollback();
      }

   }
}

public static void Commit(params ITransactionController[] txControllers)
{
   foreach (ITransactionController txController in txControllers)
   {
      if (txController != null)
      {
         txController.Commit();
      }

   }
}
   public static void DisposeAll(params object[] txControllers)
   {
```

```
        foreach (object txController in txControllers)
        {
            if (txController != null)
            {
                try
                {
                    if (txController is System.EnterpriseServices.ServicedComponent)
                    {
                        //destroy the serviced component
                        ((ServicedComponent)txController).Dispose();
                    }
                }
                catch (Exception ex){}
            }
        }
    }
}
```

The four `GetXxxTransaction()` methods are straightforward. Each returns a new instance of the serviced component whose transaction attributes match what these method names imply; for example, the `GetRequireNewTransaction()` method will return an instance of the serviced component that is marked with `[Transaction (TransactionOption.RequiresNew)]`. The following are the class declarations for these four serviced components returned by the `Controller` class:

```
[ProgId("SupportTransaction")]
[Guid("E42F5FFF-823B-4F20-AE80-B13A3C071112")]
[Transaction(TransactionOption.Supported)]
public class SupportTransaction : TransactionControllerBase
{
    //....
}


[ProgId("RequireTransaction")]
[Guid("E42F5FFF-823B-4F20-AE80-B13A3C071113")]
[Transaction(TransactionOption.Required)]
public class RequireTransaction : TransactionControllerBase
{
    //....
}


[ProgId("RequireNewTransaction")]
[Guid("E42F5FFF-823B-4F20-AE80-B13A3C071114")]
```

```
[Transaction(TransactionOption.RequiresNew)]
public class RequireNewTransaction : TransactionControllerBase
{
    //....
}

[ProgId("NoTransaction")]
[Guid("E42F5FFF-823B-4F20-AE80-B13A3C071115")]
[Transaction(TransactionOption.NotSupported)]
public class NoTransaction : TransactionControllerBase
{
    //....
}
```

With the transaction attribute marking, each new object of these classes created by the TransactionManager will create a new transaction, inherit an existing transaction, or create no transaction according to the attributes. Figure 13-7 shows the serviced components in the COM+ management console after installation.

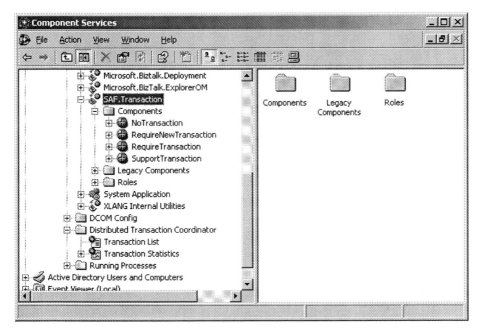

Figure 13-7. Registered SAF.Transaction *components under the COM+ console*

You can open the property page for each component to check the transaction attributes. The attribute should match what you specify in [Transaction(...)] in the class file. Figure 13-8 shows the property page for one of the SAF.Transaction components: SAF.Transaction.RequireNewTransaction.

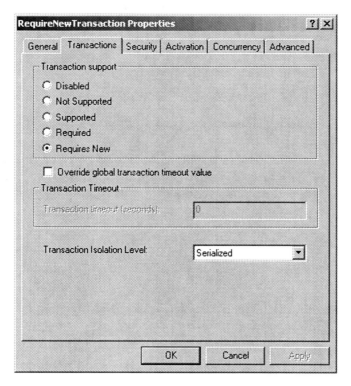

Figure 13-8. Property page of the serviced component in the COM+ console

Of course, creating an appropriate transaction on the client gets only the left part of the work done. We must also make sure that the business methods can also participate in these transactions as a single unit.

When we develop an ordinary serviced component containing some business methods that perform an update on the underlying transactional data source such as a database or message queue, the data update performed inside the method of a serviced component will participate in whatever transaction the serviced component belongs to at that time. In other words, in order to make a particular data update operation part of a transaction, this data update operation must be called from a method within a serviced component that is also part of the transaction.

Taking this behavior a little further, as long as we invoke some business methods from within the serviced component that has transactional capability, we can make those business methods participate in the transaction. Now, there are two approaches to invoking a method from within the serviced component. One approach is through defining a method inside the serviced component, which is the approach that the TransferMoney() example shown earlier has taken. This approach is not very flexible to changes and requires a number of wrapper methods, as we have discussed before. The other approach is through the use of reflection. In this approach, there is no need to define a large number of wrapper methods; instead, we will invoke all the business methods through a simple "generic" method defined in the serviced component.

TransactionControllerBase, which extends ServicedComponent, is an abstract class from which each of the four "transaction" classes inherits. It has a method called ExecuteMethod(). Here is its definition:

```
public virtual object ExecuteMethod(object o, string method, params object[] p)
```

ExecuteMethod() takes three parameters: the object that contains the business method, the name of the business method, and the parameters for the business method. When a client calls ExecuteMethod() and passes in the information about the business methods, ExecuteMethod() will invoke the business methods as part of a serviced component, and hence any transactional data updates inside these business methods will now be part of the transaction to which the serviced component belongs. The ExecuteMethod() does this with the following simple code:

```
public virtual object ExecuteMethod(object o, string method, params object[] p )
{
    try
    {
        //invoke the business method inside TransactionControllerBase,
        //a serviced component, so that it can participate in the transaction
        object ret = o.GetType().InvokeMember(method,
                                    BindingFlags.InvokeMethod,null,o,p);
        return ret;
    }
    catch (Exception ex)
    {
        //cast the vote on the transaction
        if (ContextUtil.IsInTransaction)
        {
            ContextUtil.DisableCommit();
            throw ex;
        }
    }
}
```

> **NOTE** *Because the* ExecuteMethod() *uses reflection to call the business method, there is no way for it to perform type checking at design time. As a result, you will lose type safety when using the* SAF.Transaction *service to invoke your business methods. In other words, you won't find bugs that are related to type mismatches in your program until you run the program for the first time.*

Within the "try-catch" block, the ExecuteMethod() calls the business method and passes the return value to the client. If an exception is thrown, the catch block will set the happy bit of the current transaction to false by calling the ContextUtil.DisableCommit() method, which will doom the current transaction. It then throws the exception again to bubble it up through the calling hierarchy. Regardless of whether there is an exception thrown, the client can deterministically finish the transactions it has started by calling the Commit() or Rollback() method on the TransactionManager class, which will in turn trigger either Commit or Abort on each of the transactional components. The Commit() and Abort() methods are defined in TransactionControllerBase, which is inherited by each of the four ServicedComponents, as follows:

```
public virtual void Rollback()
{
    if (ContextUtil.IsInTransaction)
    {
        ContextUtil.SetAbort();
    }
}

public virtual void Commit()
{
    if (ContextUtil.IsInTransaction)
    {
        if (ContextUtil.MyTransactionVote == TransactionVote.Commit)
        {
            ContextUtil.SetComplete();
        }
        else
        {
            ContextUtil.SetAbort();
        }
    }
}
```

Because each of the four child "transaction" classes derives from the `TransactionControllerBase` abstract class, when `TransactionControllerBase.Commit()` or `Rollback()` is called, `ContextUtil.SetComplete()` and `ContextUtil.SetAbort()` apply only to the transaction of which the child "transaction" class is part.

Let's look at a concrete example to understand better how the pieces of the `SAF.Transaction` service work together. The following is a simple client console application. This application will call some methods in a `DataAccess` component to update a data table, and it wants to group the method calls with different transactional scopes, so that some of the methods work as one unit, while others work as a second unit. When an error occurs, only the correct amount of data gets rolled back.

The following code shows the simple data access component, which does some database updating:

```
public class DataAccess
{
    public void AddNewRecord(string name, string ssn)
    {
        string connection ="...";
        SqlConnection conn = new SqlConnection(connection);
        conn.Open();
        SqlCommand command = new SqlCommand("insert into
                        employees values('" + name + "','" + ssn + "')",conn);
        command.ExecuteNonQuery();
        conn.Close();
    }
}
```

The `AddNewRecord()` method takes the employee's name and social security number and adds them to the `employee` table. The `employee` table has `ssn` as its primary key column. So we can cause the insertion to fail by adding records with a duplicate social security number.

The following console application shows several combinations of transactions being used to add records to the `employee` table:

```
public static void Main(string[] argus)
{
    DataAccess data = new DataAccess();
    //--------------Sample 1----------------------
    ITransactionController transaction_A=
TransactionManager.GetRequireTransactionController();
    try
    {
```

```
        transaction_A.ExecuteMethod(data,"AddNewRecord", "Xin","111111111");
        transaction_A.ExecuteMethod(data,"AddNewRecord","Mike","222222222");
        //this call will fail due to duplicate key error.
        transaction_A.ExecuteMethod(data,"AddNewRecord","John","111111111");
        TransactionManager.Commit(transaction_A);
    }
    catch (Exception ex)
    {
        TransactionManager.Rollback(transaction_A);
        //additional error handling code....
    }
    finally
    {
        //release the resource used by the serviced component
        TransactionManager.DisposeAll(transaction_A);
    }


    //--------------Sample 1 result ------------------
    //None of the three records is inserted into the employee table.
}
```

In sample 1, we create a transaction controller (transaction_A) for Required-Transaction, which will create a new transaction, since the console application is not running in a transaction. Then we add three employees, Xin, Mike, and John, to the table through three method calls within the same transaction. Because John's social security number is a duplicate, a database error will cause the transaction to roll back. Therefore, the end result is that no record is added to the employee table.

Sample 2 will change how the transaction is used with the business methods and will produce a different result. The following is the code for sample 2:

```
DataAccess data = new DataAccess();
//--------------Sample 2-----------------------
ITransactionController transaction_B=
TransactionManager.GetRequireTransactionController();
ITransactionController transaction_C=
TransactionManager.GetRequireNewTransactionController();
try
{
    transaction_B.ExecuteMethod(data,"AddNewRecord","Xin","111111111");
    transaction_B.ExecuteMethod(data,"AddNewRecord","Mike ","222222222");
    try
    {
```

```
        //add an important employee. Add him regardless of whether other
        //employees are added to table successfully
        transaction_C.ExecuteMethod(data,"AddNewRecord","Bill","333333333");
        TransactionManager.Commit(transaction_C);
    }
    catch (Exception ex)
       {
                  TransactionManager.Rollback(transaction_C);
       }
    //this call will fail due to duplicate key error.
    transaction_B.ExecuteMethod(data,"AddNewRecord","John","111111111");
    TransactionManager.Commit(transaction_B);
}
catch (Exception ex)
{
    TransactionManager.Rollback(transaction_B);
    //additional error handling code...
}
finally
{
    //release the resource used by the serviced component
    TransactionManager.DisposeAll(transaction_B,transaction_C);
}


//-------------Sample 2 result ------------------
//Only Bill is added to the employee table.
```

In sample 2, a new transaction (transaction_C) is added. Because transaction_B and transaction_C are two separate transactions, the rollback in transaction_B caused by the duplicate key for John shouldn't roll back the data modified by transaction_C. The same principle applies the other way around. If transaction_C had failed, it wouldn't have caused transaction_B to be rolled back. We need to add a "try-catch" block around the code for adding "Bill" so that if there is an exception during the addition of Bill, transaction_B will not be affected. The end result for sample 2 is that only "Bill" is added to the employee table. Xin, Mike, and John are not added to the table.

Sample 3 uses a different way to update the data. Some method calls participate in transactions whereas other do not, and the result reflects the behavior of the different transaction options:

```
DataAccess data = new DataAccess();
//-------------Sample 3------------------------
ITransactionController transaction_D=
                          TransactionManager.GetNoTransactionController();
```

```
ITransactionController transaction_E=
TransactionManager.GetSupportTransactionController();
ITransactionController transaction_F=
                            TransactionManager.GetRequireTransactionController();
try
{
    //the following three calls are not part of the transaction
    data.AddNewRecord("Xin","111111111");
    transaction_D.ExecuteMethod(data,"AddNewRecord","Mike","222222222");
    transaction_E.ExecuteMethod(data,"AddNewRecord","Bill","333333333");
    //this call participates in a transaction and
    //will fail due to duplicate key error.
    transaction_F.ExecuteMethod(data,"AddNewRecord","John","111111111");
    TransactionManager.Commit(transaction_D,transaction_E,transaction_F);
}
catch (Exception ex)
{
    TransactionManager.Rollback(transaction_D,transaction_E,transaction_F);
    //additional error handling code....
}
finally
{
    //release the resource used by the serviced component
    TransactionManager.DisposeAll(transaction_D,transaction_E,transaction_F);
}
//-------------Sample 3 result -----------------
//only Xin, Mike, Bill are added to the employee table. John is not added.
```

Sample 3 contains four data updates to the employee table. One is made through a direct method call to the DataAccess component. Because the console application is not running in a transaction, the first call is not part of a transaction either; therefore, it is committed automatically (through the underlying SQL server auto commit feature). The second call is made through the NoTransaction serviced component. Because this serviced component doesn't support transactions, the second is also not part of any transaction and is committed automatically. The third call is made through the SupportTransaction serviced component. SupportTransaction will participate in a transaction if it is inside one. In this example, it is not part of any transaction, since the console application is not in a transaction. The third call therefore is also committed automatically. The fourth call is different because it is made through a RequiredTransaction serviced component that is always part of a transaction, either an existing transaction or a brand new transaction. Therefore, the fourth call is part of the newly created transaction. The fourth call will throw an exception due to the duplicate key error. Because the first three calls are not part of the transaction, a failure of the fourth method will not affect them. As the rollback is called on transaction_D and transaction_E, none of the data updated by these two "transactions" is rolled back. The end result is that only Xin, Mike, and Bill are added to the employee table.

> **NOTE** *If you decide to leverage transactions at multiple layers of the application, for example the application layer and business framework layer, you must be very careful about the transaction attribute you set on each layer, since the transactional effect of one layer may be determined by the transactional effect of the layer above it. For instance,* SupportTransaction *on the outermost layers often results in no transaction context; however,* SupportTransaction *on an inner layer may either result in no transaction or part of an existing transaction context according to the transactional context of its outer layer.*

Locking and Isolation Levels

With the serviced component, it is fairly easy to create and run multiple transactions at once, and it is also fairly easy to get into trouble. A lock occurs when a transaction updates certain data in a table. Without a good analysis of how transactions are related to each other within an application, you can easily get into a situation in which multiple transactions are blocking each other indefinitely, which will cause your application to hang and time out. Contrary to popular belief, such bad locking problems are more frequent than you might expect. In fact, you can easily manufacture such situations and realize how easily transactions can be arranged into a locking problem. Using sample 2, we can create a data locking problem with a minor change. The following is partial code of sample 2:

```
ITransactionController transaction_B=
TransactionManager.GetRequireTransactionController();
ITransactionController transaction_C=
TransactionManager.GetRequireNewTransactionController();

transaction_B.ExecuteMethod(data,"UpdateRecord","Xin","111111111");
transaction_B.ExecuteMethod(data,"UpdateRecord","Mike","222222222");
try
{
    transaction_C.ExecuteMethod(data,"UpdateRecord","Bill","333333333");
}
...
```

The method call is changed from "AddNewRecord" to "UpdateRecord," which will update the social security number for a given name. If you attempt to run it again, the transaction_C.ExecuteMethod (…) call will throw an exception that reads "Timeout expired. The timeout period elapsed prior to completion of the operation or the server is not responding." You have just gotten yourself into a locking problem because both transaction_B and transaction_C have their own transactions, and are accessing the employee table at the same time, and transaction_B can't commit until transaction_C completes. However, transaction_C is waiting on transaction_B to commit to release the lock on the table (or data page) in order to update the data. You should be very careful in using mulitple transactions to update the data simultaneously.

COM+ 1.0, which comes with the Windows 2000 operating system, supports one transaction isolation level: Serializable. Serializable provides the highest level of data protection by prohibiting any data read from being updated by another transaction. Serializable transactions often result in locks on the data rows the transaction touches. If the number of rows in the table is small, serializable transactions may even result in a table lock. This will prevent other transactions from writing to and even reading from the table. The serializable isolation level provides data protection at the cost of concurrency of other transactions. However, you have more freedom on the choice of isolation level if you are using Windows XP or Windows 2003 Server, which come with COM+ 1.5. With COM+ 1.5, you have an option of choosing which isolation level to use for a given serviced component. In other words, you can now configure a component so that all the work it performs on a transactional resource is done under a specific isolation level. There are five transaction isolation levels, namely, serialized, repeatable read, read committed, read uncommitted, and any. Figure 13-8 shows these options in the bottom part of the window.

You can specify the component's isolation level either using the COM+ management console or through the transaction attribute in your class file. For example:

```
[ProgId("SupportTransaction")]
[Guid("E42F5FFF-823B-4F20-AE80-B13A3C071116")]
[Transaction(TransactionOption.Supported,
Isolation=TransactionIsolationLevel.ReadCommitted)]
public class SupportTransactionReadCommitted : TransactionControllerBase,
                                                ITransactionController{…}


[ProgId("SupportTransaction")]
[Guid("E42F5FFF-823B-4F20-AE80-B13A3C071117")]
[Transaction(TransactionOption.Supported,
Isolation=TransactionIsolationLevel.ReadUnCommitted)]
public class SupportTransactionReadUncommitted : TransactionControllerBase,

                                                ITransactionController{…}
```

You can extend what the SAF.Transaction service offers by adding a few more classes in the SAF.Transaction assembly, each with a different isolation level. Developers can then choose from a number of "transaction" serviced components to invoke the business methods with specific transaction support and transaction isolation level. For example, you can create the classes shown in Figure 13-9 to give developers freedom to choose the right transaction for the application.

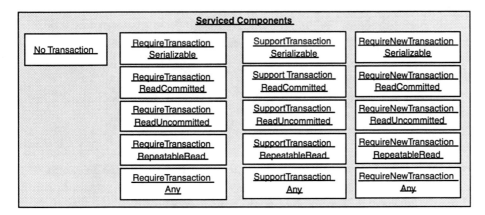

Figure 13-9. Possible extension to the SAF.Transaction *service*

After our lengthy discussion on transactions and serviced components, we should consider one reason for caution in using COM+ as a vehicle to achieve transactions throughout an application. Given the small amount of work involved in bundling multiple business methods and components in transactions, it is tempting to use COM+ for your transactions in every scenario. Although you can achieve the same result through COM+ in every scenario, you need to understand the tradeoffs. Given the extra overhead on system resources when using COM+ transactions, it doesn't always make sense to use COM+ for your transactions. For example, if your application accesses only one database, or databases that aren't strongly related, so that they are not involved in transactions across database boundaries, you don't need COM+ transactions; instead, you should use the native transaction mechanism for the underlying data source; for example, you can use System.Data.SqlClient.SqlTransaction to manage the transaction to an SQL server database, and System.Data.OleDb.OleDbTransaction to manage the transaction to an OLE DB data source, such as an Oracle database. Nondatabase products often also come with their own transactional mechanism. For example, MSMQ and MQSeries both support transactional reading and writing of messages without using COM+ transactions. However, there are situations in which you have to use COM+ transactions to ensure that multiple resource managers can participate in the same transaction, for example, writing to multiple databases or reading and writing messages in different message queue products within a single transaction. In other cases, in which performance is not the priority of your application or business users who are using the application are not sophisticated enough to notice the extra 1/10 second wait time, you should choose to use COM+ to manage the transaction throughout the application in order to simplify application development and to provide easy integration among multiple business components that need to participate in transactions. COM+ transactions provide a common denominator of transaction handling on the Windows platform, and it will make potential future application integration much easier as far as transactions are concerned.

Testing Project

The Test.SAF.Transaction project contains a console application that shows how to use the SAF.Transaction service in client applications. In order to run the demo, you must first install the SAFDemo database on the MS SQL server. The database is used in conjunction with the demo to demonstrate the data affected by the transaction.

To install SAFDemo, open SQL Server Enterprise Manager and create a database named SAFDemo and use the integrated security option for this database. After the empty database has been created, run the script inside of Setup\SAFDemo.sql under the SAFDemo database to create the tables needs for the SAF.Transaction demo application.

After you have completed the previous step, you can open the solution under Test.SAF.Transaction and hit F5 to run it. After you have successfully run the demo for the first time, the four ServicedComponents in SAF.Transaction will be shown in the Component Services management console.

Summary

In this chapter, you learned about COM+ transactions and ServicedComponent. We first looked at the basic architecture of the COM+ transaction service. We then spent a large amount of coverage on how we can leverage the COM+ transactional service in our .NET applications through the ServicedComponent. You learned how to create a serviced component and what transaction attributes are available for configuring the transactional behavior of a component. We also introduced some of the issues related to the use of transactions in ServicedComponent, such as the potential explosion of wrapper methods, the lack of class inheritance for the transactional component, and additional development and maintenance overhead. We then looked at the solution provided by the SAF.Transaction service, which provides developers with flexible ways to combine multiple business methods to form transactions more easily, eliminating the need to write wrapper methods and removing the requirement of inheriting the business component from Serviced-Component in order to support transactions.

For the past ten chapters, we have been focusing on cross-domain framework components. In the final two chapters of this book, we will be looking at two domain-specific framework components that assist the development of B2B applications with their document layer service and workflow service.

CHAPTER 14

DocumentLayer Service

BUSINESS-TO-BUSINESS (B2B) applications are all about processing business documents. The model for such applications is straightforward. Business partners send documents to the B2B application over the Internet or another channel. Our application will process the document, which involves extracting data from the document, examining it, and performing some business logic on the data presented in the document. Such processes often generate an output document or response document that contains status information about a particular document process. Although each B2B application achieves a very distinct business goal, these applications have a common architecture, one centered on the exchange of documents between business partners. This common architecture may come in different flavors and implementations, but they all more or less follow an approach that begins when a client requests some services by sending a business document to the B2B application, where the document is put through a series of layers of service, each performing a particular task based on the data in the document, and ends with some type of response document being sent back to the client to inform it of the status of the operation.

In this chapter, we will learn how to create a domain-specific framework component that simplifies the development of the business exchange in B2B applications and makes document processing in the application flexible enough to face changes in business requirements with very little additional development effort.

Motivation and Goals

As a document comes into the B2B application from the client and goes out to the client from our application, it passes through a series of tasks, each performing some specific operation on the document. For example, when a document first arrives at the system, we may want to log the incoming message so that we have a record on the original document that has been sent to us. We also want to log the response document as the document leaving our application and going back to our business partners so that we know exactly what they will receive. Sometimes, the data in the document is in an awkward data format. For example, if the data is in a different XML schema from what our application can handle, we need first to perform some XSLT processing to ensure unification of the data schema. We also want to perform a similar XSLT transformation in the reverse order to convert the response document produced by our application into a document with a schema that our partners understand. As you can see, as a document passes through a number of processing layers as it travels through the system, many of these processing layers will not only process the document as it comes in, but also as it goes out. Figure 14-1 illustrates this document processing architecture.

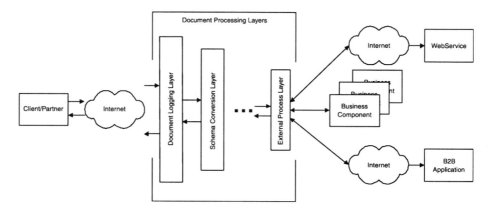

Figure 14-1. Document processing layer

The middle section of Figure 14-1 shows a chain of document processing layers. The arrows represent the direction of the document flow. As the document arrives in the system, each document processing layer has an opportunity to process the document as it enters in as well as it exits. Besides providing a comprehensive model for processing documents that involves multiple steps, this document layer architecture also provides a model that allows developers to combine multiple document layers easily into a processing chain to process the document. It also decouples each document layer from others in the processing chain so that we can add, replace, and remove a specific document layer from the existing document processing chain without affecting other document layers in the chain. This approach significantly reduces the amount of code changes developers have to support when a new requirement causes a change in the processing of business documents.

`SAF.Application.DocumentLayer` is a domain framework component that implements this type of document layer architecture. With this component, developers can easily assemble a document processing chain by putting together different document layers. Developers can also modify how a particular document is processed by rearranging the document layers in the chain through different configuration settings.

Code Sample Walkthrough

One of the challenges of implementing this type of design is figuring out how to decouple the document layers from each other, even though all the layers have to work together to process the document. The SAF.Application.DocumentLayer component resolves such design issues through the use of one of the GOF design patterns: "decorator." In the next section, we will look at more closely at the decorator design pattern. We then will look at how it is implemented in the Document-Layer service.

Design Pattern: Decorator

To quote from the GOF book, the intent of the decorator pattern is to "attach additional responsibilities to an object dynamically. Decorators provide a flexible alternative to subclassing for extending functionality."

The first sentence is another way of saying that you want to be able to add some additional services dynamically as part of a chain. The DocumentLayer service achieves this goal by allowing you to add additional layers to the document processing chain without application code change of other layers. The second sentence is just a fancy way of saying that you want to provide flexible services through delegation instead of inheritance. The DocumentLayer service meets this goal by allowing you to chain multiple document layers together to process the document. Each layer will perform a service on the document and then delegate it to the next layer in the chain for further services. Figure 14-2 shows the structure of the decorator pattern.

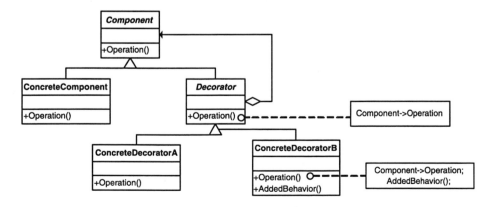

Figure 14-2. The decorator design pattern structure

In Figure 14-2, each concrete decorator is responsible for implementing the Operation method. Each concrete decorator also keeps a reference of the very next decorator through an instance variable. This relationship is expressed with the arrowhead line with a diamond at its base. This symbol indicates the aggregation of instances. In other words, each decorator holds the collective information about decorators coming behind it. Because the decorator holds the aggregated instances of other decorators, calling the Operation method on one decorator will have a cascade effect on all the aggregated instances of the decorators it holds. The cascade effect results in a chain reaction in which each layer in the chain will operate on the subject (such as the document) and then pass it to the remaining layers in the chain one by one, which will operate on the subject in the same fashion as the very first layer in the chain.

There are a number of ways the decorator pattern can be implemented to achieve its intended goal. However, there are two key concepts that every decorator pattern shares. First, there should be a well-defined interface for the decorator (or layer) object. This is necessary, since we need to know what method to invoke on each decorator as data passes through decorators in the chain. This well-defined interface can be accomplished with either an abstract class or an interface. Second, each decorator object must be able to locate the next decorator in the chain. The decorator object often has a property called Next, which holds the object reference of the next decorator in the chain. We will look at the implementation in the DocumentLayer service later in the chapter.

Even if you have not heard of the decorator pattern before, you certainly have used it without knowing it. Decorator, with its "layer" structure approach, has been implemented in many places in the .NET framework where flexibility of assembling multiple pieces of code to provide a service is the key. For example, stream objects in .NET use the decorator pattern to provide developers with an easy yet flexible way to read and write data in different forms. The following sample code shows how to chain multiple reader or writer objects to get data from one point to another:

```
StreamWriter  sw = new StreamWriter(new BufferedStream(new
            FileStream(@"c:\test.txt",FileMode.Create,FileAccess.ReadWrite)));
sr.WriteLine("test");
```

By chaining StreamWriter, BufferedStream, and FileStream together as shown in the example, whenever we use sr to write data, the data will pass through each of the three layers before it is finally written to the test.txt file. As the string "test" passes through each layer of the chain, a certain task is carried out. When the string is passed to the Write() method of the StreamWriter, the StreamWriter will prepare the string into a byte array. When the byte array is passed to the Write() method in BufferedStream, BufferedStream will put the bytes into a certain fixed-length buffer to avoid reading or writing a single byte at a time. When the byte buffer is passed to the Write() method of the FileStream, the FileStream will perform the actual disk operation to write the data to a file. Because streams in .NET are implemented using such decorator patterns, we are able to do this with one line of code. We also have the flexibility to alter the behavior of writing the string to the file by adding or replacing a stream object in the chain. For example, we can simply replace the FileStream object with a NetworkStream object to write the data to another server via a network socket.

The decorator pattern is also used in .NET remoting to provide developers with the ability to add custom channel sinks between the remoting client and server. Recall CryptoRemotingClientSink and CryptoRemotingServerSink in Chapter 12: Both sink objects can be easily plugged into the chain of the default .NET remoting channel sinks to encrypt and decrypt messages as the remoting call passes between the client and server. As you can see, the .NET remoting model relies on the decorator pattern to provide application developers the freedom to implement custom services over remoting calls.

DocumentLayer Design

The decorator design pattern provides us with a good blueprint for creating a layer-like approach to document processing. Let's take a closer look at how the decorator pattern is implemented. Figure 14-3 shows the classes and their relationships in the DocumentLayer service.

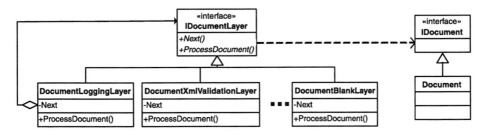

Figure 14-3. Application.DocumentLayer *service*

DocumentLayer implements the IDocumentLayer and IDocument interfaces. It also has a couple of sample concrete layer classes that are often useful for processing documents, such as one that performs document logging and another that performs XML validation on the document. Here are the definitions of IDocumentLayer and IDocument:

```
public interface IDocument
{
    IPrincipal Sender
    {
        get;set;
    }
    string Content
    {
        get;set;
    }
    object AdditionalData
    {
        get;set;
    }
}
public interface IDocumentLayer
{
    IDocumentLayer Next
    {
        get;set;
    }
    IDocument ProcessDocument(IDocument document);
}
```

The IDocument interface contains some data fields that are often needed during document processing, such as the sender information, the content of the document, and some additional objects that can vary from application to application.

The IDocumentLayer interface provides a common interface for all the decorators or layers. It has two members: a property called Next, and a method called ProcessDocument().

ProcessDocument() takes an IDocument as input, operates on the document, and then returns an instance of IDocument, which will be considered the response document. The IDocument returned from ProcessDocument() may or may not be exactly the same as the input parameter. For example, when performing document logging, the document itself shouldn't be altered in any way; on the other hand, when performing XML schema conversion, the returned document will look different from the input document.

The Next property is really the key to gluing all the layers together to form a chain. The type of the property is IDocumentLayer, which is also the interface that all the document layers have to implement. Because all the document layers have the Next property, which is supposed to point to the next layer in the chain, we are able to set off a series of actions by triggering the very first document layer in the chain. Before we look at the code for setting the Next property, let's take a look at the configuration settings needed to support the DocumentLayer service:

```
<DocumentLayers>
    <DocumentLayer name="Generic">
        <Layer type="….DocumentLoggingLayer,Application.Document">
            <Config loggingdb ="..."/>
            <Layer type="...DocumentXmlValidationLayer,… ">
                <Config incomingSchema = ".." outgoingSchema =".."/>
                <Layer type="….DocumentBlankLayer,…">
                                </Layer>
            </Layer>
        </Layer>
    </DocumentLayer>
</DocumentLayers>
```

By looking at this section of configuration settings, it is easy to see the relationships among different "layers," namely, DocumentLoggingLayer, DocumentXmlValidationLayer, and DocumentBlankLayer. The challenge is to set the Next property for each document layer to the next layer. The constructor of DocumentLoggingLayer shows how the Next property is set:

```
public DocumentLoggingLayer(XmlNode configXml)
{
    XmlNode node = configXml.SelectSingleNode("Layer");
    // retrieve possible logging specific configuration data, such as db connection
    if (node != null)
    {
        Type type = Type.GetType(node.Attributes["type"].Value);
        object[] parameters= new Object[1]{node};
        next = (IDocumentLayer)Activator.CreateInstance(type,parameters);
    }
}
```

When an IDocumentLayer object is created, an XmlNode is passed as a parameter into the constructor. The constructor is responsible for locating the child "Layer" element from the XmlNode that represents the next layer in the chain and using reflection to create the layer object by calling its constructor and passing in the element that represents this layer object. Using the constructor of the DocumentLoggingLayer class as an example, the configXml input parameter of the constructor should contain the following information:

```
<Layer type="….DocumentLoggingLayer,Application.Document">
   <Config loggingdb ="..."/>
   <Layer type="...DocumentXmlValidationLayer,… ">
      <Config incoming = "xml1.xml" outgoing ="xml2.xml"/>
      <Layer type="….DocumentBlankLayer,…">
      </Layer>
   </Layer>
</Layer>
```

Within the constructor, the node variable represents the child "Layer" element that represents the layer object that is located below the DocumentLoggingLayer object in the chain. The node variable should contain the following information:

```
<Layer type="...DocumentXmlValidationLayer,… ">
   <Config incoming = "xml1.xml" outgoing ="xml2.xml"/>
   <Layer type="….DocumentBlankLayer,…">
   </Layer>
</Layer>
```

When the constructor of the DocumentLoggingLayer tries to call the constructor of the DocumentXmlValidationLayer, it will pass in the node variable as its input parameter. Because DocumentXmlValidationLayer's constructor also uses a similar approach to that of DocumentLoggingLayer, it will locate the child "Layer" element from its input parameter and pass it to the next layer's constructor as an input parameter. This is how we can set off a chain reaction of object creation and instantiate the object with just the right information. Inside the constructor of each IDocumentLayer object, the Next property is set to the next layer object via .NET reflection. If the layer object is the last one in the chain, the Next property will be null. Later, we will see that the Next property is checked for null to determine whether it has reached the end of the processing chain.

Of course, IDocumentLayer allows you to establish a document layer chain independent of the configuration data. Sometimes the dynamic feature of being able to establish a document layer chain is not something you would greatly value; instead, you would like to provide an easy programming model, such as a .NET data stream, for developers to create a document layer chain at design time. In such cases, you can use a constructor overload to create a layer chain. This is what the overloaded constructor of DocumentLoggingLayer looks like:

```
public DocumentLoggingLayer (IDocumentLayer nextLayer)
{
   Next  =  nextLayer;
}
```

You can then create a document layer chain in a similar fashion to the way you create a .NET stream chain, as shown in the earlier example:

```
IDocumentLayer chain = new DocumentLoggingLayer (new DocumentXmlValidationLayer
                        (new DocumentBlankLayer ( ( IDocumentLayer ) null ) ) );
```

We now know how to chain multiple IDocumentLayer objects together through the use of the Next property. The next step is to find out how we can set off a chain reaction that allows each individual layer object in the chain to process the IDocument object passing through it. This is better explained by looking at the ProcessDocument() method. Here is the partial code of the ProcessDocument() method of the DocumentLoggingLayer class:

```
public IDocument ProcessDocument(IDocument doc)
{
    //...some code to log the incoming document
    if (Next != null)
    {
        doc = Next.ProcessDocument(doc);
    }
    //...some code to log the outgoing document
    return doc;
}
```

There are three blocks of code in the ProcessDocument() method. The first block is where you put your code to process the document passed in as an input parameter. In the case of DocumentLoggingLayer, it would be some code that stores the incoming document to some data store, such as a database. The second block of code is basically calling the ProcessDocument() method on the layer stored in the Next property, which is initialized in the class constructor. This will trigger a chain reaction on the ProcessDocument() methods of all the layer objects after the first one and is also the essence of the decorator pattern. The third block of code will take the return object from the Next.ProcessDocument(doc) call and perform some task on it, such as storing the response document to the database in this example. The first and the third code blocks are optional, since it is up to you how to process the document. The second block is required to keep the chain reaction going.

Before we conclude this discussion of the DocumentLayer service, let's take a look at an example of how developers can use it in their code. The following sample describes two ways to use the document layer service. The first one relies on the configuration data, and the second one relies on developers defining the relationship among the layer objects within the chain:

```
static void Main(string[] args)
{
    //set up a document object
    GenericIdentity id = new GenericIdentity("xin");
    GenericPrincipal p = new GenericPrincipal(id,new String[1]{"Administration"});
    Document d = new Document(p,@"<Test>this is test</Test>",null);

    //set up the configuration object
    Application.Configuration.ConfigurationManager cm = null;
    cm = (ConfigurationManager)ConfigurationSettings.GetConfig("Application");
    //--------------the first way (relies on the configuration file)-----------
    //ask the configuration object for the first layer object in chain
    IDocumentLayer layer = (IDocumentLayer)cm.DocumentLayerConfig
                                        .GetDocumentLayerByName("Generic");
    IDocument response1 = layer.ProcessDocument(d);
    //------------the second way (relies on a hard-coded layer sequence)---------
    //assemble a chain of layers by the developer
    IDocumentLayer chain = new DocumentLoggingLayer(new
                            DocumentXmlValidationLayer(new
                            DocumentBlankLayer((IDocumentLayer)null)));
    IDocument response2 = chain.ProcessDocument(d);
}
```

The previous sample code is based on the configuration settings shown earlier in the chapter. DocumentLayerConfig.GetDocumentLayerByName() is a method in the configuration object that returns an instance of the first layer object in the chain. Here is its definition:

```
public object GetDocumentLayerByName(string name)
{
    XmlNode pipeData = pipeXml.SelectSingleNode("DocumentLayer[@name='"
                                        + name + "']");
    XmlNode firstLayer = pipeData.SelectSingleNode("Layer");
    Type type = Type.GetType(firstLayer.Attributes["type"].Value);
    object[] parameters = new Object[1]{firstLayer};
    object Layer = Activator.CreateInstance(type,parameters);
    return Layer;
}
```

The Testing Project

The Test.SAF.Application.DocumentLayer project contains a console application that shows how to use the DocumentLayer service in a client application. If you have already set up the SAFDemo database in last chapter, there is no additional setup you need to perform to run the demo; otherwise, you need first to install the SAFDemo database, which is used by DocumentLoggingLayer to store the logging information. Please refer to the instructions under "The Testing Project" section of Chapter 13.

To run the demo, open the solution in the Test.SAF.Application.DocumentLayer folder and hit F5 to run it.

Summary

We have seen how to take advantage of a layer approach to processing a document. We also looked at how we can leverage the decorator design pattern in building such document layers, which gives developers an easy way to assemble a document process chain with the appropriate document layer objects. By using a configuration file to define the relationship among the layer objects in a given process chain, developers can change the way a particular document is processed with only configuration changes.

CHAPTER 15

The Workflow Service

IN OUR **B2B** APPLICATION, the incoming document passes through a series of layers, each of which will perform some task on the document. The tasks performed by the document layers are somewhat generic actions such as document logging and XML validation. Such tasks are commonly applied to the document regardless of the content of the document and business logic that may be involved in processing the document. However, at some point, the document has to go through a number of business components that actually process the document. Unlike the tasks performed by the document layers, the business logic involved in the business components can be quite complex and dynamic. Compared with order of the document layers, which can be generically applied to the document, the order of the components and type of components participating in processing the document can be unique and highly dependent on the content of the document itself. For example, a purchase order from a trading partner may result in a completely different set of business components due to the relationship with the trading partner, the products in the purchase order, sales promotions, etc. In this chapter, we will look at a *workflow service*, which provides the architecture for coordinating the business components involved in document processing.

Motivation and Goals

Processing a document often involves the participation of multiple business components, and sometimes the relationships and coordination among these components are so complex that this poses a challenge to the development team that is trying to develop and maintain such relationships. Figure 15-1 illustrates the document processes that are involved in a B2B application.

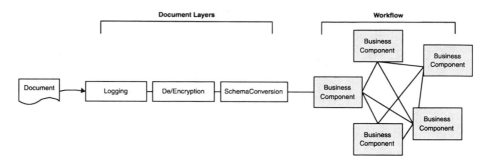

Figure 15-1. A document process scenario with complex workflow

In Figure 15-1, the document enters the system through the document layers, where the document is processed in a linear fashion. After the multiple business components have started processing the document, the relationship between the components has become difficult to manage. Because each business component will potentially interact with other business components during the processing of the document, each business component is closely coupled with other components, which leads to a cascade effect as business rules change. As we have learned from considerable past experience, close coupling among business components can make the coordination logic very complicated, and a change in one component can potentially cause other components to change as well. To avoid such coupling of business components, we can extract the coordination logic out of each component and put the task of coordination into a single component that manages the relationships among the multiple business components. Figure 15-2 shows this approach to workflow in document processing.

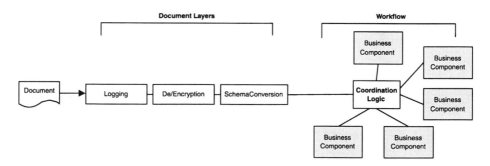

Figure 15-2. A document process scenario with coordination logic separating the business components

By introducing a component that handles the coordination logic for the business components, we can significantly reduce the number of connections each business component has to maintain. The coordination logic holds the business rules that state which components are involved in what order to process the document.

If you have used the Microsoft BizTalk Server, you will remember the concept of orchestration. BizTalk orchestration uses a similar approach to ease the complexity of business components.

> **NOTE** *BizTalk orchestration provides developers with the ability to drag and drop business components into an orchestration designer and connect them with a business rule to create a workflow for document processing. By extracting the business rules on how the business components coordinate with each other, orchestration helps reduce complexity both in developing and maintaining a workflow.*

SAF.Application.Workflow is a domain framework component that provides an architecture for processing documents using multiple business components. Using the Workflow service, developers can extract the coordination logic and put it into components that are separate from the business components. Because of this decoupling, the coordination logic and business components can change independently. For the rest of this chapter, we will look in depth at the design as well as the implementation of the Workflow service.

Code Sample Walkthrough

To better understand the design of the Workflow service, we first need to clarify our understanding of the workflow problem. In our B2B scenario, documents are processed by a set of business components, such as the component that charges the customer's account and the component for submitting an order to a backend system. However, for each individual document, different components may be involved as well as different coordination logic that describes how each component is invoked and the order of their invocation, and such coordination logic is highly dynamic and can be changed quite often based on changes to the business rules in processing the document. We may now ask ourselves a question: How can we handle a set of business components whose operations are stable, but a coordination logic for such components that can change quite often.

If you look at available design patterns, you will find that the visitor pattern provides a very nice foundation for what we want to achieve in our B2B document processing scenario.

Design Pattern: Visitor

To quote from the GOF book: "Visitor represents an operation to be performed on the elements of an object structure. Visitor lets you define a new operation without changing the classes of the element on which it operates."

Of course, if this is the first time you have read about the visitor pattern, the previous sentence may make absolutely no sense to you. It is kind of definition that one understands and appreciates only after having used the visitor pattern. To paraphrase the quotation from the GOF book, the visitor pattern makes it possible to add and change the operations that are performed on individual components without the need to change the operations of the components themselves. Figure 15-3 illustrates the class structure for the visitor pattern.

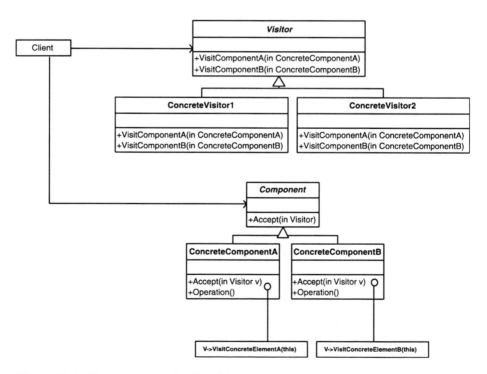

Figure 15-3. Class structure for the visitor pattern

Figure 15-3 may appear complicated, but it is really about two types of classes: visitors and components. Visitors contain the coordination logic, and components contain the business logic. The key is that ConcreteComponentA and ConcreteComponentB have no knowledge of each other. If you have certain tasks that involve the participation of both components, you place the logic on how each component is invoked inside the visitor class. In fact, you place the logic about the wiring of components into the visitor class. Of course, the visitor class must have a reference to each of the components it "operates" on or coordinates. This is achieved by the Accept method in the component. The Accept method takes the visitor object as its parameter and calls the methods on that visitor object with this as its input parameter. The keyword this represents the component itself, and this is how the visitor class can get hold of the reference to the component it wants to operate on and coordinate. The visitor class has multiple overloaded methods, each taking a different type of component as its input parameter. For example, you can create a visitor class that handles the coordination for many types of components, as follows:

```
public class MyVisitor
{
    public void Visit(ComponentA a)
    {
        a.Operation();
        //...more work
    }
    public void Visit(ComponentB b)
    {
        b.Operation();
        //...more work
    }
    public void Visit(ComponentC a)
    {
        c.Operation();
        //...more work
    }
}
```

The Accept method and a set of overloaded methods in the visitor class represent the crux of the visitor design pattern. To support the visitor pattern, each component must provide a special Accept method. The purpose of the Accept method is to bind the component with the visitor object that contains the coordination logic for how this component interacts with other components. For example, the following sample code shows the Accept method:

```
public class ComponentA : Component
{
   public void Operation()
   {
      //...some work
   }
   public void Accept(Visitor v)
   {
      v.Visit(this);
   }
}
```

If a client wants to perform some work defined in the component's Operation method, either it can call the Operation method directly, or it can get hold of the visitor object and pass it to the component's Accept method. You can see by looking at the previous two code samples that the Accept method will eventually call the Operation method. However, the difference is that when a client is calling the Accept method, the call goes through the visitor's Visit method before returning to the Operation method. This Visit method provides the opportunity to define some coordination logic, such as setting up the appropriate properties of the components and invoking additional components before and after the Operation method is called.

Now let's take a look at the Workflow service to see how it can help us develop the kind of document processing approach shown in Figure 15-2.

Workflow consists of interfaces for component and visitor classes that represent the two major elements in the visitor pattern. The IComponent interface defines the methods and properties a class must implement to participate as a component in the workflow.

The following code segment shows the IComponent interface:

```
public interface IComponent
{
   IDocument Request{get;set;}
   IDocument Response{get;set;}
   IComponent NextComponent{get;set;}
   void Accept(IVisitor v);
}
```

The Accept method will trigger the actual processing of the document. The NextComponent property keeps track of which component object is next in line to do its part in processing the document.

If you plan to have multiple business components participate in document processing at one point or another, you need to create component classes for each business component that is involved. The following shows an example of a component class:

```
public class ComponentChargeAccount :  IComponent
{
    public bool success;
    //….some code omitted…
    public override void Accept(Visitor v)
    {
        //perform the transaction on the account
        //set the success flag accordingly.
        v.Visit(this);
    }
}
```

ComponentChargeAccount is a component that performs some of the necessary work to charge a client's account. Within its Accept() method are some database calls, and if the operation is successful, the success flag will be set to true. Otherwise, it will be set to false. As you can imagine, there may be a number of components that need to be invoked after the client's account has been charged, but the kind of components involved may vary, depending on the outcome of the transaction for charging the client's account. For example, if the client's account is successfully charged with a given amount, the component that handles the shipment of the product will be called. On the other hand, if the client's account doesn't have adequate funds, a different component may be called to cancel the purchase and send notification to the client. Of course, in the real world, the situation may be much more complex than that. Notice that the Accept() method doesn't contain code that determines the next component that needs to be called. Instead, it calls v.Visit(this). This is really the heart of the visitor pattern, which is to separate the coordination logic from the component itself. Now let's take a look at what the visitor object is like in this case:

```
public class Visitor
{
    public void Accept (ComponentChargeAccount cca)
    {
        //make decision on what to do next
        if (cca.success ==true)
        {
            ComponentShipGoods csg = new ComponentShipGoods();
```

```
        csg.Request = cca.Request;
        cca.NextComponent = csg;
    }
    else
    {
        ComponentCancelOrder cco = new ComponentCancelOrder();
        Cco.Request = cca. Request;
        cca.NextComponent = cco;
    }
}
public void Accept(ComponentA a){...}
public void Accept(ComponentB b){...}
}
```

When v.Visit(this) is called, the corresponding overload of the Accept() method will be invoked, in this case public void Accept(ComponentChargeAccount cca). A decision is made as to which component will next handle the document by examining the success flag. The previous sample shows only the simplest form of coordination logic between the components.

One of the great things about the visitor pattern is that you have one Accept() method for each type of component, which helps in partitioning the coordination logic on a component-by-component basis.

In my example, the Accept() method only sets the NextComponent. In order to make sure that the document is processed by all the necessary components, we need to set up a loop to ensure that all the components are invoked in the correct order. The following code does exactly that from the client side:

```
IVisitor v = new Visitor();
IComponent chargeAccount = new ComponentChargeAccount();
chargeAccount.Accept(v);

Component nextComponent = chargeAccount.NextComponent;
while (nextComponent != null)
{
    nextComponent.Accept(v);
    nextComponent = nextComponent.NextComponent;
}
```

In a B2B scenario, the component that processes the document should start when all the document layers have finished their jobs on the document. We need to create a document layer class whose sole purpose is to link the document layers and the workflow. DocumentWorkFlowLayer, which is often located at the bottom of the document layer chain, does exactly that. Here is some of its code:

```csharp
public class DocumentWorkFlowLayer  : IDocumentLayer
{
    private IDocumentLayer next;
    private IComponent nextComponent;
    private IVisitor v;

    public DocumentWorkFlowLayer(XmlNode configXml)
    {
        XmlNode node = configXml.SelectSingleNode("Layer");
        string initialComponent = configXml.SelectSingleNode("Config/
                                      InitialComponent").Attributes["type"].Value;
        string visitor = configXml.SelectSingleNode("Config/
                                          Visitor").Attributes["type"].Value;
        //use reflect to create the processing unit and visitor object
        nextComponent = (IComponent)Activator.CreateInstance(Type.
                                          GetType(initialComponent),null);
        v = (IVisitor)Activator.CreateInstance(Type.GetType(visitor),null);
        //set the Next property to the next document layer if there is one.
        if (node != null)
        {
            Type type = Type.GetType(node.Attributes["type"].Value);
            object[] parameters= new Object[1]{node};
            next = (IDocumentLayer)Activator.CreateInstance(type,parameters);
        }
    }

        public IDocument ProcessDocument(IDocument doc)
        {
            IDocument request = null;
            IDocument response = null;
            nextComponent.Request = doc;
            //Start each processing unit by calling the Accept(v) method
            while (nextComponent != null)
            {
                //trigger the process flow logic
                nextComponent.Accept(v);
                request = nextComponent.Request;
                response = nextComponent.Response;
                //set the next processing unit
                nextComponent = nextComponent.NextComponent;
                //if this is the last processing unit, retrieve
                //the request and response document
                if (nextComponent != null)
```

```
            {
                nextComponent.Request = request;
                nextComponent.Response = response;
            }
        }
        //if next document layer exists, proceed with the next layer.
        if (Next != null)
        {
            response = Next.ProcessDocument(response);
        }
        return response;
    }
}
```

DocumentWorkFlowLayer relies on the configuration file for creating the initial business component object and the visitor object during its construction. In its ProcessDocument() method, it will invoke the Accept() method on the initial business component and use the loop to invoke each of the participating business components through their Accept() methods. The following configuration settings show how DocumentWorkFlowLayer is used to link the processes of the document layers and the processes of the business components:

```
<Layer type="Application.Document.DocumentLoggingLayer,Application.Document">
    <Layer type="….DocumentXmlValidationLayer,Application.Document">
        <Layer type="….DocumentWorkFlowLayer,Application.Document">
            <InitialComponent type = "….ComponentInitial,…"/>
            <Visitor type = "….Visitor,Application.WorkFlow"/>
        </Layer>
    </Layer>
</Layer>
```

The Testing Project

The Test.SAF.Application.Workflow project contains a console application that demonstrates how to create components and visitor objects for the Workflow service and how to set up the workflow. There is no additional setup if you have already installed the SAFDemo database according to the instructions in Chapter 13. One of the components (TestWorkflow.SendConfirmationEmail) in the demo sends out e-mail via SMTP. You need to turn on the SMTP service in the Internet Information Services Manager. Please refer to IIS on-line help for more instruction.

The demo will function even if you don't get SMTP running properly. It will just not send the e-mail.

To run the demo, open the solution in the `Test.SAF.Application.Workflow` folder and hit F5 to run it.

Summary

In this chapter, you have learned how to make document processes more flexible by decoupling the business logic from the coordination logic that controls the sequence of the process flow. We also looked at the visitor pattern, which provides a foundation for such a decoupling between the business logic and coordination logic. Through the example of the `SAF.Application.Workflow` service, you have learned how to implement this pattern in .NET and how it can be integrated into the document processing layer in our B2B application.

Index

X

JOIN THE APRESS FORUMS AND BE PART OF OUR COMMUNITY. You'll find discussions that cover topics of interest to IT professionals, programmers, and enthusiasts just like you. If you post a query to one of our forums, you can expect that some of the best minds in the business—especially Apress authors, who all write with *The Expert's Voice*™—will chime in to help you. Why not aim to become one of our most valuable participants (MVPs) and win cool stuff? Here's a sampling of what you'll find:

Data drives everything.

Share information, exchange ideas, and discuss any database programming or administration issues.

Unfortunately, it is.

Talk about the Apress line of books that cover software methodology, best practices, and how programmers interact with the "suits."

Try living without plumbing (and eventually IPv6).

Talk about networking topics including protocols, design, administration, wireless, wired, storage, backup, certifications, trends, and new technologies.

Ugly doesn't cut it anymore, and CGI is absurd.

Help is in sight for your site. Find design solutions for your projects and get ideas for building an interactive Web site.

We've come a long way from the old Oak tree.

Hang out and discuss Java in whatever flavor you choose: J2SE, J2EE, J2ME, Jakarta, and so on.

Lots of bad guys out there—the good guys need help.

Discuss computer and network security issues here. Just don't let anyone else know the answers!

All about the Zen of OS X.

OS X is both the present and the future for Mac apps. Make suggestions, offer up ideas, or boast about your new hardware.

Cool things. Fun things.

It's after hours. It's time to play. Whether you're into LEGO® MINDSTORMS™ or turning an old PC into a DVR, this is where technology turns into fun.

Source code is good; understanding (open) source is better.

Discuss open source technologies and related topics such as PHP, MySQL, Linux, Perl, Apache, Python, and more.

No defenestration here.

Ask questions about all aspects of Windows programming, get help on Microsoft technologies covered in Apress books, or provide feedback on any Apress Windows book.

HOW TO PARTICIPATE:

Go to the Apress Forums site at **http://forums.apress.com/**.

Click the New User link.

Printed in the United States
118146LV00005B/87-90/A